Take
Two

Take Two:

Adapting the Contemporary American Novel to Film

edited by

Barbara Tepa Lupack

Bowling Green State University Popular Press
Bowling Green, OH 43403

A shorter version of "Adapting *The Color Purple*: When Folk Goes Pop" first appeared in *Literature/Film Quarterly*.

"*The World According to Garp*: Novel to Film" first appeared in *The Bennington Review* and is reprinted here with permission of Bennington College.

A shorter version of "The Waking Nightmare of Mike Nichols' *Catch-22*" first appeared in *The New Orleans Review*, as did an earlier version of "Chance Encounters: Bringing *Being There* to the Screen."

"One Flew, Two Followed: Stage and Screen Adaptations of *Cuckoo's Nest*" contains material from *Ken Kesey* (New York: Ungar, 1981) and is reprinted here with the permission of the author.

Portions of "*Tough Guy* Goes Hollywood: Mailer and the Movies" originally appeared in substantially different form in *New Hampshire College Journal*.

Library of Congress Catalogue Card No.: 93-72985

ISBN: 0-87972-641-5 Clothbound
      0-87972-642-3 Paperback

Cover art by Gary Dumm

Design by Dumm Art

In memory of my father,

George W. Tepa
(1908 - 1992)

A good man, a wise man, a brave man
who did not go gentle into that good night

Acknowledgments

My thanks to all of the contributors to this volume, especially to Jerry Klinkowitz, whose groundbreaking work in American literature continues to surprise and inspire me, and to Barry Leeds, whose keen insights into literature and culture have been exceeded only by his friendship and support.

Several essays in this volume grew out of papers presented at the Popular Culture and American Culture Associations' National Meetings. Pat Browne and Ray B. Browne have been tireless in their efforts to foster the study of popular culture and to make the scholarly community aware of its scope and significance; I am indeed in their debt, as are many contemporary scholars.

I am grateful to Andrea Diehl and to Virginia Sandy, Department of Communications, Bennington College, for their assistance in securing necessary permissions for material from *The Bennington Review*; to those of my colleagues who read portions of the manuscript, suggested topics for me to pursue, or simply listened to my ideas; and to Christy Schurmann for her expertise and technical assistance on this project.

The George Eastman House/International Museum of Photography proved invaluable in my research: I am grateful to Ed Stratmann, Becky Simmons, and especially Kaye MacRae. I am particularly indebted to Tracey Lemon, who helped me to locate countless reference materials necessary for my work.

The University of Rochester's Rush Rhees Library also provided me with numerous materials and services.

Finally, I wish to express my thanks to Jane H. Tepa, for her encouragement and support. And to my husband, Alan Lupack, whose judgments I rely on and whose opinions I trust beyond all others: as always, this is not only for you but also *because* of you.

Contents

On Adapting the Contemporary American Novel

Barbara Tepa Lupack

My task which I am trying to achieve is, by power of the written word, to make you hear, to make you feel—it is, before all, to make you see.

Conrad, Preface,
The Nigger of the Narcissus

The task I'm trying to achieve is above all to make you see.

D. W. Griffith

"Sound cinema is literate," wrote Geoffrey Wagner in *The Novel and the Cinema*. "It therefore partakes of literature" (9). Hollywood, however, has rarely been noted for its literacy. Yet, as Joy Gould Boyum observed in *Double Exposure: Fiction into Film*, "from its very beginnings, it has turned to literature for inspiration and persisted in the practice of translating books into film" (3).

Revolutionary French film artist and magician Georges Méliès, who was the first to exploit the medium of film as a means of personal expression, was also the first to adapt a work of literature for the screen. His *A Trip to the Moon* (1902), based on Jules Verne's *From the Earth to the Moon*—the scenario for which was written by Méliès himself—lampooned the scientific and mechanical interests of the new century by wittily depicting the lunar dream world of the professors and the futuristic hopes of some of the scientific societies (Jacobs 27). (See Figure 1.) For years afterwards, Méliès continued to surprise moviegoers with similar "fantastic fantasies"; his best-known works included titles such as *Gulliver's Travels* (1902); *Robinson Crusoe* (1902); *The Damnation of Faust* (1903), based on Berlioz's celebrated song poem; and *The Legend of Rip Van Winkle* (1905).

Following the lead of Méliès and of other French and Italian filmmakers who looked to literature (especially to the novels of Balzac, Hugo, Dickens, Bulwer-Lytton, and Sienkiewicz) for story material, Americans began turning routinely to novels as well as to poems, plays, and short stories. Edwin S.

1

Figure 1. A scene from Méliès' *A Trip to the Moon* (1902), considered to be the first film adapted from a literary work. (Photo credit: Eastman House)

Porter, generally acknowledged today as the father of the story film and credited with the introduction of the principles of film editing, became a dominant figure in the film industry with innovative works such as *The Life of an American Fireman; The Great Train Robbery* (which surpassed Méliès' *The Impossible Voyage* in popularity and established Porter as the leading filmmaker of his day); and *Uncle Tom's Cabin*, the largest and most expensive picture made until that time in America. (Produced for Edison, *Uncle Tom's Cabin* ran the extraordinary length of 1,100 feet and included fourteen scenes and a prologue and, according to its own advertisement, departed "from the methods of dissolving one scene into another by inserting announcements with brief descriptions" [Jacobs 42].) After leaving Edison, Porter pioneered with Adolph Zukor's Famous Players Company and directed their first motion picture, *The Count of Monte Cristo*, and went on to make other features, such as *The Prisoner of Zenda*—though his later work did not deliver fully on his early promise.

The tremendous demand for stories caused other moviemakers to turn their attention increasingly to literature and the stage for available material. One-reel screen presentations soon abounded, including, among many others, *Parsifal, The Lady or the Tiger, Ben Hur, As You Like It, Hiawatha, Evangeline, Dr. Jekyll and Mr. Hyde, The Merry Widow, Monsieur Beaucaire, The Scarlet Letter, The Last of the Mohicans, The Three Musketeers, Treasure Island, Martin Chuzzlewit, The Merchant of Venice, Alice's Adventures in Wonderland*, and *A Curious Dream* (the last of which was accompanied by an interesting testimonial, no doubt the first of its kind in motion pictures: "Gentlemen: I authorize the Vitagraph Company of America to make a moving picture from my 'Curious Dream.' I have their picture of John Barter, examining his gravestone, and find it frightfully and deliciously humorous" [Signed] Mark Twain [Jacobs 76]). The adaptation of fiction and plays was quickened by the censorship attacks that flared up in 1907-1908,[1] since producers felt fairly certain that material taken from decorous literary works would ensure a kind of substantiveness and respectability which might discourage critics from attacking their productions.

The most revered and influential film artist of his day and perhaps of all film history, D. W. Griffith, also looked to literature, both high and low, to help forge the distinctive language of American film. Further refining the art of Méliès and of Porter through his own new techniques,[2] he adapted, among others, works by Jack London, Shakespeare, Hood, Tolstoy, Poe, O. Henry, Maupassant, Stevenson, and Tennyson; in one year alone, the hundred or more pictures which he produced included *The Taming of the Shrew, The Song of the Shirt, Edgar Allan Poe, The Cricket on the Hearth, The Necklace*, and *The Lover's Tale*. These earliest pictures were followed by such important films as *Pippa Passes*, which was greeted enthusiastically by *The New York Times* (Browning "is being presented to the average motion picture audiences, who have received it [*Pippa*] with applause and are asking for more" [10 October 1909]); *Ramona*; a remake of *Enoch Arden* (the first "two-reeler"); *Orphans of the Storm*, adapted from the play *The Two Orphans*; and, of course, his remarkable *The Birth of a Nation*, based on Thomas Dixon's racist bestseller *The Clansman* and now hailed as the first film classic.

Griffith, in turn, was soon followed by other talented, if lesser known, men with literary proclivities:[3] Sidney Olcott, whose spectacular *Ben Hur* (1907) made a huge amount of money for its manufacturer (and, notably, forced the resolution of the copyright problem when the courts determined, in 1912, that literary rights existed in all filmed works);[4] Frank Lloyd, renowned for his screen adaptations of literary classics (*The Gentleman from Indiana*, *A Tale of Two Cities*, *David Garrick*); John Stuart Robertson, brought to prominence with his *Dr. Jekyll and Mr. Hyde* (1920); James Cruze, remembered for satires like *Ruggles of Red Gap* (1923) and *Beggar on Horseback* (1923), adapted from a stage play by the same name; and the foreign invasion (particularly Sergei Eisenstein, the Soviet director whose brief tenure in Hollywood yielded an early script for *An American Tragedy*; and Sweden's Victor Seastrom, singled out in 1927 as one of Hollywood's top ten directors, largely because of the success of his adaptation the previous year of *The Scarlet Letter*).

Early movies were met with praise not only for their innovation but for the promise they offered in educating their audiences. In fact, critic Stephen Bush, writing in *The Moving Picture World* in 1911, suggested that the introduction of the literary classics to the masses might be the very mission of the new medium of the motion picture:

> It is the masterpiece of the ages that especially invites filming, and the reason for it is very plain. An epic that has pleased and charmed many generations is most likely to stand the test of cinematographic reproduction.... After all, the word "classic" has some meaning. It implies the approval of the best people in the most enlightened times. The merits of a classic subject are nonetheless certain because known and appreciated by comparatively few men. It is the business of the moving picture to make them known to all. (qtd. in Boyum 4)

Jack London likewise believed that motion pictures could batter down "the barriers of poverty and environment" and provide "universal education." "The greatest minds," he wrote in *Paramount Magazine* (1915), "have delivered their messages through the book or play. The motion picture spreads it on the screen where all can read and understand—and enjoy."[5]

Film adaptation remained popular in the following decades (so much so, in fact, that André Bazin,[6] in "The Evolution of the Language of Film," observed—with some overstatement—that "the film-maker [of the 1930s and 40s]...is, at last, the equal of the novelist" [40].) But it reached some kind of zenith in 1939, when nearly every film competing for the Academy Awards was an adaptation: *Of Mice and Men; Goodbye, Mr. Chips; The Wizard of Oz; Wuthering Heights;* and *Gone with the Wind*—and when even the winner of the Oscar for best short subject was an adaptation, Walt Disney's version of Hans Christian Andersen's "The Ugly Duckling."[7]

Furthermore, writes Morris Beja in *Film & Literature* (1977), "If the Academy Awards tell us anything about the American film industry or its sense of itself, then it is interesting that (according to my calculations) since their inception in 1927-28, more than three-fourths of the awards for 'best picture' have gone to adaptations; and of those, about three-fourths were based on either novels or short stories. The figures would be roughly the same for the New York Film Critics Award for 'best motion picture,' which began in 1935" (78). And George Bluestone, noting that no precise record has been adequately kept, estimated in his important study of *Novels into Film* (1957) that between 17 and 50 percent of total studio productions are "filmed novels" (3).

Adaptation continues to be a lively art, as even the most cursory glance at Hollywood and independent films—particularly films recent, current, or in development—demonstrates: *The Last of the Mohicans; Of Mice and Men; The Remains of the Day; A River Runs Through It; Howard's End; Ethan Frome; The Custom of the Country; The Age of Innocence; The Buccaneers; The Witches of Eastwick; The French Lieutenant's Woman; Terms of Endearment; The Sheltering Sky; In Country; Cannery Row; Tender Mercies; My Left Foot; Deliverance; Passage to India; A Room with a View; Trial; Tess; Naked Lunch; Less Than Zero; Postcards from the Edge; The Hotel New Hampshire; Heartburn; The Book of Daniel; Wide Sargasso Sea; This Boy's Life; Jurassic Park.* Today's adaptations, moreover, are not restricted to literary classics, and embrace many genres: mysteries and thrillers (*Silence of the Lambs, The Hunt for Red October, Patriot Games, The Pelican Brief*); horror tales (*The Shining, Carrie,* and Stephen King's other works—a virtual category of their own); crime stories and sagas (*Goodfellas; The Godfather; The Firm*); even Americanized remakes of foreign films (*Sommersby*).

Yet adaptation has always had more than its share of detractors. Vachel Lindsay, as long ago as 1915 in *The Art of the Moving Picture*, the first important book of cinema criticism in the United States, was passionately taken with the new medium and championed "film as art"; but he argued against adaptation on the grounds that it worked against the film's uniqueness. A decade later, in "The Movies and Reality" (1926), Virginia Woolf expressed a similar view: alliance between cinema and literature, she held, was "unnatural" and "disastrous" to both forms. Books especially would be hurt, becoming "unfortunate victim" as the "parasite" movies preyed on them with "immense rapacity." "All this, which is accessible to words, and to words alone," she wrote, "the cinema must avoid."[8] And, later still, Hannah Arendt came to the defense of the high culture she felt was being diminished by the popular arts:

> The entertainment industry is confronted with gargantuan appetites, and since its wares disappear in consumption, it must constantly offer new commodities. In this predicament, those who produce for the mass media ransack the entire range of past and present culture in the hope of finding suitable material. This material, however, cannot be offered as it is; it must be prepared and altered in order to become entertaining.... The danger is...precisely that it may become very entertaining indeed; there are also many great authors of the past who have survived centuries of oblivion and neglect, but it is still an open question whether they will be able to survive an entertaining version of what they have to say. (qtd. in Boyum 7)

More recent filmmakers and commentators, while less concerned with the distinctions between high and low art, have often been equally vocal in expressing their disdain for adaptations. "It is hard to think of a truly revolutionary film that was derived from a novel" (38), argued George W. Linden in his text *Reflections on the Screen* (articulating a view quite common among many academics and some filmmakers as well). "Film has nothing to do with literature," Ingmar Bergman contended (though his works, especially in their symbolism and ambiguity, are quite literary); "the character and substance of the two art forms are usually in conflict." Bergman concluded that "we should avoid making films out of books" (Wagner 29). Alain Resnais agreed that he would not want to shoot an adaptation: "I think that the writer has completely expressed himself in the novel," he said, "and that wanting to make a film of it is a little like re-heating a meal" (Richardson 16, citing Armes). And Jean-Luc Godard (forgetting, at least momentarily, his own attempts at adaptation) noted that the only way he could think of filming a novel would be to show it, page by page, on the screen.[9]

Still other critics and commentators have attacked adaptation on the grounds that it is a lesser art which lacks the novelty and impact of the original. George Bluestone, in *Novels into Film*, concluded that, despite superficial similarities, novels and movies are essentially antithetical forms, and that adaptations, even at their best, are lesser works of art than their sources—"disappointing lead" rather than "surprising deposits of gold" (219). (Boyum [8] demonstrates, however, that Bluestone's analysis, published in 1957, *is* largely correct in terms of American films of the 1950s. During that time, threatened by the loss of their audiences to television and devastated by the Supreme Court ruling that forced studios to divest themselves of their theaters, movies—she writes—were at their absolute nadir, both financially and aesthetically, with beach blanket teen-flicks and 3-D horror films abounding.)

Yet the arguments against adaptation are more often arguments against movies themselves or against film-as-it-was rather than film-as-it-is—"about film when it was synonymous with Hollywood and had to submit to the taste of the moguls, the strictures of the star system, and the censoring eye of the Hayes office; about film when it was more of a mass medium than it is today and, consequently, operated with very different notions as to the nature of its audience" (Boyum 18). Today, as film has evolved (its evolution in many ways paralleling that of the novel and resulting in a relation so close that Marshall McLuhan remarked of it: "Film, both in its reel forms and in its scenario and script forms, is completely involved with book culture" [Beja 51-52]), film's very aesthetic has changed; and, accordingly, so have film adaptations.

Ironically, many contemporary authors, rather than helping to quell the literary backlash against the movies, have themselves added to it.[10] Joseph Heller seemed to speak for a number of novelists when he observed: "I can't think of any film ever adapted from any work of literature that I or other people feel has any quality to it that even approaches the original work of literature that was its source" (Wagner 6).

Not surprisingly, the attitudes of contemporary writers towards films and towards the film industry are in large part shaped by their own relationship with Hollywood. Some authors, like J. D. Salinger, whose fine story "Uncle Wiggily in Connecticut" was made into *My Foolish Heart*, a tear-jerking, sudsy vehicle for Susan Hayward, were so traumatized by their experiences that they decided never to become involved again. Fortunately, however, few have gone to the lengths which Willa Cather did. Upset by the way Hollywood had twice, in 1924 and 1934, mangled her novel *A Lost Lady* (1923), she made a point of eschewing any further contact with the cinema while she lived. And she provided in her will that after her death the executors should "not...release, license or otherwise dispose of my literary properties for any dramatization whether for the purpose of the spoken stage or otherwise, motion picture, radio broadcasting, television (or any other) mechanical reproduction whether by means now in existence or which may hereafter be discovered or perfected" (Fosburgh 1).

Generally, though, writers—if no less averse philosophically to Hollywood—are more pragmatic in their dealings. John Updike and Saul Bellow, for example, allow their work to be sold—yet they profess to be quite glad when the films from their works are never made. Updike received about $400,000 almost two decades ago for *Couples*; he banked some of the money, spent some, and—when the film fell through—affirmed that such an arrangement was "the best of all possible worlds" (Fosburgh 1). Similarly, Bellow, saying he was completely indifferent to the machinations of Hollywood, added, "I'm delighted to say that I've received money for two pictures and the pictures were never made. It's the perfect situation" (Fosburgh 1). But perhaps most realistic in his attitude and in his assessment of the writer's relationship with the film industry was Bernard Malamud. While appalled by several of the movies based on his novels, he acknowledged that it is important for a writer to remember that he takes the money in order to get on with his work. "When you think about it that way, you really have nothing to complain about" (Fosburgh 1).

Still other writers actually find some fascination in the adaptation of their own works. William Styron—though far from delighted by the film as a whole—admits to liking parts of the movie, *Sophie's Choice*; but he deliberately remained uninvolved in the process of bringing the book to the screen. To explain his decision, Styron borrowed "an ugly old phrase of some writer...who said that writing a script from his own novel would be like a dog eating its own vomit. I don't feel quite that vividly about it, but it would be going over terribly familiar ground" (Morris 69). Conversely, Kurt Vonnegut, who wrote that he loved both Director George Roy Hill and Universal Pictures for making "a flawless translation" of *Slaughterhouse-Five* which was harmonious with what he felt when he wrote the book (though he participated only marginally in the movie), concluded that ultimately he doesn't like film. It "is too clankingly real, too permanent, too industrial for me."[11]

And still other contemporary authors have gained respect, even admiration, for the film medium. Jerzy Kosinski, for many years adamantly opposed to the filming of his fiction ("to transfer my novels into a film would strip them of the very power they have" [Fosburgh 13]), eventually wrote the prize-winning screenplay for *Being There*, undertook the writing of screenplays for other of his works, and even appeared on the Hollywood stage as a presenter at the Academy Awards. Writers like E. L. Doctorow and Norman Mailer have also demonstrated their continuing interest in film adaptations of their works. Doctorow, who concedes that he doesn't know "how anyone can write today without accommodating eighty or ninety years of film technology" (McCaffery 40), applauds the fact that film introduces his stories to a whole new audience; while Mailer, who said once in an interview that, "Film and literature are as far apart as, say, cave painting and song" (Wagner 28), has himself tried his hand at movie work. Mailer has gone so far as to write, direct and produce some features, memorable largely for their failure, as well as appearing in a cameo role in one of the adaptations of Doctorow's novels before directing his own script of *Tough Guys Don't Dance*, a major commercial release. (Even James Joyce was interested enough in cinema to become involved in opening the first movie house in Dublin, which ultimately failed. And, at Sergei Eisenstein's instigation, Joyce met with the filmmaker to discuss Eisenstein's ideas about cinema—e.g., that film was more able to make mental processes, such as interior monologue, accessible, comprehensible and vivid than literature. An impressed Joyce later remarked to a friend that he could imagine Eisenstein succeeding in his wish to bring *Ulysses* to the screen.)

Nevertheless, as film adaptations—both good and bad—continue to appear, the debate about their merits continues as well.[12] Popular novelist Larry McMurtry admits that he himself has tried to get a hold of the "slippery relationship" between the film and the novel since 1957 (the year of Bluestone's classic study), but it had squirmed out of his reach. In his essay, "The Situation in Criticism: Reviewers, Critics, Professors," McMurtry asks "What [then] is the relationship? Are the two arts sister arts, or merely cousins by marriage? Or could it be that something darker is suggested? Perhaps the relationship of film to movie is that of whore to customer, of mortician to cadaver, of cannibal to meal? On the other hand, perhaps the relationship is only that of near neighbors" (75). Film critic Pauline Kael, wondering "who started the divide and conquer game of aesthetics in which the different media are assigned their special domains like salesmen staking out their territories—you stick to the Midwest and I'll take Florida," suggests an excellent starting point for discussion: "What motion picture art shares with other arts," she writes, "is perhaps even more important than what it may, or may *not*, have exclusively" (Beja 59).

Most of the novels represented in this volume—*Slaughterhouse-Five, One Flew Over the Cuckoo's Nest, Catch-22, The World According to Garp,* and *Being There,* for example—are extraordinary in that they virtually defined their ages and provided not only catchphrases for but also concepts significant to the popular culture. All are novels which address important and often controversial contemporary issues, from loss of a sense of self to the institutionalization of a bureaucracy which represses individualism, from the politics of sexism and gender to violence and insanity as metaphors for modern life. And the adaptations of those novels, especially by some of the most talented filmmakers of our time—Mike Nichols (*Catch-22*); Milos Forman (*One Flew Over the Cuckoo's Nest*); George Roy Hill (*Slaughterhouse-Five, Garp*); Hal Ashby (*Being There*); Hector Babenco (*Ironweed*); Steven Spielberg (*The Color Purple*); Alan J. Pakula (*Sophie's Choice*); Robert Benton (*Billy Bathgate*)—are at times equally compelling. They confirm the fact that the uniqueness of a film does not necessarily have to be undermined by the fact that it has been adapted and that film deserves to be treated as a distinctive art form—even when good novels do not always make good films.

Graham Greene once commented that "there is no need to regard the cinema as a completely new art; in its fictional forms it has the same purpose as the novel" (Beja 51). William Kennedy recognized similar possibilities inherent in film (and particularly in translating his own work for the screen): he wrote about adaptation as a juggling act which involved reduction but which could still produce "the nugget."[13] This, then, is the purpose of the current volume: to examine the nuggets—the visions of both novelists and filmmakers—and to discover how, in their fictional forms, those visions converge and diverge. For, as Boyum writes, in assessing an adaptation we are not really comparing book with film but rather interpretation with interpretation—the novel that we ourselves have re-created in our imaginations, out of which we have constructed our own individualized "movie," and the novel on which the filmmaker has worked a parallel transformation.

> For just as we are readers, so implicitly is the filmmaker, offering us, through his work, his perceptions, his vision, his particular insight into his source. An adaptation is always, whatever else it may be, an interpretation. And if this is one way of understanding the nature of adaptation and the relationship of any given film to the book that inspired it, it's also a way of understanding what may bring such a film into being in the first place: the chance to offer an analysis and an appreciation of one work of art through another. (61-62)

The essays in the volume help us to do just that—not only to hear, feel, and see the words of the contemporary American novelist adapted to the screen but also to understand more about the complex, sometimes controversial relation of book to film.

NOTES

[1]"Family values" is hardly a recent issue. Jacobs notes that, as far back as 1907, *The Chicago Tribune* condemned the nickelodeon for "ministering to the lowest passion of children.... Proper to suppress them at once...influence wholly vicious.... They cannot be defended. They are hopelessly bad." Declaimed the *Christian Leader* that same year, "A set of revolutionists training for the overthrow of the government could find no surer means than these exhibitions [of early movies]" (63).

The chief motive for the flood of such abuse was essentially economic and not ideological: "Movies had suddenly become a competitor of the church, saloon, and vaudeville.... Confronted with such a formidable competitor, several such social institutions cloaked their economic fear in moral censure." But George Kleine of Kalem Pictures and other powerful men of early motion pictures fought back against the attacks, soon winning much public support—even from some unlikely sources. In Philadelphia, for instance, a prominent pastor, Dr. McClellan, went so far as to suggest that the movie might be utilized by the church to attract non-churchgoers; and *Harper's Weekly* affirmed that "many moral lessons are to be had from these brief moving picture performances." Eventually, "the opposition, realizing they were waging a losing battle, changed their tactics: instead of fighting their competitor, they formed an alliance with it" (64-65). But regulation nevertheless became the norm:

the first National Board of Censorship of Motion Pictures (later renamed the National Board of Review) was formed in 1909. Still, controversies over censorship issues continued to erupt.

Robert Sklar pointed out in *Movie-Made America: A Social History of American Movies* (18) that at the heart of the moral and social uneasiness over early movies was the fact that the movies represented a working class pastime which had appeared without the control—or even the knowledge—of the middle-class guardians of culture.

To lessen the uneasiness, observed Joel W. Finler in *The Hollywood Story*, often "early film-makers turned to uplifting subjects. They adapted literary and stage works for the screen, and adopted the middle-class values of the period which stressed the sanctity of home and family, embraced Christian values, and were strongly anti-trade union and heavily patriotic—especially in response to America's involvement in World War I" (10).

[2]In his adaptation of Tennyson's *Enoch Arden*, for example, Griffith introduced his new device, the close-up (which had been used before, in passing, by Porter in his *Great Train Robbery*). The close-up brought a new concept into the technique of editing, as did Griffith's use of cross-cutting, which ironically brought a torrent of abuse down upon the experimenter.

Jacobs explains:

> "It's jerky and distracting! How can people tell a story jumping about like that? People won't know what it's all about!"
> Griffith was ready for all dissenters.
> "Doesn't Dickens write that way?"
> "Yes, but writing is different."
> "Not much. These stories are in pictures, that's all." (103)

(The anecdote is first cited by Mrs. D. W. Griffith [Linda Arvidson]. Sklar [50-51] refers to it as well.)

Another of Griffith's adapted films, *Ramona*, was the first to use "distant views," the model for all later panoramic shots. For a brief discussion of Griffith's innovations, see Thomas and Vivian C. Sobchack's *An Introduction to Film* (Boston: Little, Brown and Company, 1980) or Paul O'Dell's *Griffith and the Rise of Hollywood* (New York: A. S. Barnes, 1970). For a more complete discussion of Griffith's innovations, see Tom Gunning, *D. W. Griffith and the Origins of American Narrative Film* (Urbana: University of Illinois Press, 1991).

[3]And not only directors but also many of Hollywood's best producers are remembered for the literary adaptations on which they left their special stamp: Pandro S. Berman (*Of Human Bondage*); Samuel Goldwyn (*Dodsworth*, *Wuthering Heights*); Arthur Hornblow, Jr. (*Ruggles of Red Gap*); Albert Lewin (*The Good Earth*); Kenneth Macgowan (*Little Women*); Robert F. Sisk (*The Plough and the Stars*); Hunt Stromberg (*The Thin Man*); and Darryl F. Zanuck (*Les Misérables*).

[4]Mrs. D. W. Griffith (Linda Arvidson) demonstrated the rather cavalier attitude of early filmmakers concerning literary copyrights. In *When the Movies Were Young* (1925; rpt. New York: Dover, 1969), she wrote of Griffith's film company, Biograph: "As the days went by we produced many works of literary masters—Dickens, Scott, Shakespeare, Bret Harte, O. Henry, and Frank Norris. We never bothered about 'rights' for the little one-reel versions of five-act plays and eight-hundred-page novels. Authors and publishers were quite unaware of our existence" (90).

[5]Opinions about the medium's educational merits changed. G. K. Chesterton ("About the Films," from *As I Was Saying* [London: A. P. Watt & Son, 1936]), for instance, saw limits to the educational value of cinema. He perceived, in particular, "a real danger of historical falsehood being popularized through the film"—a criticism still raised by viewers and critics today.

Along a similar line, George Bernard Shaw (in Archibald Henderson's *Table-Talk of G. B. S.* [London: Chapman & Hall, 1925]) saw the enormous development of the film industry as detrimental, especially to the dramatic arts. Films must aim "at the average American millionaire and a Chinese coolie, a cathedral-town governess and a mining-village barmaid." A "huge national audience makes mediocrity compulsory," he concludes. "[D]emocracy always prefers second-bests."

And James T. Farrell, in *The League of Frightened Philistines* (New York: Vanguard, 1945), noted that films "tell huge masses of people how and what to believe"; the constant struggle to reach the widest possible audience means "there is no time for costly experiments for educating the tastes of this [heterogeneous] audience. Staple commodities in art, based on the lowest common denominator of the mentality and the emotional life of the audience, must be produced." (Cited in Harry W. Geduld, ed., *Authors on Film* [Bloomington: Indiana University Press, 1972]: 115; 118-19; 225; 238).

[6]André Bazin was not only an important critic in his own right but also a significant influence on many younger French critics who went on to become prominent film directors: François Truffaut (who once remarked, "I don't want to make films for people who don't read" [Beja 73]); Jean-Luc Godard; Claude Chabrol.

[7]By that time, many writers, including Fitzgerald, Faulkner and Steinbeck, had already gone to Hollywood, sometimes to adapt their own works but more often to write screenplays directly for film; others, like Truman Capote, soon followed. (The observation about the zenith of adaptations in 1939 is Boyum's.)

[8]Woolf's comments are often quoted in relation to film adaptation. Geduld reprints her article, originally published in *New Republic* (4 August 1926); Boyum refers to Woolf's ideas in her analysis, as do Beja (78) and others. (Beja, in particular, makes the point that Woolf wrote her essay before the advent of sound film and suggests that her perspectives on film might have been different had she had the opportunity to see the medium's progression.)

[9]As with Woolf's comments, Godard's remark is one familiar to those who write about or study adaptation. It has been quoted often, by Wagner (28), Boyum (14), and others.

[10]The most recent, perhaps, is Michael Crichton. Interviewed about *Jurassic Park*, Crichton denied that he wrote the novel with a movie in mind. "They're different forms," he says. "If you want a movie, write a screenplay"—which is just what he did, for the movie *Westworld*. ("Author Interview," [Rochester, NY] *Democrat and Chronicle*, 11 June 1993, 4C.)

[11]Kurt Vonnegut, *Between Time and Timbuktu* (New York: Delacorte Press/Seymour Lawrence, 1972) xv. For a fuller discussion, see Jerome Klinkowitz's essay, "*Slaughterhouse-Five*: Fiction into Film," in this volume.

[12]Some of the earliest include the following: William A. Brady, "Have the Movies Ideals?" in *The Forum* (1918); Elbridge Colby, "Literature and the Movies," in *American Review* (1924); Alec Waugh, "Film and the Future," in *The Fortnightly Review* (1924); John Erskine, "No Plot is Needed in Moving Pictures," in *Theatre Magazine* (1927); M. Willson Disher, "Classics into Films," in *The Fortnightly Review* (1928); and "Galsworthy on the Talkies," in *The Living Age* (1930).

[13]David Thompson, "The Man Has Legs: William Kennedy Interviewed," *Film Comment* 21.2 (March-April 1985): 56. For a fuller discussion, see Benedict Giamo's essay, "*Ironweed* and the Snows of Reduction," in this volume.

WORKS CITED

Armes, Roy. *French Cinema Since 1946*. 2 vols. London: Zwemmer, 1966.

Bazin, André. "The Evolution of the Language of Cinema." *What Is Cinema?* 2 vols. Trans. by Hugh Gray. Berkeley: University of California Press, 1967.

Beja, Morris. *Film & Literature: An Introduction*. New York: Longman, 1979.

Bluestone, George. *Novels into Film*. Berkeley: University of California Press, 1957.

Boyum, Joy Gould. *Double Exposure: Fiction into Film*. New York: Universe Books, 1985.

Finler, Joel W. *The Hollywood Story*. New York: Crown Publishers, 1988.

Fosburgh, Lacey. "Why More Top Novelists Don't Go Hollywood." *The New York Times* 21 Nov. 1976, Sect. 2: 1, 13-14.

Geduld, Harry W., ed. *Authors on Film*. Bloomington: Indiana University Press, 1972.

Griffith, Mrs. D. W. (Linda Arvidson). *When the Movies Were Young*. 1925. New York: Dover, 1969.

Gunning, Tom. *D. W. Griffith and the Origins of American Narrative Film*. Urbana: University of Illinois Press, 1991.

Jacobs, Lewis. *The Rise of the American Film: A Critical History*. 2nd ed. New York: Teachers College Press, 1968.

Linden, George W. *Reflections on the Screen*. Belmont, CA: Wadsworth, 1970.

London, Jack. "The Message of Motion Pictures." *Paramount Magazine*, 1.2 (Feb. 1915).

McCaffery, Larry. "A Spirit of Transgression." *E. L. Doctorow: Essays and Conversations*. Ed. Richard Trenner. Princeton, NJ: Ontario Review Press, 1983. 31-47.

McMurtry, Larry. *Film Flam: Essays on Hollywood*. New York: Simon and Schuster, 1987.

Morris, Robert K. "Interviews with William Styron." *The Achievement of William Styron*. Ed. Robert K. Morris with Irving Malin. Rev. ed. Athens: University of Georgia Press, 1981. 29-69.

O'Dell, Paul. *Griffith and the Rise of Hollywood*. New York: A. S. Barnes, 1970.

Richardson, Robert. *Literature and Film*. Bloomington: Indiana University Press, 1969.

Sklar, Robert. *Movie-Made America: A Social History of American Movies*. New York: Random House, 1975.

Sobchack, Thomas and Vivian C. *An Introduction to Film*. Boston: Little, Brown and Co., 1980.

Wagner, Geoffrey. *The Novel and the Cinema*. Rutherford, NJ: Fairleigh Dickinson University Press, 1975.

SUGGESTIONS FOR FURTHER READING

Bálazs, Béla. *Theory of the Film: Characters and Growth of a New Art*. London: Dobson Books Ltd., 1952.

Braudy, Leo. *The World in a Frame: What We See in Films*. Garden City, NY: Anchor Press/Doubleday, 1976.

Cagin, Seth and Philip Dray. *Hollywood Films in the Seventies: Sex, Drugs, Rock'N'Roll, & Politics*. New York: Harper & Row, 1984.

Cohen, Keith. *Film and Fiction*. New Haven: Yale University Press, 1979.

———. *Writing in a Film Age: Essays by Contemporary Novelists*. Niwot, CO: University of Colorado Press, 1991.

Eisenstein, Sergei. *Film Form*. New York: Harcourt, Brace, Jovanovich, 1949.

Enser, A. G. S. *Filmed Books and Plays: A List of Books and Plays from Which Films Have Been Made, 1928-1967*. London: Deutsch, 1968.

Gifford, Denis. *Books and Plays in Films, 1896-1915: Literary, Theatrical and Artistic Sources of the First Twenty Years of Motion Pictures*. London: Mansell, 1991.

Harrington, John, ed. *Film and/as Literature*. Englewood Cliffs, NJ: Prentice-Hall, 1977.

Horton, Andrew, and Joan Magretta, eds. *Modern European Filmmakers and the Art of Adaptation*. New York: Frederick Ungar, 1981.

Jinks, William. *The Celluloid Literature: Films in the Humanities*. Beverly Hills, CA: Glencoe Press, 1971.

Langman, Larry. *Writers on the American Scene: A Guide to the Adaptations of American and Foreign Literary Works*. New York: Garland, 1980.

Limbacher, James L. *Haven't I Seen You Somewhere Before? Remakes, Sequels, and Series in Motion Pictures and Television, 1896-1978*. Ann Arbor: Pierian Press, 1979.

Magill, Frank N. *Cinema—The Novel into Film*. Pasadena: Salem Press, 1980.

Marcus, Fred Harold. *Film and Literature: Contrasts in Media*. Scranton: Chandler Publishing Company, 1971.

Murray, Edward. *The Cinematic Imagination: Writers and the Motion Pictures*. New York: Frederick Ungar, 1972.

Peary, Gerald and Roger Shatzkin, eds. *The Modern American Novel and the Movies*. New York: Frederick Ungar, 1978.

Quart, Leonard and Albert Auster. *American Film and Society Since 1945*. New York: Praeger, 1984.

Scholes, Robert, and Robert Kellogg. *The Nature of Narrative*. New York: Oxford University Press, 1966.

Slide, Anthony. *Early American Cinema*. New York: A. S. Barnes, 1970.

Spiegel, Alan. *Fiction and the Camera Eye: Visual Consciousness in Film and the Modern Novel*. Charlottesville: University Press of Virginia, 1976.

Welch, Jeffrey Egan. *Literature and Film: An Annotated Bibliography, 1909-1977*. New York: Garland, 1981.

The Waking Nightmare
of Mike Nichols' *Catch-22*

Robert Merrill and John L. Simons

There are a number of reasons why we should take another look at Mike Nichols' *Catch-22* (1970). The first is the continuing popularity of Joseph Heller's *Catch-22* (1961), the novel on which Nichols' film is based. The subject of more than two hundred published discussions as well as a conference at the Air Force Academy in 1986 honoring the twenty-fifth anniversary of the novel's publication,[1] *Catch-22* has rather obviously become one of the standard texts for anyone interested in post-World War II American fiction. A second reason is the continuing vitality of the film itself. Nichols' movie, which received mixed notices when it first appeared, almost twenty-five years later is still shown and discussed as a serious effort by one of our more important contemporary directors. Yet a third reason involves the study of film in general. One of the more interesting strands of film criticism is the comparison of a film and its literary source. Here such comparison is especially interesting, for the source is extremely well known and notoriously intractable to adaptation. Nichols' film teaches us once again that film is a truly independent medium even when it draws its materials from another source. The reassessment to follow should also confirm that Nichols' *Catch-22* is a flawed but highly underrated movie, one of the more important American films of the last twenty-five years.

I

If *Catch-22* the film differs significantly from *Catch-22* the novel, Heller would say that this is as it should be. "Most films that are adaptations of novels and plays don't succeed as films," Heller notes, "and one reason they don't succeed is because they try to do little more than to photograph, in the case of a novel, to photograph a work that is mainly literary, to put literary values into visual terms. *Catch-22* as a movie doesn't do that; it's non-literary" (Heller, "On Translating" 359). Strict fidelity to Heller's novel would have produced "a twelve-hour picture that everybody would find interminably dull and pretentious and verbose, and that would really not be a reflection of the book" (349). Heller's remarks are supported by the least effective—but most "faithful"—moments in Nichols' film. Buck Henry's

16

script seldom rises above cheap imitation when it draws its dialogue from the book, especially dialogue that tries to capture the loony "catch-22" conundrum. The movie succeeds when it develops visually a basic metaphor from Heller's book: the nightmarish and omnipresent danger of death in war.

Nichols' film does not so much reprise the novel's truculent satire on American capitalism as tell a story about the traumatizing fear of death, a fear that confuses the brain and blunts the conscience. Though he occasionally indulges satire on the Air Force and contemporary American society, Nichols builds his cinematic structure around the idea of death and the motif of a deranged dream, a nightmare state. Yossarian (Alan Arkin) is terrified of dying, and because he is terrified, he can think of nothing else but death. As the film demonstrates, however, Yossarian cannot confront the reality of death until he re-imagines his own death through that of his imagined double, Snowden (Jon Korkes). The surreal and oneiric Snowden scenes are therefore crucial to the film's circular action, its great bending arc that keeps returning, dreamlike, to Snowden's agonizing death-throes, an agony that can be transcended only after Yossarian *lives* through it.

Nichols' reformulation of Milo Minderbinder (Jon Voight) is also crucial. The Milo of the film is not so much the well-intentioned capitalistic expropriator of Heller's novel as he is a Nazi-like, all too Aryan angel of death, destroyer of youth, perverter of the life impulse. That Milo should be played by blond, baby-faced Jon Voight only enhances the viewer's perception that youth is destroying itself in the world Nichols projects. This is why Yossarian is haunted by two deaths: Snowden's and the boyish Nately's (Art Garfunkel). These three boys, Milo, Snowden, and Nately, are really children rather than men. Their perversities (Milo) and their innocence (Snowden and Nately) combine in the wounded Yossarian's mind to stigmatize him with guilt: he cannot act against the insane system represented by Colonels Cathcart (Martin Balsam) and Korn (Buck Henry). When he is stabbed by Nately's whore (Gina Rovere), Yossarian therefore experiences the blow as Snowden's wound and Nately's death. Death is the nightmare from which Yossarian cannot awaken until the end of the film, through the novel/film's mediation of Orr's escape to Sweden.

The film's opening scenes are essential to what we have called its cinematic structure. To engage his viewers, many of whom were no doubt jaded by familiar memories of Heller's book, Nichols took a daring risk: he began his *Catch-22* in blackness and in silence. No soundtrack, no music, nothing but titles appearing out of darkness, then vanishing into darkness—a brilliant contrast to the book's raucous cacophony of voices. As the beginning gradually turns into a depiction of approaching dawn—silhouetted mountains, the soft chirping of birds, a dog's distant bark—it appears that we are watching someone wake up. The engines of airplanes are slowly turned on and a deafening daylight roar replaces the silent darkness of night and dream. But what we are really comprehending—and the viewer's confusion here is a fruitful one, for he or she has been defamiliarized from the extremely familiar text of the novel—is the dream *content* of Yossarian's nightmare. Once "real," this scene is now taking place in the past, in Yossarian's feverish mind after he has been stabbed by Nately's whore and taken to the hospital. We are therefore trapped in the waking nightmare of Yossarian's life, his experience of a United States Air Force which he rightly deduces is trying to kill him.

Nichols maintains the quality of a dream even though it appears we have simply observed morning emerge from night. The bombers' roar drowns out all other sounds, including those of Yossarian, whom we originally view in a long shot, hands in his pockets, standing on the second floor and staring out of a bombed-out building. As the camera draws closer, we see that Yossarian is talking but cannot tell if he is talking to anyone. The effect is disturbingly dreamlike: something is happening, but we cannot deduce its significance. As the camera moves closer, we hear Yossarian talking but cannot tell what he is saying. Finally, the camera turns round him where two figures are standing and smiling sinisterly. In the filming of the shot, these figures seem to come out of the man standing on top of that broken building; that is, they seem to emerge *from* Yossarian. Are they real? In one sense they are obviously real, for they are Colonel Cathcart and Colonel Korn. But they are also dark presences that inhabit Yossarian's nightmare world. Lurking in back of him, they threaten him from behind. Indeed, they represent the unseen forces that are trying to kill Yossarian.

After he shakes hands with Cathcart and Korn (we do not know why) and moves down the stairs of the gutted building, Yossarian appears to be somewhat refreshed but circumspect. Amid the deafening din of the engines, he pauses to remove his airman's wings and throw them into the sand. A soldier, his back to Yossarian, moves his rake across the parched ground. As in a nightmare the figure frightens us because we cannot see its face (which allies it with the hidden or absent figures of Cathcart and Korn). The figure moves quickly toward Yossarian and stabs him in the side, then disappears around a building. Yossarian clutches his side and utters a muted cry, "Help, help," before falling to the ground. As Yossarian lies on the sand, holding his side and sinking out of consciousness, two shadows pass over him, the shadows of the planes he has sworn he will never fly again, death shadows that cross over him like knife-cuts from the blade of Nately's whore. Thus Yossarian's guilt for Nately's death twines itself with his guilt for making the deal with Cathcart and Korn; and soon this guilt will merge with the horrifying death of the young gunner Snowden, a scene that will be repeated no fewer than five times. (See Figure 2.)

Suddenly a blinding white light suffuses the screen, a light that glares so harshly it obscures rather than illuminates. Like an overexposure, it draws Yossarian out of his subsidiary nightmare and into his central horror. Echoing Yossarian's cry for help, a voice calls through the intercom, "Help him." Then

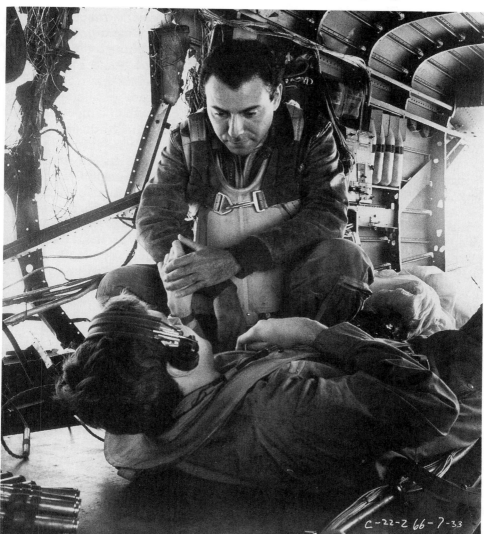

Figure 2. Yossarian (Alan Arkin) tries to help the dying gunner Snowden, an episode which recurs no fewer than five times. Copyright © 1970 by Paramount Pictures Corporation.

something startlingly surreal occurs. A blurring motion, that of a human figure who was once lying down and now suddenly sitting up, sweeps from the lower left corner of the screen to pass diagonally through the rest of the screen and disappear. What is it? At first glance it seems to be Yossarian himself, sitting in the bomb bay after having risen up. But that is impossible. Yossarian has been sitting up all the time, and in any case the shape has risen from a supine and not a prone position. A ghostly white blur, it is almost certainly the spirit of Snowden, more broadly the spirit of death, entering Yossarian's consciousness.

If the scene is phantasmagorical, its meaning is not. As the spirit enters Yossarian, we hear a bomb explode. The bomb and the spirit are thereby linked, and each symbolizes the terrifying reality of death for Yossarian. Snowden is therefore an especially crucial figure, and Nichols proceeds to construct his film around Yossarian's subsequent shock over Snowden's death. As Nichols has said in an interview, "You must understand that *Catch-22* is about a character blocking out a traumatic event, coming in contact with it, and finally collapsing as a result—just like a classical analysis of a hysterical, psychoanalytical situation—and coming out of it to make a decision" (qtd. in Thegze 12). Yossarian must pass through and accept Snowden's death before he can make the crucial decision that he will not die senselessly for Cathcart and Korn.

These opening scenes focus on Yossarian's nightmarish struggle against a world that threatens everyone but especially the innocent. Indeed, the theme of innocence, its saintliness and its corruption, dominates Nichols' film even more than Heller's novel. Among the characters explored in this light are the chaplain (Anthony Perkins), Major Danby (Richard Benjamin), Nately, Snowden, and Milo (the embodiment of a perverse innocence). In order to give cinematic coherence to this subject, Nichols needed a unifying motif, something associated not just with innocence but with the temptations of childhood. For it is not just death that the film mourns, but the deaths of young men, of boys. The metaphor Nichols chose is sweets or candy, specifically chocolates. This metaphor may have been suggested by Milo's referring to his consortium as M & M Enterprises, for that "&" does not fit Milo's name but rather the sugarcoated chocolates favored by children—and movie audiences.[2] Or it may be that Heller's description of the inanimate soldier in white as "hollow inside, like a chocolate soldier" (*Catch-22* 375), spurred Nichols and Buck Henry to apply that metaphor to the corruption of children through death, a corruption that links the soldier in white with Snowden's famous secret, i.e., divorced from spiritual concerns and moral action we are nothing more than matter (see 450).

After the first Snowden nightmare Yossarian flashes back, presumably from his hospital bed, to a scene in which he sits in the pilots' mess saying that everybody is out to kill him. One of the first voices we hear in response is that of Milo Minderbinder, who, in Buck Henry's script (his lines are not in the book), assures Yossarian, "No one's trying to kill you, sweetheart. Now, eat your dessert like a good boy." Those words, "sweet" (in the compound word "sweetheart"), "dessert," and "boy," anticipate Nichols' primary figure. It is perfectly appropriate that they should be uttered by Milo, the Moloch figure in this film, the baby-faced killer, the blond assassin. In later scenes we watch the puerile, almost childish Major Danby (a real alteration from the book and played by the innocuous Richard Benjamin) talking like a superannuated boy scout and sporting a Baby Ruth candy bar in his shirt pocket. Later we see Colonel Cathcart eating a box of Cracker Jacks, and, in a psychologically related scene, we watch him defecate before the chaplain. Critics have pointed out that Lyndon Johnson was fond of talking to his aides, even his cabinet officers, while sitting on the john. It is possible that Nichols intended that in-joke about Johnson and America's involvement in the Vietnam War. But the scene also works within the film, which clearly associates candy and excrement. Young men, almost children, are being killed in this film. The connection between candy, or children, and death, or excrement, is one meaning of Cathcart's eating the Cracker Jacks and then defecating before the embarrassed chaplain. (Nichols was in therapy for years and obviously knows his Freud.) This also ties in with the novel's celebrated soldier in white scenes, where the nurses substitute the bottle that collects waste for the in-take bottle, as if the two were interchangeable. In his own way Cathcart does not differ much from the hollowed out soldier in white, whom Heller describes in language equally applicable to the amoral Cathcart who "takes matter, he absorbs it, he excretes it or uses it up, and this is a natural process in which he is just one tiny phase of the whole cycle" ("An Impolite" 279). Nor should we ignore the connection between Cathcart's defecation and the slow, grisly spilling of Snowden's guts later in the film. This is Snowden's secret, of course: viewed only as matter, man is little more than a vegetable or an animal.

But it is through Milo Minderbinder himself that the theme of sweets and death is most forcefully presented. One of the most crucial moments in both film and novel occurs during Snowden's funeral service. Isolating himself from the socially corrupt world of the Air Force, Yossarian sits naked in a tree watching Snowden's funeral service. (See Figure 3.) As we are told in the novel, this tree is analogous to the Garden of Eden, to "the tree of life and of knowledge of good and evil, too" (Heller, Catch-22 269). But the tree also represents Yossarian's Rousseauistic rejection of social man, of the corrupt institutions of ownership and private property. Naked as natural man, shorn of the Air Force uniform Snowden bled all over, Yossarian renounces the uniform's meaning, its attempt to regiment his life (and to take it away). Milo invades this Edenic world with his latest lucrative scheme, for making money is the sexless Milo's single passion. This point is even more sinister because Nichols' Milo is, in the film's darkened treatment of him, the prototype of the inhuman Nazi master race, except that his god is not Die Volk, or race, but

Figure 3. Yossarian, naked, watches Snowden's funeral service. Copyright © 1970 by Paramount Pictures Corporation.

capitalism, free enterprise. It is not that Milo is unsympathetic toward Snowden; he simply cannot comprehend the idea of death itself. "Look at that. Looks like a funeral," Milo remarks. Yossarian responds, "It is. That's the kid who got killed in my plane last week." "Oh, what happened to him?" Milo asks offhandedly. The survival of his syndicate means everything to Milo, the death of the "kid," Snowden, means nothing. Milo's serpentine purpose for being in the tree is to entice Yossarian to ingest inedible chocolate-covered cotton, which Yossarian and the other men must eat because Milo has cornered the world's supply. Yossarian refuses and returns to watching Snowden's funeral. Alone, naked as a baby, he listens as the chaplain reads the following words over Snowden, the slaughtered innocent, the sacrificial lamb: "The Lord is my shepherd, I shall not want."

As photographed by cinematographer David Watkin, Snowden's funeral captures the ambiguity of Yossarian's traumatizing response to death. Yossarian is in the tree because he wishes to return to some kind of natural love and affection, some sort of lost innocence that Snowden embodied before he was killed. Yet Milo invades Yossarian's fantasy world. We see this in both the discussion about Snowden's death and the incident of the chocolate-covered cotton. Yossarian on one limb and Milo on another are separated yet joined, linked in the cinematic shot by an opening between the branches that creates a window-framed image of Yossarian's dilemma. Through that gap in the trees we observe the funeral taking place while they talk. Yossarian has yet to comprehend Milo's responsibility for Snowden's suffering and death—a responsibility both indirect (Milo is making money off this war) and direct (Milo has replaced Snowden's morphine with a "share" in M & M Enterprises). In addition, by not finding Milo guilty, Yossarian is evading his own responsibility for the death, as he will finally acknowledge when he refuses to make a deal with those secondary Satans, Cathcart and Korn, then decides to desert from the Air Force. Snowden is the link that ties Yossarian to Milo. Until Yossarian breaks that link and wakes from his nightmare, he will co-exist with Milo in a kind of guilty collusion, unable to act against his nightmarish fear of death and unwilling to affirm a genuine rebirth of consciousness and conscience.

Milo Minderbinder really makes two entrances into the world of the film. The first is the scene discussed above in which he functions as a member of a chorus of voices, introducing the theme of childhood and sweets. But we initially see him introduced as Lieutenant Minderbinder when Colonel Cathcart encounters him at the foot of his headquarters, holding up between his thumb and forefinger a shiny white hen's egg. (See Figure 4.) Milo brandishes the egg because his syndicate is about to buy and sell eggs for profit. How Milo can buy them for seven cents and sell them for five cents is one of the funniest plays upon logic and economic wheeler-dealing in the novel. But the film makes little of that motif. Rather, it establishes Milo's financial finagling within the context of young aviators flying off to lose their

Figure 4. The capitalistic Milo (Jon Voight) explains his latest scheme to Colonel Cathcart (Martin Balsam). Copyright © 19_0 by Paramount Pictures Corporation.

lives. Milo's egg (new life) underscores the theme of lost youth, the senseless, violent deaths that accompany Milo's mad capitalistic schemes. This is made even clearer when a returning plane blows up, killing the pilot and crew, while the indifferent Milo and Cathcart continue to discuss Milo's enterprises. As satire the scene is heavyhanded, but it points once more to the film's pervasive *kindertoten* motif, the theme of splattered youth.

For Milo human existence is a commodity. In the film he is so egregiously baby-faced because he has in no way grown up, has no comprehension of the temporal process of birth, life, and death. When the equally cherubic Nately dies as a result of Milo's mission against his own base (in the book Nately is killed on a raid), Milo cannot comprehend why Yossarian is so grievously upset. For Milo it is not even a rationalization when he tells Yossarian that Nately died for a noble cause, the growth and advancement of the syndicate. But Nately is dead, Yossarian replies. "Then his family will be rich," Milo responds. "They're already rich!" Yossarian shouts. "Then they'll understand," Milo says succinctly. Milo appears so monstrously inhuman because he fails to realize that a human life is nothing unless it is lived toward a higher end. After Yossarian finds the stock certificate for M & M Enterprises while searching for Snowden's morphine, Nichols cuts to Milo standing by the water counting and documenting a group of male Greek statuary, bleached and inanimate sculpture he is preparing for shipment.

Heller has said that Nichols omitted the pivotal moment in his book, the revelation of Snowden's secret, because there was no way to convey it within the visual medium of film (see "On Translating" 359). We disagree. By focusing on the death of Snowden and Milo's insidious if indirect responsibility for that death, Nichols lays bare the truth of Snowden's secret as Heller defines it: "It was easy to read the message in his entrails. Man was matter, that was Snowden's secret. Drop him out a window and he'll fall. Set fire to him and he'll burn. Bury him and he'll rot like other kinds of garbage. The spirit gone, man is garbage. That was Snowden's secret. Ripeness was all" (*Catch-22* 450). The real human "garbage" in *Catch-22* is Milo, not Snowden, for it is Milo, the ruthless war profiteer and dealer in human as well as material commodities, who demonstrates better than anyone else the truth of Snowden's secret. His spirit gone, Milo is the one who "spill[s] all over the messy floor" (450).

Nichols has explained why Yossarian runs away at the end of the film: "It all has to do with Snowden, that is, with fully understanding another person's death, which is in fact the thing which changes life when you understand it, and makes you decide to live your life differently. Because it means that you fully understand that you will die, and time spent not living your life as you feel you should becomes more and more expensive because you've understood that you will die. And that's what happens to Yossarian" (qtd. in Thegze 11). Once he awakens from the nightmare of Snowden's death and accepts the fact that life is not an absolute value in itself, that "living your life as you feel you should" is more important, Yossarian can take control over his own life and determine not to kill anymore in a war that is effectively over and that he continues to participate in only because of perverse, self-seeking orders from Cathcart and Korn. Acting on his own and taking responsibility for his own actions, Yossarian no longer feels immobilized by death and guilt. But he refuses to traffic with the devil after he is stabbed by Nately's maternal/erotic whore. His near-fatal wound in the side symbolizes his guilt over Nately's death as well as his anguish over Snowden's death. In classic Freudian terms, Yossarian must go back and re-experience Snowden's death, that traumatizing nightmare event, before he can be cured and go forward in the world. In the last of the five dreamlike Snowden scenes, Yossarian sees the shocking wound and understands what it means, but he nevertheless comforts Snowden, responds to the dying boy's "I'm cold, I'm cold" with traditional words of maternal comfort, "There, there. There, there," and covers Snowden with the nylon blanket of a parachute.

We deliberately invoke the image of the maternal or the Pietà figure because Yossarian gives birth to his own freed self after he wakes from the fearful Snowden dream. It is a long process and involves moving through a birthlike passageway that assimilates the womb-of-death metaphor Heller applies to the corridor Yossarian must pass through to reach the stricken Snowden. No longer willing to be the bombardier, squatting over the bomb bay and dropping eggs of death upon the cities and towns of Europe, Yossarian chooses life and moves through a different opening, the window in his sick-bay room, out into the blue world of the sea and freedom. Earlier, the wounded Yossarian gazed toward this window while talking to the chaplain about the dangerous profession of flying missions. Though Yossarian looked toward the chaplain, the figure at the center of the frame was a silhouetted soldier sitting in the window and staring sideways. We believe that shadowy black figure blocks Yossarian's release because it represents the ghostly, deathlike presence of Snowden, a presence Yossarian can overcome only when he has learned Snowden's secret. Now, after that truth has come to him, the window that separates Yossarian and the chaplain (as well as Danby) opens onto a sapphire sky. Yossarian learns about the escape of Orr (Bob Balaban), the dwarfish bombardier who ditches so many planes he is finally given up for dead and who is therefore, in the "catch-22" logic of book and film, sufficiently alive to escape to Sweden, a neutral country. Yossarian suddenly realizes that he can do the same thing. He leaps out the window and into space. (See Figure 5.)

Initially we do not know what the free-falling Yossarian is leaping into, nor does he. There will always be danger and the fear of death, but Yossarian has known these things with his own people, and most of his friends are already dead. His is not so much a desertion as a liberation. It is

Figure 5. Inspired by Orr's escape, Yossarian leaps to freedom. Copyright © 1970 by Paramount Pictures Corporation.

also a challenge to the timid chaplain and Danby, good but weak men, to emulate in some way his rebellion. Like a child, Yossarian leaps through the window onto the sand of the beach and goes running toward the sea. Nichols has said that he wanted the movie's conclusion to have an "unreal" quality to it. On a realistic level the chaplain and Danby cannot possibly hear Yossarian as the distance widens between them and the Air Force band blares "Stars and Stripes Forever"; as Nichols has argued, however, "We're not talking about something literal here; we're talking about a moral decision" (Thegze 11).

In the novel Yossarian decides to go to Rome to find and rescue Nately's whore's kid sister, then to undertake a seemingly impossible flight to Sweden. In the film the change from death to life, from Snowden to Sweden, from snowy death to an imagined Eden, returns us full circle to the image of man as child, but not to Milo or the leering, regressively infantile Cathcart and Korn; instead, we witness man re-fathering and re-mothering himself, as he is reborn into a life of resistance and moral action. The re-birth motif, so crucial to Nichols' psychoanalytical approach to *Catch-22*, echoes even as it reverses the famous poem about birth into death, Randall Jarrell's "The Death of the Ball-Turret Gunner" (1945). Heller may have had this poem in mind when he wrote *Catch-22*, for it perfectly recapitulates what happens to Snowden.

> From my mother's sleep I fell into the State,
> And I hunched in its belly till my wet fur froze.
> Six miles from earth, loosed from its dream of life,
> I woke to black flak and the nightmare fighters.
> When I died they washed me out of the turret with a hose.

A different kind of "nightmare fighter" himself, Yossarian wakes from the brutal dream of the turret gunner's death to a new life. It is therefore appropriate that Yossarian escapes into the sea in a tiny inflatable life raft with a paddle so small and fragile that it looks like a children's toy. This contributes to Nichols' fantasy theme of redeemed childhood. Yossarian rows off toward an uncertain future, but one he no longer dreads because he has decided to act on his own.

As Yossarian rows a few feet off shore, the camera pulls farther and farther away from his diminishing form. This suggests a crucial ambiguity. What can one small man do against the large worldly forces that militate against him? Not much, the speck-sized figure of Yossarian seems to indicate. But the important thing is Yossarian's break, not his subsequent success or failure in reaching Sweden. Once Yossarian has made this break, the action is effectively complete. Indeed, once the camera has withdrawn so far that Yossarian nearly vanishes, a quick cut thrusts the audience back into the very darkness and dreamlike silence with which the film began. A mother's womb? The interior of the human mind, Yossarian's or the viewer's? The darkened theater as seed-bed, birthplace of dreams? All these possibilities present themselves as the film's credits pass slowly by. It is left to the viewer, in his or her subjective state, to internalize the significance of Yossarian's decision, to give birth to his or her resolve regarding the forms of authority that function as the enemies of life, the betrayers of the innocent Snowdens in this world.

In short, the audience carries the dream of the film with them as they leave the theater. Nichols has taken the noisiest, most garrulous of recent American novels and reduced its "catch-22" language, its self-negating logic-chopping, to silence. "Silence is the essence of inwardness, of the inner life," writes Kierkegaard. "Only someone who knows how to remain essentially silent can really talk—and act essentially." For Kierkegaard, to act essentially is to live for truth, not to reduce truth or action to language games: "Talkativeness is afraid of the silence which reveals its emptiness" (Kierkegaard 69). *Catch-22* is full of Kierkegaardian talkativeness. Those who live so zealously "outside themselves," as Kierkegaard remarks, objectify their language in the same way they objectify, reify, and ultimately commoditize others. It is Yossarian's task—and his achievement—to distance himself from these people. His "There, there. There, there," coming out of the silent re-dreaming of Snowden's pathetic death, his wasted life, affirms Yossarian's rejection of their talky world.

II

Catch-22 is about "dying."
Mike Nichols (qtd. in "Some Are More" 345)

Catch-22 is about "the contemporary regimented business society."
Joseph Heller (qtd. in "Joseph Heller Replies" 30)

We do not wish to overemphasize the thematic differences between Heller's novel and Nichols' movie. Heller himself has praised what Nichols did to his book: "He caught its essence. He understood" ("Some Are More" 345). Presumably this "essence" is Yossarian's struggle to grasp Snowden's secret and to act accordingly, the central narrative line in both novel and film. Nonetheless, there are important differences that both suggest the limitations of Nichols' adaptation and underline the complexity of Heller's literary achievement. By ending with these differences we mean to point out what Nichols did not do as well as what he did.

Wayne C. Miller has already remarked upon the first important difference between novel and film. As Miller says, "Yossarian is not merely trying to escape the war. He is trying to escape the culture that produced the war and the traditions that produced the culture. Heller's satire is aimed at those traditions, at the institutions that capitalize on them, and at the individuals who adjust to the system and thrive within it." Miller argues that Nichols "missed" the novel's social and cultural satire, "the most important dimension in the novel" (Miller 384). We agree that Nichols downplays the novel's satirical elements, though we doubt that this was done because Nichols "missed" them. By eliminating Chief White Halfoat, Captain Black, Colonel Cargill, Lieutenant/Colonel/General Scheisskopf, Major Major Major's father, Corporal Whitcomb, ex-P.F.C. Wintergreen, Major Sanderson, the story of Doc Daneeka's untimely demise, and the several interrogation scenes, Nichols has indeed stripped away most of the novel's concern for the larger social context represented in the film almost entirely by Milo. In part this was done through necessity, as Nichols and Buck Henry whittled away at the forty-odd characters of some importance in Heller's novel. But we believe it was also done because Nichols took *Catch-22* to be *about* a character blocking out a traumatic event. Nichols seems to have read Heller's book as a psychological study of Yossarian. While Miller exposes the limitations of this approach, it should be acknowledged that Nichols' *Catch-22* has its own integrity as a psychological portrait that is not exactly Heller's but which does derive from the "essence" of Heller's novel.

A second and more important difference between novel and film involves their respective structures. As we noted earlier, Nichols begins with an ominous silence that is finally broken by the loud noise of planes being prepared for a mission. This is followed by the stabbing of Yossarian, the first Snowden flashback, the fierce battle scene in which Yossarian is wounded, and the second Snowden flashback. Finally, Yossarian wakes up in the hospital staring up at the chaplain, a moment similar to that with which Heller opens his novel. These first scenes focus almost entirely on Yossarian and the violence that surrounds him. By contrast, Heller's novel opens with a series of comic vignettes that surround and all but camouflage such serious moments as the death of the soldier in white and the first reported battle scene. In the first chapter alone we are given Yossarian's infatuation with the chaplain, the Texan's quaint political theories, the firemen who abandon a fire in the hospital kitchen to return to the air field where another fire *might* occur, and the colonel in Communications who is visited daily by "a gentle, sweet-faced woman with curly ash-blond hair who was not a nurse and not a Wac and not a Red Cross girl" (*Catch-22* 15).[3] Indeed, it is to the point that Yossarian is only pretending to be sick in Heller's first chapter, whereas in the film he is actually wounded. Throughout the first two hundred pages Heller continues to surround the more serious episodes with what seems Keystone Kops material and to describe the supposedly serious moments in comic fashion. Thus the book's well-deserved reputation for hilarity. Nichols includes a few of these comic touches, but, as his opening sequence strongly suggests, the dominant tone of his film is exceedingly grim.

Heller's novel embodies an elaborate "tonal structure" (see Burhans 42) that no film could be expected to duplicate (except perhaps that twelve-hour monster Heller invoked when sympathizing with Nichols' problems). The novel shifts gradually from a comic to a relatively earnest to a deadly serious representation of events. The events in question are often the same ones, repeated more or less often—a technique the film does not honor except in the crucial Snowden sequence. To achieve this gradual shift in representation and perspective, as well as to accommodate the large number of repetitions, Heller required a broad fictional canvas. Indeed, we would argue that Heller's novel, so often attacked for its excessive length, could hardly have been much shorter than it is. The great impact of the final Snowden scene, as well as the crucial Eternal City chapter, derives largely from the gradually developed contrast with earlier representations of the same event (Snowden's death) or the same material (wartime Rome). Heller's novel literally depends on its strange mixture of comic and tragic effects to achieve his announced purpose: "I tried consciously for a comic effect juxtaposed with the catastrophic. I wanted people to laugh and then look back with horror at what they were laughing at" ("So They Say" 234). We are first made to laugh at the novel's bizarre absurdities (even Snowden's death and the book's most insensitive figures, Milo and Aarfy); then we are shown these same events and characters in a different, rather more serious light; and finally we are exposed to these materials frontally, so to speak, so that we might be forced to gaze upon their catastrophic reality.[4] The effect is very different from the one Nichols creates, for the world of Nichols' film is always catastrophic. From its first moments the film validates Yossarian's fear that he is in deathly danger. The only significant tonal shift occurs at the end, where Yossarian achieves roughly the same enlightenment as in the book.

It is hard to avoid the conclusion that Nichols' film is simply less complex than Heller's novel. To understand what Heller has done we might consider a similar example of simplification, Milos Forman's 1975 adaptation of a novel often compared with Heller's, Ken Kesey's *One Flew Over the Cuckoo's Nest* (1962).[5] Both Kesey's novel and Forman's film focus on the battle of wills between Randle Patrick McMurphy, an inmate in a mental hospital, and Nurse Ratched, the ward's head nurse. In Kesey's novel, however, this contest goes through a series of stages no film could fully reproduce within a reasonable time frame (Forman's film is over two hours long as it is). For our purposes, the crucial stage is the one depicted in Part Two, where McMurphy discovers that he will be confined to the ward until Nurse Ratched agrees to release him. In Kesey's novel (but not in Forman's film) this discovery leads McMurphy to abandon his fight with the Big Nurse, and this in turn leads to the complete collapse of the patients' rebellion. Finally, when he can no longer stand his feelings of guilt, McMurphy sticks his fist through Big Nurse's window and the game is on again. This time it is not really a game, however, for McMurphy now understands that the consequences of his attack on the Big Nurse will be very serious indeed. Part Two is crucial to Kesey's meaning because it makes clear that McMurphy *chooses* to help the men on the ward, knowing full well (as he did not at first) the great risk to himself.[6]

Forman chose to eliminate almost everything from this crucial middle section of the story and to present the contest between McMurphy (Jack Nicholson) and Nurse Ratched (Louise Fletcher) as one uninterrupted action. He includes materials from this section but incorporates them into a different structure. Thus McMurphy is told at the swimming pool about Nurse Ratched's power over him, and later he puts his fist through her window. But in the film these two events occur within a few minutes of each other, and there is no chance for McMurphy to first retreat from his fight with Big Nurse and then consciously renew the struggle in the wake of Cheswick's suicide (deleted from the film), the ward's general demoralization, and his own uneasiness with his decision. Indeed, there is no time for any decision to be made, and when McMurphy punches out Nurse Ratched's window, it is made to seem an act of frustration at events on the ward instead of a calculated moral choice.[7] By effectively eliminating the middle stage of McMurphy's moral progress, Forman drastically simplifies his protagonist and renders him a far less impressive figure than Kesey's.

Other changes in Forman's film reinforce this unfortunate revision of Kesey's character. In the movie, for example, the basketball game and the fishing trip occur fairly early and are relatively lighthearted episodes, whereas in Kesey's novel they occur relatively late, *after* McMurphy reengages Nurse Ratched, and their humor is qualified by McMurphy's sense of impending doom. The fishing trip is especially affected by this change. In the film the trip is entirely improvised, as McMurphy impulsively escapes from the hospital, steals a bus with a number of patients aboard, and heads off to the sea. In the book, by contrast, the fishing trip is elaborately planned by McMurphy as a crucial step in the alternative therapy he offers the men. Not only does he not steal a bus, he has to go through the bureaucratic hassle of arranging for the transportation of a dozen patients on an officially sanctioned excursion. The fishing trip marks an important step in McMurphy's increasingly successful—but personally debilitating—effort to "save" the men from themselves. The episode is climaxed by Chief Bromden's discovery that, despite the apparent success of the trip, McMurphy has begun to look "dreadfully tired and strained and frantic, like there wasn't enough time left for something he had to do..." (Kesey 245). This expression is appropriate toward the end of McMurphy's struggle with Nurse Ratched and of course has no place (early or late) in Forman's film.

Like Forman, Nichols can move episodes around because the simplified version of his source aims at somewhat different effects. A good example is the scene in which McWatt flies too low over a raft and cuts Hungry Joe in half, then flies his plane into a mountain.[8] Nichols could move this event forward from its relatively late place in Heller's novel because in the film it is simply one more example of the pervasive violence we have been acutely aware of from the first frame. In the novel this grisly scene belongs in its late position because it contributes to the darkened effect Heller seeks toward the end. Here as elsewhere, Nichols simplifies Heller's tonal structure for the practical reasons that no doubt influenced Forman as well. We would add that Nichols simplifies his source no less thoroughly than Forman simplifies his, but the effect is less objectionable because Nichols does not thereby alter Heller's conception of Yossarian. With all his changes, Nichols continues to tell the "essential" story he found in his source.

A third important difference between Heller's novel and Nichols' film concerns their respective endings. Nichols follows Heller in most details, but he merely alludes to Yossarian's final refusal to fly more missions. By not depicting Yossarian's final rebellion, Nichols also deletes the sympathetic response of the other men, many of whom begin to question Cathcart's policies for the first time. Indeed, even the gung ho Havermeyer comes to Yossarian's tent to congratulate him on his gutsy stance. Nichols' decision to omit the effects of Yossarian's rebellion again parallels what Forman did at the end of *One Flew Over the Cuckoo's Nest*. Like Nichols, Forman follows his source in many details but elects to omit the most crucial effect of his hero's final rebellion. In the novel McMurphy's final physical attack on Big Nurse and her subsequent use of extensive shock treatment expose the nature of the ward so blatantly the men can no longer rationalize their voluntary participation; most of the men, including key figures such as Harding, check out of the hospital. We suspect that Forman omitted this feature of the ending for the same reason Nichols omitted Yossarian's influence on the other flyers: neither director could bring himself to be quite so optimistic in the crucial last moments of his film. Indeed, both Heller and Kesey seem to imply that the actions of their protagonists are anything but futile, for these actions have unmistakably positive effects upon the very men Yossarian and McMurphy are trying to influence. Nichols and Forman retain a few of these effects—Yossarian inspires the chaplain and Danby, and the inmates cheer Chief Bromden as he makes his escape after smothering McMurphy. But their endings are much less assertive than those in their sources. Nichols' decision to emphasize the small Yossarian in his tiny boat is an especially clear instance of directorial revision, and Forman allows only Chief Bromden to leave the hospital at the end of his film. We would not go so far as to speak of "Forman's pessimism regarding the possibilities for human growth" (MacDonald 172), but we do think Forman shares with Nichols the more chastened views about personal transformation characteristic of the 1970s, the era in which their adaptations appeared.

Such revision should not be attacked because it violates a sacred text. Certainly we have not intended to question Nichols' film because it deviates from Heller's novel. Nonetheless, even as we praise Nichols' adaptation as a superior film we think it is important to note that Nichols omits the crucial satirical features in his source, simplifies the narrative considerably, and alters the ending subtly but decisively in the direction of ambiguity. The result is no doubt predictable: *Catch-22* the film is less powerful than *Catch-22* the novel. Given the extraordinary problems in adapting this complex book, however, Nichols deserves our respect for succeeding as well as he did. Indeed, his film deserves to be ranked with the better American movies of the last twenty-five years, an achievement nourished by Heller's famous text but ultimately independent of it.

NOTES

[1]Indeed, our paper was first read at this conference.

[2]M & M candies were invented by the Mars candy company during World War II so that soldiers could eat candy without getting their hands sticky with chocolate.

[3]Several lines in this paragraph first appeared in Robert Merrill, "The Rhetorical Structure of *Catch-22*," *Notes on Contemporary Literature* 8 (May 1978): 9-11.

[4]For a more detailed discussion of the novel's rhetorical structure, see Robert Merrill, *Joseph Heller* (Boston: Twayne, 1987) 33-54.

[5]The two works were first paired soon after their respective publications. See especially Joseph J. Waldmeir, "Two Novelists of the Absurd: Heller and Kesey," *Wisconsin Studies in Contemporary Literature* 5 (1964): 192-204.

[6]As Barry H. Leeds notes in *Ken Kesey*, McMurphy "makes the clear moral choice to abandon self-interest and fight the Combine once again" (New York: Frederick Ungar, 1981) 33.

[7]Leeds makes much the same point (52).

[8]In the novel it is Kid Sampson who is cut in half. We can see no obvious reason for this minor change.

WORKS CITED

"An Impolite Interview with Joseph Heller." *A "Catch-22" Casebook*. Eds. Frederick Kiley and Walter McDonald. New York: Thomas Y. Crowell, 1973.

Burhans, Clinton S., Jr. "Spindrift and the Sea: Structural Patterns and Unifying Elements in *Catch-22*." *Critical Essays on Joseph Heller*. Ed. James Nagel. Boston: G. K. Hall, 1984.

Heller, Joseph. "On Translating Catch-22 into a Movie." *A "Catch-22" Casebook*. Eds. Frederick Kiley and Walter McDonald. New York: Thomas Y. Crowell, 1973.

_____. *Catch-22*. 1961. New York: Dell, 1962.

"Joseph Heller Replies." *The Realist* 50 (1964): 30.

Kesey, Ken. *One Flew Over the Cuckoo's Nest: Text and Criticism*. Ed. John C. Pratt. New York: Viking, 1973.

Kierkegaard, Soren. *The Present Age*. Trans. Alexander Dru. New York: Harper & Row, 1962.

MacDonald, George B. "Control by Camera: Milos Forman as Subjective Narrator." *A Casebook on Ken Kesey's* One Flew Over the Cuckoo's Nest. Ed. George J. Searles. Albuquerque: University of New Mexico Press, 1972.

Miller, Wayne Charles. "Heller's Portrait of American Culture—The Missing Portrait in Mike Nichols' Movie." *A "Catch-22" Casebook*. Eds. Frederick Kiley and Walter McDonald. New York: Thomas Y. Crowell, 1973.

"So They Say: Guest Editors Interview Six Creative People." *Mademoiselle* 57 (August 1963): 234.

"Some Are More Yossarian than Others." *A "Catch-22" Casebook*. Eds. Frederick Kiley and Walter McDonald. New York: Thomas Y. Crowell, 1973.

Thegze, Chuck. "'I See Everything Twice': An Examination of *Catch-22*." *Film Quarterly* 24 (Fall 1970): 11, 12.

One Flew, Two Followed: Stage and Screen Adaptations of *Cuckoo's Nest*

Barry H. Leeds

Ken Kesey's first novel, *One Flew Over the Cuckoo's Nest* (1962), has been enormously popular for three decades, in large part because the central thematic thrust of the novel strikes even closer to the heart of the American experience now than it did when it was first published. The questioning of a monolithic bureaucratic order, the rejection of stereotyped sexual roles, the simultaneous awareness that healthy sexuality and a clear sense of sexual identity are prerequisites for human emotional survival, the recognition and rejection of hypocrisy, the devotion to the expression of individual identity: all establish the continuing social relevance of Kesey's work and illuminate the depth of Kesey's mastery of such aspects of novelistic form as symbolism and structure.

Randle Patrick McMurphy, the protagonist, is a man who has consistently resisted the strictures of society. Having decided that life on a psychiatric ward will be preferable to hard labor on the county work farm where he has been serving a sentence for assault and battery, McMurphy feigns insanity. This brings him into dramatic confrontation with "Big Nurse," a representative of the most repressive aspects of American society. Big Nurse is backed by the power of a mechanistic "Combine," a central agency for that society's suppression of individuality.

During his stay on her ward, McMurphy fights a constant guerrilla action against Big Nurse and her aides. He rallies the other patients behind him as he introduces gambling, laughter, and human vitality to the ward. He leads the patients on a therapeutically rejuvenating deep-sea fishing trip which restores their manhood and teaches them to rely on themselves as well as on each other for support. In a penultimate rebellion, he smuggles whores and liquor onto the ward for a hilarious party.

Against this humorous backdrop, the struggle between McMurphy and Big Nurse continues to escalate. In the climactic final scenes, she is able to provoke him into outbursts of violence which provide the excuse to "treat" McMurphy with electroshock therapy (EST) and ultimately with a lobotomy.

36

In the moving conclusion, McMurphy's friend Chief Bromden mercifully smothers him to death and makes his own escape. Although McMurphy is ultimately destroyed, he is not defeated. His courage and humor are never broken. Even after his death, his spirit pervades the ward; it is clear that he has beaten Big Nurse and damaged the Combine.

It is not just McMurphy's own struggle which is at issue in the novel. For one thing, McMurphy comes to represent the only hope for salvation open to his fellow inmates, a salvation which he brings about through the tutelage of example, making them aware of their own manhood in the dual senses of masculinity and humanity. Also, the novel's first-person narrator, Chief Bromden, assumes during the course of the novel a rebel role similar to that of McMurphy.

In a narrative structure analogous to that employed by F. Scott Fitzgerald in *The Great Gatsby*,[1] Kesey places Chief Bromden in a pivotal position. In both novels, the narrator is a man closely associated with the protagonist and torn by ambivalent feelings of disapproval and admiration for him, who, during the course of the novel, learns and develops through the tutelary example of the protagonist's life and ultimate death, and who, in recounting the story of his friend's life, clarifies his own development to the point where he takes on both the strengths of the protagonist and an awareness of how to avoid a similar downfall and death. Bromden and Nick Carraway both become syntheses of their own latent strengths and abilities and the best aspects of McMurphy and Gatsby. This narrative structure provides the novelist with the advantages of both the first-person point of view (within which the narrator can be revealed in terms of his own internal cerebration) and a third-person (hence more credibly objective) view of the novel's central figure.

The progressive development of the characters of McMurphy and Bromden cannot be said to parallel one another; a more accurate geometric metaphor is that of two intersecting oblique lines: as McMurphy's strength wanes, Bromden moves toward the ascendant. But the two developments proceed simultaneously and are integral to one another, until the transfer of power from McMurphy to Bromden is complete.

Bromden is an American Indian, a 280-pound, 6-foot 8-inch former high school football player and combat veteran of World War II who has been robbed of identity and sanity by the combination of pressures brought to bear on him by twentieth-century American society. At the outset of the novel, he is literally cut off from even the most rudimentary communication. He is so fearful of the dangers of dealing with people that he has learned to feign total deafness and has maintained absolute silence for years. Considered incurable by the medical staff, he is forced to perform menial janitorial work by the orderlies, who ridicule him with the title "Chief Broom."

That experience, and others from his past, all of which rob him of his masculine pride and his racial identity—and ultimately of his very humanity—are revealed in the novel in brief flashbacks, each precipitated by McMurphy as he persists in forcing Bromden to leave his fortress of silence and forgetfulness and reenter by stages the external world. As McMurphy makes friendly overtures toward him, Bromden begins to remember and understand episodes from his past. In persistently attempting communication with Bromden, McMurphy functions as a sort of combination lay psychiatrist and confessor, precipitating more and more painful and traumatic memories out of Bromden's mind until the Chief is able to face his own problems and begin the trip back to manhood.

Each of Bromden's hallucinations forms part of a complex system of recurrent symbols, and each is ultimately shown by Kesey to grow out of Bromden's previous experiences. Bromden, for example, crushes a tranquilizer capsule and sees (in the split second before it self-destructs upon contact with the air and turns to white powder) that it is a miniature electronic element, intended by the Combine to control the man who swallows it. The transistor metaphor later becomes part of a more comprehensive theory of Bromden's that the Combine exerts direct control over the citizenry through electronic devices; and the reader is not surprised when later still Bromden remarks in passing that he has studied electronics in the army and in his one year of college.

In fact, the psychological verisimilitude employed by Kesey in establishing these image patterns as natural outgrowths of Bromden's experience is so painstakingly precise that even the briefest metaphors used by Bromden can always be traced to their source. For example, one morning Bromden is served a "canned peach on a piece of green, torn lettuce." Later, relating the story of how orderlies forcibly administered medication to an inmate, Bromden describes the scene in the same terms: "One sits on his head and the other rips his pants open in back and peels the cloth until Taber's peach-colored rear is framed by the ragged lettuce-green."

Perhaps the most frightening product of Bromden's hallucinatory perception is the Combine itself. He defines it as a "huge organization that aims to adjust the Outside as well as the Big Nurse has the Inside." The Inside, as Bromden sees it, is different from the outside world only in the degree of control which must be exerted over its inhabitants. The Combine, committed as it is to the supremacy of technology over humanity, extends its influence by dehumanizing men and making them machines. But as the novel progresses, it becomes clear that Kesey envisions emasculation as a preliminary step in the dehumanization process. Ultimately, a pattern emerges: The Combine functions on two levels, mechanistic and matriarchal. The two are fused in the Big Nurse, Miss Ratched, who is a "high ranking official" of the Combine.

Big Nurse herself is conceived in mechanistic terms. Even her name, "Ratched," sounds like a kind of wrench or machine component, and the association with "rat" makes its sound very unpleasant. Bromden sees her as an expensive piece of precision-made machinery, marred in its functional design only by a pair of oversized breasts. Despite her annoyance at being forced to carry them, and despite Bromden's feeling that they mark an obvious flaw in an otherwise perfect piece of work, their presence is not inconsistent with the symbolic irony intended by Kesey. Miss Ratched's breasts are ironic reminders of the sexuality she has renounced. At the novel's end, they will be exposed by McMurphy as the palpable symbol of her vulnerability. Finally, they are her badge of membership in the Smothering Mother cadre of the Combine.

Using the sounds of laughter and song and the threat of his own sexual vitality, McMurphy manages to break down the barriers which Ratched and the Combine impose. He runs his hand, the symbol of his potency, through the protective glass of her nurses' station, which separates Big Nurse from the men at the same time that it allows her to spy on them. He raises his powerful hand in a vote against her authority and convinces most of the other inmates to do the same. And ultimately, in his final, physical attack on Big Nurse, he uses his hands to rip her starchy uniform off, tearing down her insulation as he did her glass wall and exposing her large, fleshy breasts, an action by which he demonstrates that she is no invincible machine but simply a woman, a human being with all the attendant human vulnerability and fallibility. Though the assault costs him his own lobotomy (perhaps the ultimate castration in a novel full of emasculation and castration imagery), he nevertheless triumphs in bringing about the complete disintegration of Miss Ratched's rule: she will never again command absolute power over the inmates. And his example emboldens his most successful disciple, Bromden, who picks up the control panel which McMurphy had earlier attempted to lift, smashes it through a window, and makes his escape. In this way Bromden surpasses his teacher in the capacity to survive in American society and to maintain personal identity in spite of the Combine.

Yet Kesey makes it clear that one need not have the physical prowess of a McMurphy or a Bromden to renounce "rabbithood" and become a man. He suggests that someone like the sensitive, almost effeminate Dale Harding has a real chance to thwart the Combine; and, in the end, Harding signs himself out of the hospital to try again with his wife, Vera, armed with a new honesty derived from his contact with McMurphy. Even the slow and virginal Billy Bibbit is able to go part of the way. But Billy fails. Barraged by Big Nurse's recriminations until the old habit patterns of guilt and dependence are reawakened in him, he commits suicide by cutting his throat. Kesey's feeling, however, is clear: it is better to be destroyed in the attempt to fight the Combine than to accept the role of rabbit for life.

For precisely this reason, Kesey's Randle Patrick McMurphy is a compelling figure. Into the sterility of Bromden's world and the stifling American society it represents, he brings a breath, a breeze, a wind of change. In the wasteland of the ward, his sexuality makes him loom as a figure of mythic proportions. Yet the most important part of the legacy he has left Bromden and his fellows is that he was just a man. And that, finally, is enough.

The dramatic power of Kesey's novel clearly made it a desirable prospect for stage and screen adaptation. But its sophistication and complexity, particularly in point of view and symbolism, presented major obstacles to translation to these media.

On November 13, 1963, a stage adaptation of *One Flew Over the Cuckoo's Nest* written by Dale Wasserman opened at the Cort Theatre in New York. The production starred Kirk Douglas as McMurphy, with Joan Tetzel as Nurse Ratched and Gene Wilder as Billy Bibbit. The play received unfavorable reviews and closed after three months. In 1969, a revised version opened in San Francisco and enjoyed far greater success, as did the 1971 off-Broadway production at the Mercer-Hansberry Theatre, starring William Devane and Janet Ward. Since then, Wasserman's play has been performed by various amateur and professional companies around the country to great popular success. Kirk Douglas had bought the movie rights to *Cuckoo's Nest* from Kesey in 1962 for $18,000. For years, rumors circulated that the making of the film was imminent. Finally, Douglas turned the rights over to his son, Michael. Michael Douglas and Saul Zaentz produced the movie in 1975. At the 1976 Academy Awards it won five Oscars: best picture, best director (Milos Forman), best actor (Jack Nicholson as McMurphy), best actress (Louise Fletcher as Nurse Ratched), and best screenplay adapted from another medium (Lawrence Hauben and Bo Goldman).

This last award carries some irony for Kesey and his admirers. Kesey himself had been hired to write the screenplay, but after the initial drafts he and the producers parted company under less than amicable circumstances. Kesey's subsequent successful lawsuit was based on the premise that he had not consented to the use of his name in connection with the final version of the film (Riley 25); but the primary artistic disagreement seems to have been over the producers' decision to shoot the film from a realistic, almost documentary point of view, even to the extent of casting some real patients in minor roles and Dean Brooks, director of Oregon State Hospital in Salem, where the movie was shot, as Dr. Spivey. Kesey had wanted to retain the hallucinatory point of view of Chief Bromden (25). I believe that this shift in point of view is the essential weakness in a movie that has many strengths. As Jack Kroll wrote in *Newsweek*:

> The result is a well-made film that flares at times into incandescence but lacks ultimately the novel's passion, insight and complexity....
> Kesey's novel was filtered through the paranoid consciousness of his Indian narrator, Chief Bromden. By opting for a style of comic realism, Forman loses much of the nightmare quality that made the book a capsized allegory of an increasingly mad reality.

Bromden's point of view is central to the novel's thematic message and narrative force. This significance was recognized by Dale Wasserman when he wrote the stage version. At frequent intervals in the play, Chief Bromden stands alone on a dark stage as a single shaft of light falls on him and "vague and milky light-patterns wreathe and intertwine across the stage" while his inner thoughts (represented by his voice on a tape) address his dead father:

> Papa? They're foggin' it in again.... You hear it, Papa?
> The Black Machine.... They're puttin people in one end and out comes what they want.... You think I'm ravin' 'cause it sounds too awful to be true, but, my God, there's such a lot of things that's true even if they never really happen! (Wasserman 6)

This emphasis on Bromden and his madness, including a reference to the fog machine and a paraphrase of Bromden's words from the novel, is symptomatic of the greater fidelity of the play to the novel. The movie departs more radically and frequently from the novel, but director Forman has thus succeeded to a greater degree in presenting a work of some originality and artistic merit in its own right.

Both Forman (with screenwriters Goldman and Hauben) and Wasserman made various alterations, compressions, and omissions of necessity in adapting *Cuckoo's Nest* to the limitations and strengths of their chosen media. Some characters are omitted in each version (e.g., George Sorensen appears in neither) and others are combined (as in Wasserman's effective merging of Ruckley with Ellis). Some clearly recognizable characters have undergone inexplicable changes of name. Thus, in the play, Ratched's assistant, Nurse Pilbow, becomes Nurse Flinn, and Aide Washington becomes Williams. In the movie, Pilbow and Washington retain their original names, but Aide Geever becomes Miller, and Sandy becomes Rose. More puzzling is the large role written into the movie for Taber (Christopher Lloyd), a character who did not live on the ward during McMurphy's stay but is remembered by Bromden as an unsuccessful precursor to McMurphy, a less forceful rebel who was ultimately defeated by the Combine. The Combine is not even mentioned in the movie, and Taber is a loud, exuberant psychotic whose barely contained violence clearly is less controllable than McMurphy's. Perhaps he represents that true madness which McMurphy never evinces; ironically, he survives McMurphy's destruction to give the exultant shout of triumph at the film's conclusion when Bromden escapes.

Along with their limitations, both stage and screen media enjoy some advantages over fiction. The visual immediacy of Bromden smothering McMurphy in both versions, the graphic representation of McMurphy's EST convulsions, particularly in the movie close-up, and the appearance of the patients are very effective. The play's success with audiences lies in the essential dramatic power of the plot situation itself, which sweeps one along in its own forceful movement, despite such omissions as the fishing trip.

Excellent casting is one of the movie's great strengths. In addition to the verisimilitude lent by the use of real patients and psychiatrist in a real hospital, casting directors Mike Fenton and Jane Feinberg filled most roles almost perfectly. Among the patients, Brad Dourif is superb as Billy Bibbit. Almost as good are Sydney Lassick as Cheswick (although the character does not commit suicide in either adaptation) and William Redfield as the intellectual Harding. Will Sampson is everyone's idea of Chief Bromden, and Scatman Crothers is a fine Turkle, disarmingly humorous in his vices.

Jack Nicholson and Louise Fletcher give excellent performances as McMurphy and Ratched, effectively overcoming the preconceptions of faithful readers of the novel, despite the fact that neither is a physically accurate representation of Kesey's character. For one thing, neither is big enough. Nicholson is not the broad, muscular McMurphy who inspires Bromden to think a giant has come to save him. Fletcher is too slender and attractive to suggest the invincible machine that Ratched is to Bromden. Thus, we are not tempted even briefly to see these characters as mythic figures, larger than life, the revelation of whose human vulnerability is so important to the novel's conclusion. Nonetheless, Nicholson's enormous, infectious vitality makes his McMurphy a forceful, engaging creation. And Fletcher, her pompadour resembling horns, uses subtle facial expressions— smug self-righteousness, rigidly controlled rage, a smirk half hidden by a hand—to evoke a Ratched whom anyone can hate.

In their ages, too, the characters differ from their counterparts in the novel. Ratched is no longer fifteen years older than McMurphy. Rather, Forman seems intentionally to have made them contemporaries. This, coupled with Fletcher's undeniably attractive appearance, heightens the sexual tensions between the antagonists, particularly the graphically sexual suggestion of the climactic strangulation scene, when Nicholson lies on top of the struggling Fletcher.

Finally, it should be noted that in casting Louise Fletcher for the role, Forman has robbed the character of a primary ambiguity of motive that enriched the novel. Kesey's Big Nurse appears an invincible monster to Bromden. The climactic scene in which McMurphy reveals her humanity by exposing her breasts in full view of the other men holds great import for Bromden and the reader, and it opens the further question of whether the nurse is a consciously evil character or a self-deluding bureaucrat who believes that she is doing good. In showing Fletcher as a rigid, tight-lipped, but clearly human woman—with a first name, Mildred—Forman imposes his own resolution of this interesting ambiguity, showing her as a misguided person who believes in her own good intentions. Jack Kroll points out that "Most of the characters are thinned out...Big Nurse, deprived of most of her mythic dimension, seems much more of a sexist concept—Woman as

Castrator" (113). Thus, paradoxically, the humanization of Ratched does not add a more humanistic dimension to the film.

I have said that Wasserman's play is more faithful to the novel. Not only is Bromden's hallucinatory perspective maintained, including his references to the fog machine and the Combine, but the wild geese, a central symbol in the novel of freedom and transcendence, pass overhead in the scene during which he begins to find himself. In the movie, Bromden's character is simplified: He is not insane but merely a cunning Indian who has fooled the medical staff for years by pretending to be deaf and dumb. His first speech, upon accepting a stick of Juicy Fruit gum from McMurphy to replace the old gum removed from under his bed by an aide, is played largely for laughs (see Figure 6); and the development of his relationship with McMurphy seems less credible, sudden rather than gradual.

The play also retains references to lobotomy as castration, to Nurse Ratched as a destructive mother, and to the Christ imagery of the EST scene. Many passages are taken almost verbatim from the novel, including the children's rhyme of the title, which is spoken as Bromden undergoes EST. Some speeches are retained but shifted to a different point in the action. Because of this, in at least one case a line is quoted entirely out of context, thus garbling Kesey's intention: McMurphy tells Bromden, "You growed half a foot already" (Wasserman 58), but the preceding passage about young women has been shifted to a later point so that the bawdy but significant double entendre is lost.

In departing dramatically from the novel, Milos Forman has taken some chances. Often he succeeds in doing something as well as or better than Kesey. The fishing trip (of necessity omitted from the play) enables Forman to use the advantages peculiar to his medium. The contrast between the constriction of the locked ward—in which almost all camera shots are tightly framed close-ups—and the enormous expanse of an incredibly blue sea in an extreme long shot state far better than words the polarity between the repression of Nurse Ratched's ward and the freedom McMurphy offers the men. These two settings suggest too the dual strengths of Forman's work. He is able to present both a dispassionate, depressing docudrama and an exultant fictive story.

Similarly, Forman moves the basketball game (which marks the beginning of the men's growing camaraderie and foreshadows the more serious competition which will soon take place) outside, from the ward in which Kesey set it to an exercise yard which, while fenced in, is open to the sky. (See Figure 7.) The surrounding trees and the image of a squirrel running atop the fence suggest that this is an interim stage between imprisonment and freedom. Indeed, McMurphy later escapes from the yard to steal a bus and take his fellow inmates fishing. And it is in the exercise yard, in two different basketball scenes, that Bromden's movement toward confidence and freedom under McMurphy's tutelage is implied. In the first

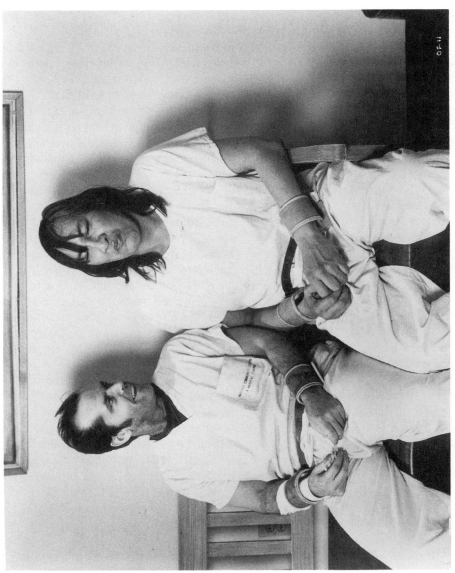

Figure 6. McMurphy (Jack Nicholson) and Bromden (Will Sampson), about to undergo EST treatment as punishment. Copyright © 1975 by United Artists Corporation.

Figure 7. McMurphy teaches Bromden how to sink a basket. Copyright © Fantasy Films and United Artists Corporation.

scene, McMurphy is able only to get Bromden to raise his hands with the basketball, not to dunk it, though he demonstrates by climbing onto Bancini's shoulders. Here, McMurphy literally shows Bromden how to be big, as he looks down on him. The scene is effectively bracketed by two shots of Nurse Ratched looking silently down on both of them, framed ghostlike and forbidding by the ward window. In the second basketball scene, the actual game with the aides, Bromden gradually blossoms until he becomes the star of the game, obviously delighted with himself.

The first basketball scene suggests a juxtaposition of two symbols from the novel: hands and windows. In the novel, the two are linked when McMurphy shatters the window of the nurses' station with his hand, and the recurrent symbolism of the hand as an index of male potency radiates outward from that center. Forman does less with hands, but he creates a pervasive and effective pattern of windows and television sets. Upon McMurphy's first appearance on the ward, Forman uses a wide-angle lens for a tightly framed shot of his manacled hands from below. (See Figure 8.) They seem red and very large, and the implicit phallic symbolism is emphasized when McMurphy hooks one finger in his fly. Later, as McMurphy leans against the window of the nurses' station, Ratched tells him, "Your hand is staining my window." (See Figure 9.) In addition to raising his hands with the basketball, Chief Bromden raises one hand to vote for the World Series after McMurphy suggestively exhorts him, "All the guys have got 'em up...Show her that you can still do it, Chief."

McMurphy's shattering of Nurse Ratched's window is less effective in the movie than in the novel. Kesey presented it as a conscious act, dispassionately chosen by McMurphy to mark a new stage in the escalation of his rebellion. Forman loses much of its significance, presenting it as a sudden, impulsive act of frustration, wedged into a series of telescoped events which move the plot along rapidly, achieving compression at the expense of emphasis. Within a few minutes, McMurphy learns he is committed indefinitely, momentarily considers acting cagey, is faced with Nurse Ratched's withholding of cigarettes and Cheswick's tantrum about that issue, and breaks the window. This precipitates his fight with Washington, ward orderly Warren's interference, Bromden's aiding of McMurphy, their assignment to the EST room, the first conversation between McMurphy and Bromden, and their decision to escape to Canada together.

Forman is more subtle in his recurrent use of windows. In addition to the scenes already mentioned, windows figure in a pattern of escapes and attempted escapes. McMurphy's prostitute friends Candy and Rose enter through a window, promising both figurative and literal escape through the same window. Ultimately, Bromden does escape by shattering the window. Finally, television sets are seen as pseudo-windows. When Nurse Ratched refuses to allow McMurphy to watch the World Series, he is shown looking disconsolately at his reflection in the dead TV screen. Remembering who he

Figure 8. Hands bound, McMurphy enters the asylum. Copyright © 1975 by Fantasy Films and United Artists Corporation.

Figure 9. McMurphy confronts the Big Nurse, Miss Ratched (Louise Fletcher). Copyright © 1975 by Fantasy Films and United Artists Corporation.

is, he perks up and begins cheering. Soon he is joined by Martini (Danny DeVito), and both their faces are reflected. When the others join them, they all momentarily escape Big Nurse's rule through the television set. Later, on the fishing trip, the men look fearfully and hungrily out of the bus windows at the outside world. Each is framed in his own window, isolated. They pass an appliance store outside which, in a palpably ironic shot, several older people are comfortably seated, looking through the store window at a daytime television show. Despite their ostensible freedom, these people have chosen to watch flickering shadows rather than participate in life. But the patients themselves soon choose life in the fishing episode which follows.

It is in this choice of life, freedom and vitality, clearly implicit in the beautifully photographed fishing sequence, that Forman most effectively captures the exuberant hope of Kesey's vision. And the film's conclusion, when Bromden laboriously rips the hydrotherapy machine which McMurphy had earlier attempted to hoist from its moorings, lifts it with palpably gathering confidence, crashes it through the window, and gradually disappears into the breaking dawn, his white pajama legs moving ethereally like wings, is easily as moving as the same conclusion in Kesey's words. It is far more effective than Wasserman's conclusion, in which, after shorting out the hospital's power by lifting the control panel, Bromden leaves through a window that Harding unlocks for him.

Although neither adaptation can consistently approach the level of artistic success achieved in the novel, both have virtues and lapses. Ultimately, however, Wasserman's play, with all its gestures toward fidelity to the original, is relatively pedestrian and unimaginative in conception, while Forman's movie, its omissions and departures from the novel notwithstanding, is more admirable as an independent and original work of art.

Unfortunately, the same cannot be said of the movie version of Kesey's second novel *Sometimes a Great Notion* (1964), which merits no more than a brief mention. Released in 1971, the film stars Paul Newman as Hank Stamper, Henry Fonda as Henry, and Lee Remick as Viv, with Michael Sarrazin as Lee and Richard Jaeckel as Joby. In compressing the massive, complex novel into a two-hour movie, director Paul Newman made no apparent attempt to create more than an entertaining cinematic plot summary. Because of this unpretentious approach and its excellent cast, the movie is moderately successful as an entertainment; but it bears only the most superficial resemblance to Kesey's fine work. Further liberties were taken when the movie came to network television. The title was changed to *Never Give a Inch*, and so many plot transitions were cut to make room for commercials that the movie became incomprehensible to viewers unfamiliar with the novel or the full-length version. Particularly ill served was the potentially fine role of Viv, which was cut and simplified to the point where even the considerable talents of Lee Remick could not make the character's motivation clear. In short, this movie is no more than a simplistic popularization of a magnificent novel which, in its experimental structure, shifting point of view and powerful thematic thrust, is more ambitious, more innovative, and ultimately more successful artistically than even *One Flew Over the Cuckoo's Nest*.

NOTE

[1]Other obvious structural analogies are suggested by Robert Penn Warren's *All the King's Men* and Norman Mailer's *The Deer Park*.

WORKS CITED

Kroll, Jack. "You're All Right, Jack." *Newsweek* 24 November 1975: 113.

Riley, John. "Bio: Novelist Ken Kesey Has Flown the 'Cuckoo's Nest' and Given Up Tripping for Farming." *People Weekly* 22 March 1976: 25.

Wasserman, Dale. *One Flew Over the Cuckoo's Nest: A Play in Two Acts from the Novel by Ken Kesey*. New York: Samuel French, Inc., 1970.

Slaughterhouse-Five: Fiction Into Film

Jerome Klinkowitz

Does Kurt Vonnegut's novel *Slaughterhouse-Five* transpose effectively to the screen? One of the first authorities to answer that question was Vonnegut himself. Early in 1972, as the film itself was being seen by audiences across the country, Vonnegut prefaced the script of a National Educational Television special drawn from his works and published as *Between Time and Timbuktu* (New York: Delacorte Press/Seymour Lawrence, 1972) with some comments on the issue:

> I love George Roy Hill and Universal Pictures, who made a flawless translation of my novel *Slaughterhouse-Five* to the silver screen. I drool and cackle every time I watch that film, because it is so harmonious with what I felt when I wrote the book.
>
> Even so—I don't like film.
>
> Film is too clankingly real, too permanent, too industrial for me. As a stingy child of the Great Depression, I am bound to complain that it is also too fucking expensive to be much fun. I get the heebie-jeebies every time I hear how much it will cost to fix a scene that doesn't work quite right. "For God's sake," I say, "leave it just like it is. It's *beautiful!* Leave it be!" (xv)

The author is speaking from experience. In the two previous years he had abandoned fiction for stage and screen work. The sudden wealth and fame occasioned by *Slaughterhouse-Five* (1969), his first bestseller after a twenty-year career of virtual anonymity, had shocked him. Coinciding with the break-up of his twenty-five year marriage and move away from his familiar village surroundings in tiny West Barnstable, Massachusetts, to a bachelor apartment in New York City, this new stature moved him to a style of direct spokesmanship he found most amenable outside the novel. He wrote many personal essays and spoke on behalf of important social and political issues (at one point even risking his life traveling to the blockaded nation of Biafra to report the carnage and starvation there). Away from his rambling house on Cape Cod where he could tap away at his manual typewriter in happy isolation, he now sought company in New York—and found it in the communal aspects of working on a play, *Happy Birthday, Wanda June*, which ran successfully for most of the 1970 Broadway season. The following year he served as screenwriter for its film adaptation. Meanwhile his next novel, *Breakfast of Champions*, sat unfinished; unfinishable, Vonnegut claimed, announcing that he was done with the form forever. Having his work digested for public television was simply a logical next step as a former novelist.

His Preface, however, finds him turning away from movies and back to novels, and not just because of the expense:

> I have become an enthusiast for the printed word again. I have to be that, I now understand, because I want to be a character in all my works. I can do that in print. In a movie, somehow, the author always vanishes. Everything of mine which has been filmed so far has been one character short, and the character is me. (xv)

As more than one viewer has remarked, the most apparent difference a reader of *Slaughterhouse-Five* notes when being shown the film is that there is no one saying, "So it goes." That phrase, repeated precisely one hundred times in the novel and uttered on the occasion of any death whatsoever, human, animal, or vegetable, was Vonnegut's own breakthrough to understanding the prevalence of death in the story he had to tell. Nor was the notion of having himself present in the novel an idle thought; since 1966 (and a new Introduction for the second edition of the novel, *Mother Night*) Vonnegut had begun each work with an autobiographical note explaining his own part in the action to follow, and in *Slaughterhouse-Five* these candid remarks would be incorporated even more directly as the novel's first and last chapters, framing the narrative in which the author himself appears another three times.

On the other hand, film itself has within its very nature many of the techniques *Slaughterhouse-Five* as a novel seeks to emulate: quick-cutting across time and space in order to juxtapose distinct images in a way that prompts new associations; reinforcement of sight and sound, often so that one can cue the other; and the ability to show quite graphically what a character is thinking. As a novelist, Vonnegut pushes his work beyond limits of convention and creates a technical masterpiece worthy of the innovative 1960s (in the company of Jerzy Kosinski's *Steps*, Anais Nin's *Collages*, Ronald Sukenick's *Up*, and Clarence Major's *Reflex and Bone Structure*), all as a way of forcing the printed word to do what film does most naturally. And so at the very least one expects a trade-off between the merits of page and screen, which is just what happens in making *Slaughterhouse-Five* almost as good a film as it is a novel, albeit that convention serves the movie in place of the innovation so necessary within the book.

One change is that the film's central character is asked to carry a greater burden of both theme and technique. In Kurt Vonnegut's novel, he himself is the writer, identifying himself as such and functioning that way in setting up shop during Chapter One. The film of *Slaughterhouse-Five*, of course, opens with a scene showing Billy Pilgrim as a writer, striking those manual typewriter keys in the same style of rambling, waterside house Vonnegut had occupied when writing the novel (a situation he describes *in situ* within the concluding Chapter Ten, typing these last pages as the news reports tell him of Robert Kennedy's assassination). For the substance of Billy's writing, film provides the ideal technique for explication: cross-cutting from the little marks on the page to the equally tiny figure of Billy Pilgrim wandering across the snowfield screen, searching for his unit lost during the Battle of the Bulge.

Having Billy as the writer and using film's customary techniques to convey the notion of time travel tightens up the work, but at the expense of Kurt Vonnegut's involvement as a real person in the fiction he creates. Much of the novel's first chapter dealt with the difficulty of writing such a work; of how hard it was for Vonnegut to avoid the romantic clichés of war literature, and of how the nature of a massacre itself defied any sense of articulation. In the film, Billy Pilgrim has it much easier: though suffering the loss of his wife (see Figure 10), he feels confident in writing letters to the editor that explain the new state of knowledge he has achieved, thanks to the Tralfamadorians and their theories of time, space, and volition. Indeed, these were the devices Vonnegut construed as a way to solve his own writing problems when facing the matter of Dresden; for Billy as a writer, they are already solved.

In similar manner cinematic form lends itself quite handily to the time travel techniques that are so crucial to the novel's action. In the novel, they indicated that Billy was experiencing life much like a movie; now he is a character in a movie, and to the viewer seems much more in place. The most obvious point of the novel's innovation was its sudden, initially inexplicable jumps in space and time; in the film, these jumps are devices familiar to every moviegoer and are no more radical in format than the simplest cartoon. What is radical and disjointed in a novel thus appears normal in a movie, thanks to the reinforcements sight, sound, and motion provide to the otherwise more difficult thematic links. The quick-cut from Billy's white sheet of typing paper to the snowfield in Luxembourg is just the first of many such jumps, most of which are cued by visual elements obvious to the viewer (novelistic transitions, depending upon repeated words, demand more of readers in terms of attention to language—language that for some melts away into represented action). Once in the film an even more traditional technique is used: the dissolve, in which the foreboding, inhuman, and totally other-worldlike surface of Tralfamadore blends into the moonscape of Dresden in the aftermath of firebombing.

Film provides aural links for quick-cutting. The most obvious is Billy's shriek when subjected to electric shock treatment, a piercing sound that is

Figure 10. In happier times: Billy (Michael Sacks) gives his wife Valencia (Sharon Gans) a Cadillac for her birthday. Copyright © by Universal Pictures.

actually represented by something from the next scene, a train whistle at the prisoner-of-war camp. Sound is used again when the applause Billy receives when being named president of the Ilium Lions Club causes him to clap (all by himself) when Edgar Derby is elected leader of the American P.O.W.s. Before, light had been a similarly linking device, as the flash bulb of a publicist at the opening of Billy's optometry clinic prompts him to smile broadly, only this time for a German propagandist's wartime photo of a supposedly pitiful American soldier captured in the ruins of battle. (See Figure 11.)

In his novel, Vonnegut had used light and colors to link scenes vastly separated in time. The faces of the Russian prisoners are said to glow like the dials of radium-treated wristwatches; a few pages later Billy, as a little boy, is told the cave he's visiting is totally dark, yet notices the glowing radium dial of his father's watch. In wartime Germany, the prisoner-of-war train is striped in the same colors as the caterer's tent for a party at Billy's postwar home. And so on. The difference is that Vonnegut's novelistic links are subliminal, so subtle and displaced that the reader is less likely to note them consciously than to have the general feeling that for some reason this wildly disjointed narrative is hanging together. In the film, the links are not only more obvious in themselves but are mutually reinforcing, such as having not just the sights but also the sounds and even the movements of Billy's postwar life appear identical with those of his P.O.W. experience.

Links in terms of motion are the most effective bonding of these two lines because as action they qualify as narratives themselves. As the P.O.W. showers turn on, Billy is suddenly back in the shower room of the YMCA, where his father is about to teach him to swim by the old sudden immersion method; then, after the war, Billy returns home to mount the bedroom stairs with the same sense of loss in which he climbs the air raid shelter stairs in Dresden after the bombing. Motion also lends three-dimensionality to individual scenes. In one of the film's best, Edgar Derby is led off by a firing squad and shot while in the foreground two Nazi officers walk away, totally disregarding the man they have condemned while handling and then discarding the tiny Dresden figurine they've caught Derby purportedly looting. Since Griffith and Eisenstein filmmakers have understood the instructional value of such parallels; shooting a scene like this moves beyond theatrical blocking, for the viewer's position is allowed to change as well. In *Slaughterhouse-Five* it is a ballet of motion, in which motion itself tells the story, just as clearly but without the expositional obviousness of the more writerly device used in subsequent cross-cutting, where Edgar Derby's story is part of a wedding anniversary tale in which Billy's wife tells how the diamond he is giving her dates back to Billy's fortunes as a prisoner (in which he found a diamond and survived, while Edgar Derby found a china figurine and was shot).

Kurt Vonnegut did not write the screenplay. That was done by Stephen Geller, and Vonnegut pledged to stay out of his way, perhaps because of his own unhappy experience in adapting *Happy Birthday, Wanda June* for the

Figure 11. Billy recreates his capture for German photographers. Copyright © Universal Pictures.

screen (which Vonnegut himself admits was one of the worst screenplays in film history). But he can claim credit to one line in the film. Present on the set when Billy's hospital room meeting with Air Force historian B. C. Rumfoord was being filmed, Vonnegut saw the trouble director George Roy Hill was having in ending this episode: the dialogue and action just didn't provide an easy way out of the scene. And so, on the spot, Vonnegut contrived one, having Rumfoord answer Billy's repeated "I was there" with the gruff admonition, "The hell with him, let him write his own book."

One wishes Kurt Vonnegut had been present in a few other scenes: the ones where Billy lives in his cage-like canopy on the alien planet Tralfamadore. (See Figure 12.) In a sense these scenes are appropriately Vonneguttian: photographed in garish color, overplayed lighting, and constructed like a 1930s Buck Rogers epic, they mock the claptrap of space opera that Vonnegut himself often uses to satirize science fiction (such as having Tralfamadorians resemble plumbers' helpers). But the final scene where fireworks fill the sky at the birth of Billy's new son seems overly tawdry and especially unsuitable as the ending to the film; think of how much more tellingly (and, for that matter, sweetly) the novel ends, with the war over and Billy waking up in the suburbs to hear nature's birdsong almost magically restored. Even more regrettable is the device of having the film's disembodied Tralfamadorian voice—so deeply authoritative and commanding, no plumber's helper here—be the carrier of the novel's philosophy. In the novel, Billy discovers it in literary terms, through the format of Tralfamadorian fiction. In the film, it is boomed out in a way that sounds unconvincing, especially in the medium of film. "The best way to handle life is to think about the good times and ignore the bad"—trivial indeed, even more so twenty years later when the film appeared on cable television via the Arts & Entertainment Network, whose sponsor, Michelob Beer, peppered the viewing with commercials advising to "drink Michelob, because some days are better than others."

Tralfamadorian philosophy does prompt the most important question about the film's adequacy. When Billy Pilgrim encounters literature described as the Tralfamadorian novel, he encounters something less otherworldly than quite pertinently contemporary: for this style of otherworldly fiction emulates the innovative novel of the American 1960s, in which fragmentation and antirepresentation demanded a style of reading in which chronology, development, and above all the suspension of disbelief were discarded in favor of an immediacy and totality of comprehension. As a novel, *Slaughterhouse-Five* refuses to make sense in a cumulative way; instead, its fragmentary scenes float as if in solution until all of them are read, at which point meaning coalesces. One finds the method used in Jerzy Kosinski's *Steps*, Richard Brautigan's *Trout Fishing in America*, and Donald Barthelme's *Snow White*, all published within a year or two of Vonnegut's novel. The author's own contribution to this innovative trend was including

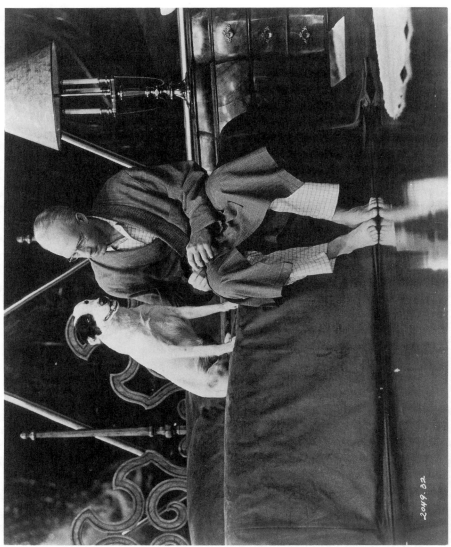

Figure 12. Billy with his faithful Spot in their cage-like canopy on the planet Tralfamadore.

himself as the novel's creator, present and willing to discuss just how he did it. When the novel ends, it is not just because the war is over and Billy is hearing the birds, but because it is June 1968 and a very real Kurt Vonnegut has finished typing it just as Robert Kennedy has died (a key historical event that prompts readers to recall where they were when Kennedy died).

As a film, *Slaughterhouse-Five* does not have this self-apparent sense of its own making. The novel had it partly because it was a novel striving to be a film. Director George Roy Hill's film already is one, and he wisely discarded any intentions of taking it a parallel step farther and including the cinematically self-reflective devices being used in such current films as *Medium Cool* and *Coming Apart*. To do so would have changed *Slaughterhouse-Five* into something else, into a personal work by the director as something uniquely his own. *Slaughterhouse-Five* can only be a record of Kurt Vonnegut's own struggle to write it. The book is its success, and the film notes that fact—but cannot recreate it, for that action happens only in the novel.

Chance Encounters: Bringing *Being There* to the Screen

Barbara Tepa Lupack

Few novels lend themselves more naturally to analysis of their adaptation to film than does Jerzy Kosinski's *Being There*. That is, in large part, because few novels have as their subject the effects of a medium so closely related to film—a medium, moreover, powerful enough to render individuals incapable of intelligent and free choice and thus to create a force as collectively supreme as the Combine in *One Flew Over the Cuckoo's Nest* and as totalitarian as the military machine in *Catch-22*.

Being There (1971), Kosinski's third novel, is on one level a simple story of chance. On another level, it is the story of simple Chance, an innocent Gulliver possessed of a Lilliputian intellect, a contemporary Candide who wants only to cultivate his own garden. His knowledge of the world is restricted to the television set which he watches in his room and the yard which he tends at the home of his benefactor, known only as the Old Man. Although never specified, Chance's origins are somewhat suspicious: there is the suggestion that he is the Old Man's son by one of the domestics. Once the Old Man dies and his house is closed, Chance is thrust onto the street, where almost immediately he is struck by EE Rand's limousine, which pins and injures his leg. The Rands become his new benefactors, and numerous interesting adventures follow. Those adventures, usually the result of others' mistaking Chance's simplistic recitations of gardening lore as profundity, take Chance to the pinnacle of American-popular-cultural superstardom. He becomes a media darling and eventually a candidate for high office (Vice-President in the novel, President in the film).

Through Chance, Kosinski decries the contemporary condition of video idiocy—Kosinski called it "videocy"—which affects young and old Americans alike, who allow the artificial world of TV to become their only reality. Such passive response, according to Kosinski, also leads easily to the usurpation by others of the privacy and integrity of the self, a concern central to all of his fiction beginning with his celebrated first novel. But, as John Aldridge noted, whereas *The Painted Bird* (1965) was a parable of demonic totalitarianism, "of that form of Nazi bestiality which is not a politics but a violence of the soul and blood, *Being There* has to do with a totalitarianism of a subtler and

60

more fearful kind, the kind that arises when the higher sensibilities of a people have become not so much brutalized as benumbed, when they have lost both skepticism and all hold on the real, and so fall victim to those agencies of propaganda which manipulate their thinking to accept whatever the state finds it expedient for them to accept" (26).

Kosinski was personally familiar with the adverse effects of both totalitarianism and propagandism. Born in Lodz, Poland, in 1933, he survived the war by eking out a meager existence among the often primitive and sometimes brutal peasants, events which he fictionalized in *The Painted Bird* and to which he alluded in other novels. The repressive atmosphere of postwar Stalinism made him determined to escape his native land; and, after concocting an elaborate plan (premised upon a fictitious "Chase Manhattan Bank Fellowship"), he arrived in the United States in 1957, where he worked a series of low-paying jobs. After securing an actual grant, from the Ford Foundation, he wrote and published two nonfiction books, *The Future Is Ours, Comrade* (1960) and *No Third Path* (1962), based on his experiences as a college student in Russia. The books, well-received in an era of cold war, generated much fan mail, including a letter from Mary Hayward Weir, the widow of American steel magnate Ernest T. Weir. Mary and Kosinski soon met (after she played a trick on him by impersonating her own secretary—a trick fictionalized and recounted in *Blind Date* [1977]) and married. Once Kosinski became a part of Mary's world of wealth and power, he discovered a life as sensational as that of fiction. "I had lived the American nightmare," he said, "now I was living the American dream" (Lavers 6). And he used many of those American-dream experiences, especially in creating the privileged world of Ben Rand, a character based loosely on Ernest Weir, just as he endowed Chance with his own perspectives as a foreigner, an outsider observing with wonderment the sociopolitical landscape of his new world.

It is not Chance, though, whom Kosinski targets for his parody and criticism; rather it is Chance's society, a people so visually oriented that they thrive on the superficial, so easily swayed by others' opinions that they become dupes of the collective forces of television and the media. Chance is assumed to be a wealthy businessman because he is attractive and well-dressed. Though his only assets are that "he's personable, well-spoken, and he comes across well on TV" (Kosinski 116), he is soon reputed to be a Presidential advisor whose many attributes include great intelligence, linguistic ability, impeccable manners, and social presence.

The fact that Chance never responds directly to the specific question posed to him is easily overlooked; ironically, his evasiveness is hailed as directness and lauded as a political and social virtue. He has, says his dinner companion, an "uncanny ability of reducing complex matters to the simplest of human terms" (Kosinski 106). Similarly, his inability to contemplate or calculate is praised as a naturalness lacking in most public figures. Like the media, who make him their golden boy, the various audiences who watch

Chance perform become quickly enamored of him since he is the fulfillment of their shallow expectations. Hungry for balms, they seize his literal remarks and transform them into profound metaphors; yet his purportedly insightful comments—that spring follows winter and that gardens need tending—are no more than echoes of their own hollowness and superficiality. (Kosinski documented this tendency of Americans to accept without question or challenge what others offer to them as reality. One week, in a course on Creativity and Reality which he taught at Yale University, he announced that, at the next class, teachers from a professional dance studio in New Haven would come and show the students how to tap dance; after the dance session, he would have a point to make. As Adrienne Kennedy, a student in that course, recalls: "The following week the dance teachers came and gave us lessons in basic tap steps. We practiced for more than an hour. When the lesson was over, Mr. Kosinski told us we had just had a lesson in reality. He pointed out that, as inept as the teachers had been, *because* he told us they *were* dance teachers, none of us, not one, had even questioned it. The dance teachers were, in fact, undergraduate students at Yale. It had all been staged" [A. Kennedy 20].)

An instant celebrity, Chance becomes the quintessential screen upon which others try to act out their own drama, a mirror which (while lacking depth itself) reflects and duplicates the images it is presented. His ability to reflect what he observes is emphasized by the many mirror images in the novel.

And Chance also serves as a mirror for the book's other characters in the novel. He shows EE (or at least EE believes that he shows her) how to evoke her "innumerable selves" by unleashing her sexuality and thus her individual identity (Kosinski 74). (In fact, he merely mimics the actions of television lovers.) On the Gary Burns late-night talk show, "the viewers existed only as projections of his own thoughts, as images," and Chance in turn "became only an image for millions of real people" (65). And he becomes Ben Rand's protégé, a reflection of his mentor's views on business and life, so completely that Chance is expected to fill the dying man's place. In one version of the screenplay which he wrote for the film, Kosinski added an even more pointed mirror image: Ben explains, "When I was a boy, I was told that the Lord fashioned us from his own image. That's when I decided to manufacture mirrors" (Kosinski and Jones 103). And much of Chance's conversation is nothing more than an aural reflection of what others have said to him.

The mirror images are particularly appropriate, given the mythic dimension of the protagonist. As a contemporary Narcissus, he echoes the shallow and narcissistic values of his society. While it is the other viewers who become enamored of his image, Chance is drawn to his television as Narcissus was drawn to his pool of water; he uses the TV to inform his behavior. When dining with the Rands, for example, he chooses to imitate "the TV program of a young businessman who often dined with his boss and the boss's daughter" (Kosinski 39).

Narcissus is not the only archetype upon which *Being There* draws; an equally important mythic dimension in the book is the biblical one. Kosinski's novel, a kind of contemporary parable, is written in seven parts and occurs over a period of seven days, paralleling the seven days of creation. The Old Man, in whose home Chance for many years resides, is portrayed as a distant but god-like figure; after he dies, Chance is expelled from his garden paradise into the fallen world, where he meets EE—whose full name is Elizabeth Eve (changed simply to "Eve" in the film)—who, like her biblical counterpart, tries to corrupt her innocent companion. And Chance himself is cast quite deliberately as Kosinski's "American Adam," to borrow R. W. B. Lewis's popular term, an archetypal man in his new world garden, fundamentally innocent in his very newness—a type of the creator, who creates language itself "by naming the elements of the scene about him" (Lewis 5).

At the same time, though, the Adamic Chance is an outsider, estranged from the society of *Being There*. His estrangement is not simply physical but also linguistic: he is incapable of true communication with anyone, from the Old Man's maid to the President of the United States. Words simply mean something different to him than they do to others. When the Old Man's lawyer asks him to sign a legal document, Chance says, "I can't sign it.... I just can't" (Kosinski 24). It is the lawyer who assumes that he refuses to withdraw his claim against the Old Man's estate; Chance means that he does not know how to write words and therefore is unable to sign anything. When EE visits Chance in his bedroom late one night and he tells her, "I like to watch" (114), he means precisely that: he enjoys watching television. It is EE who concludes that he is interested in kinky sex and who obliges him—and herself—by masturbating while he looks on. And when his Soviet dinner companion Skrapinov says to him that "We are not so far from each other," and Chance responds literally, "We are not.... Our chairs are almost touching" (89), his response is greeted as a fine metaphor when in fact there is no subtlety to it whatsoever. Similarly, when he is extended the recognition of an honorary doctor of laws degree, he dismisses it because "I do not need a doctor."

Although these exchanges, like so much of the novel's sharp and witty dialogue, read almost like a movie script, Kosinski insisted he did not write *Being There* to be a motion picture. He claimed repeatedly to have rejected offers to film the story since its 1971 publication. On a number of occasions he stated that he would *never* allow any of his works to be filmed. As William Kennedy observed, Kosinski's literary integrity is immense, "another way of resisting collectivization," and he tells all comers that "the books were written as novels, not scenarios" (W. Kennedy 12). At a panel in 1975 on "Making Movies Out of Books," Kosinski offered another reason for not wanting to film his novels. "I do like movies, and have known of many excellent screenplays," he explained, "but the book and the film have little in common. Movies are a much more dynamic industry; so much is done so quickly it diminishes those who write" ("Press Panels" 49). In a subsequent interview with *The New York Times*, he elaborated on his position. Films "are basically about plot and action," he said, "and to transfer my novels to film would strip them of the very specific power they have, and that is to trigger in the reader his own psychological set-up, his own projecting. Film has the very opposite effect. It doesn't trigger anything from within. It sets things from without and you, the viewer, are there to be an observer, not a participant" (Fosburgh 13).

Kosinski nevertheless experienced a change of heart with *Being There*. Reportedly, one studio had ordered a script based on Kosinski's characters to be written. Fearing a quick, cheap version in which he would have no authorial or financial control, he began to reconsider. At the same time, Peter Sellers, who ultimately won the lead role, was escalating his own campaign.

Sellers had read Kosinski's book shortly after it had been published and decided that he was the only actor who could play Chance. He saw in the role an opportunity to bring his career to its culmination (a curious ambition for a man whose reputation and popularity rested largely on his portrayal of multi-charactered and multi-voiced roles, usually in a staggering array of makeups) (Schickel 64). More importantly, though, Sellers, who had already suffered several heart attacks, felt that the novel expressed his philosophy that life was dictated by chance.

Sellers also believed that the trauma of his heart condition gave him a unique point of identification with Chance. "They later told me that I did not suffer any brain damage [as a result of the heart attacks], but I have reason to believe I did. My mind has deteriorated since then." Citing absent-mindedness and a general vagueness, he said, "I think I'm probably going a little soft in the head, which is why I have something in common with Chance" (Schickel 68).

Desperate to play the role, Sellers began sending Kosinski cryptic telegrams which read, "Available my garden or outside it. C. Gardiner" (DeSalvo 1). A telephone number—Sellers'—was always included. Sellers tried other stunts, too: he would spend long portions of his meetings with Kosinski portraying Chance, sometimes sitting for hours in front of a blank screen. Kosinski recalled: "Once we were in a hotel suite with a lot of guests, and he physically moved them to one side so he could turn on the television. Nobody ever caught on to what he was doing, just as nobody in my novel ever realized that Gardiner was a frail man behind a facade, that he had no substance" (Harmetz 19).

Even while giving interviews, Sellers would refer to Kosinski's novel. On one occasion, appearing on a TV show before he started work on *Being There*, Sellers was told, by a figure no less auspicious than Kermit the Frog of

The Muppet Show, to "just relax and be yourself." He responded that that would be altogether impossible. "I could never be myself...because there is no me. I do not exist." He confided further, "There used to be a me. But I had it surgically removed" (Schickel 64). His good joke, on the one hand an expression of his profound fear (and perhaps every actor's insecurity) that the real man has no personality apart from the particular fictive self he adopts at any given time, is also an explanation of why he so coveted the role of Kosinski's protagonist, who is nothing more than the image of him which others have created. On another occasion, Sellers provided a similar insight; he said that his whole life "has been devoted to imitating others. It has been devoted to the portrayal of those who appear to be different from what they are. If I were to tell you that Chauncey Gardiner was the ultimate Peter Sellers, then I would be telling you what my whole life was about. If I don't portray him, he will ultimately portray me" (Schickel 67).

Sellers won the role he so doggedly pursued after Kosinski finally agreed to allow the film to be made and even to write the screenplay for it—a screenplay which eventually garnered awards from the Writers Guild of America and the British Academy of Film and Television Arts. Kosinski had already written a first version of the screenplay in the early 1970s when he was teaching at Yale in order to illustrate the difference between a screenplay and a novel. (A novel, he explained, is an "internalizing" medium; it "describes." A screenplay, on the other hand, as an "externalizing" medium, "announces" situations that are eventually going to be described in images by someone else.) Kosinski subsequently wrote two more versions of the screenplay; the film used portions of all three (DeSalvo 2).

Although the book is set in New York City, for the final version Kosinski moved the setting to Washington, D.C. The move was appropriate, he claimed, since—in the decade between the time the book was published and the movie was made—America's real power base had shifted accordingly (Arlen 57). Indeed, he said, the Watergate scandal was another manifestation of the situation he predicted in *Being There*—that of the corrupting influence of television, which gives politicians the confidence to try anything, even the manipulation of the media. Similarly, before Carter's election, Kosinski considered Jimmy Carter the perfect media candidate, because he had no known past, no negative viewer recognition, prior to 1975 when his media persona appeared on network television. And, while Kosinski did not live to witness the ultimate Chance-like candidacy of H. Ross Perot, conducted largely via television time purchased with his own millions, he surely must have appreciated the irony of actor Ronald Reagan's two telegenic terms in office as well as understudy George Bush's subsequent lackluster performance in the White House.

When *Being There*, the movie, was released in late 1979, it was not the first film to examine the impact of television on modern life: *The China Syndrome* (1979) had already explored TV's power in current affairs, and

Network (1976) had caricatured the people who run the broadcasting empires. But *Being There's* vision of television viewers as passive empty victims was in marked contrast to Paddy Chayefsky's "mad-as-hell" audiences who refused to take it anymore (Broeske 147); conversely, Chance's society can't seem to get enough of a bad thing. *Being There's* subtlety and understatement were also notably different—cinematically as well as thematically—from the special effects used so widely in other films that year (including *The Invasion of the Body Snatchers; Superman: The Movie; The Black Hole; Battlestar Galactica; Buck Rogers in the 25th Century; Alien;* and *Apocalypse Now*). "I'm elated to see such a literate movie succeed," film critic Nora Sayre wrote of *Being There;* "its wit challenges the flying cutlery and sooty holes and mirthless farces of midwinter" (70).

Much of the credit for the film's success belonged to director Hal Ashby, best known for his critically and commercially successful *Coming Home* (1978) and for cult hits like *Harold and Maude* (1971) and *Shampoo* (1975). With *Being There*, though, Ashby was faced with an especially complex directorial challenge—sustaining a single, though witty, joke for almost two hours. "This is the most delicate film I've ever worked with as an editor," Ashby admitted. "The balance is just incredible. It could be ruined in a second if you let it become too broad. Peter's character is a sponge. He imitates everything he sees on television and everyone he meets. In one scene, he imitated the voice of a homosexual. It was very funny, but we couldn't allow it. It would have destroyed the balance" (Harmetz 29). Some of the outtakes seen as the credits roll at the end of the film show the exercise of a similar control.

Ashby chose to direct *Being There* with a deliberate, slow pace to amplify the dulled emotions of the deadpan Chauncey and to give the film the languid and removed quality of a dream (Broeske 147, Champlin 1) (much as Mike Nichols did in portions of *Catch-22*). Kosinski initially feared that Ashby's film "would give all the answers. That would have been the death of my vision." But eventually he recognized that "Hal made the exact cinematic equivalent of my novel, a film where the observer is inside the film looking out. You take Chauncey Gardiner's place. You are there" (Harmetz 19).

Given the main character's spiritual and emotional nullity, a film so pensive and interior could have been quite soporific. But Ashby's use of the TV screen keeps it nimbly dramatic: absurd and hilarious fragments of random programs punctuate the blankness of Sellers' demeanor (Sayre 123). Whereas in the book Kosinski rarely described the shows Chance watches, for the movie film-researcher Dianne Schroeder carefully selected TV show clips to further the message. The selections were crucial. As Colin Westerbeck observed, in *Being There* the opportunity existed to use television sets as if they were telegraph keys, as a way to flash urgent signals to the audiences. But "the comments that the television insertions make to the movie are more oblique and imaginative" (Westerbeck 118).

Ashby knew the importance of such seemingly simple visual statements. In his earlier film *Coming Home*, he used television to create especially poignant and meaningful moments: for instance, when Jane Fonda turns on a set late on the night that her husband has shipped out for Vietnam, a picture of the American flag appears on the screen; as the sound of the "Star-Spangled Banner" plays in the background, the screen suddenly goes blank. In *Being There*, there are a number of scenes in which the characters' actions are cleverly linked to or even foreshadowed by television programs. For example, when Chance goes up to see the Old Man, lying pale and dead in his bed, he has little reaction to the death. Turning his back to the corpse, he clicks on the TV and watches a commercial for Sealy Posturepedic; the unapproachable young woman on the mattress is a more attractive reality than the stiff Old Man on whose bed he is still sitting. Later, as Chance prepares to leave the Old Man's home, he tunes in a show about a widow grieving at the cemetery; "she" turns out to be Agent Maxwell Smart in disguise. The scene not only prefigures Chance's relationship with soon-to-be widow Eve Rand (played by Shirley MacLaine) but also suggests that only through television can Chance ever "Get Smart." Later still, at the Rand home, while talking to *New York Times* reporter Courtney on Mrs. Aubrey's phone, Chance gets a glimpse of an exercise program; unable to flex any mental muscles, he instead resorts to the most literal of responses and flexes his pecs. And after appearing on the Gary Burns show and delivering several powerful—though unintentional—verbal punches to the President, Chance views a martial arts demonstration on the limousine's set on the way home.

But the best use of television clips occurs when Eve stops by Chance's bedroom late one evening. Having just watched the amiable "Mr. Rogers" chatting with neighbor Mr. McFeely, Chance is now tuned in to a late-night love story. As Eve enters his room with the intention of seducing him, Chance begins to mimic the screen lovers' actions; he grabs Eve and—in a particularly comical play on the name McFeely[1]—kisses her and twirls her around the room while romantic music from the TV show plays in the background. But the TV picture dissolves in the passionate clinches and Chance cannot consummate the act. With no idea what to do next, he responds to Eve's frustration by telling her he would rather watch. Misunderstanding, she masturbates on the floor below him. (See Figure 13.) Chance's attention span, though, is short; and as he loses interest in Eve, he becomes engrossed in a program of yoga exercises on the screen. As Eve climaxes, he imitates the exercise hostess by standing on his head—a fitting symbol for himself and for the inverted values of his society.

In still another scene, this one a significant departure from the novel, Chance's accident occurs as he is watching a TV screen in a department

Figure 13. EE Rand (Shirley MacLaine) allows Chance to watch. Copyright © by United Artists.

store window: looking at an image of himself being filmed by a camera in the store, he backs off the curb, only to be struck by the Rands' chauffeur-driven car. Thus, he actually observes his own accident by means of the television screen—a marvelous example of his detachment from reality and of the "screen[s] thrown between the self and awareness" (Tucker 222).

To emphasize Chance's dependence on TV, in the film Ashby has him carry a remote control, which he always keeps close by; when he is uncomfortable in a particular situation (as in the scene—original to the film— with the black youths, Lolo and Abbaz, who taunt him and accuse him of having been sent by Raphael), he clicks it and hopes to change his surroundings. Sellers' brilliant exaggeration of this remote-reflex—one of many comic touches original to the movie—affords a further comment on Americans today, who, with the touch of a button, expect to tune out any unpleasant reality. In another nice coupling of plot and television clip, Chance loses his remote as he is being driven to the Rand home after his accident; on the limo television is a commercial which urges people to protect themselves with a remote-controlled radar-tracking device called a "fuzzbuster."

Just as sights are important to the film, so are sounds. In the novel Chance realizes that people usually have two names and that Chance alone "didn't seem to be enough" (Kosinski 31). So he adds that he is Chance— the gardener. EE hears "Chauncey Gardiner" and assumes immediately that he must be related to her old friends, Basil and Perdita Gardiner. The assumption of this new identity is handled more elaborately and even more cleverly in the film. As he is drinking the cognac which Eve has offered him, Chance starts to introduce himself. But he has never tasted alcohol before and it stings his throat; he chokes out his name, garbling the words "Chance-Chance-the gardener."

Colin Westerbeck writes that in the film, though not in the book, there is an irony in the fact that the acceptance of Chance among all his fabulous new friends results from their having gotten his name wrong. "The film explores an irony missed by the book when Sellers endows Chance with the social grace of never making a mistake like this. Chance gets everyone's name right the first time and remembers it from then on. The way Sellers emphasizes this knack Chance has, it might be the only talent possessed by an *idiot savant*, a single way he has discovered that he can get approval from the world. Chance repeats everybody's name a bit too insistently, just as he thanks people for small amenities a bit too effusively" (Westerbeck 119). In similar fashion, Sellers as Chance ingratiates himself to others by repeating what they have said. He parrots back the end of their sentences and other snippets of their conversations; his listeners, unaware that they are hearing only the echo of their own opinions and prejudices, are struck by the profundity of his remarks. For example, after Chance says that the lawyers have closed his house, Ben (Melvyn Douglas) assumes he means that legal complications have brought about the demise of his business. The doctor (Richard Dysart) concurs and says that lawyers will soon legislate even the medical profession out of existence. Sounding quite knowledgeable, Chance responds, "Yes. Right out of existence."

As with the naming scene discussed earlier, many of the most humorous moments in the book occur as a result of some misunderstanding. In the film, precisely because they can be seen and heard, Chance's silly gestures and remarks are even more effective than in the novel; still others, just as effective, are original to the script. For instance, before going to breakfast, Chance hears a meteorologist's prediction that there is a lot of snow in the forecast. "What a morning!" the TV weatherman warns. At breakfast, Louise the maid (Ruth Attaway) informs Chance that the Old Man has died; "Oh Lord, What a mornin'!" she says. Chance associates her comment with the weatherman's and repeats instinctively, "Yes, Louise, it looks like it's going to snow." After watching a black slave on a TV show tip his hat to his white mistress, Chance (in an interesting racial reversal) greets Louise the same way on the following morning. When he is brought for treatment of his injury to the Rand estate, Chance is wheeled into an elevator by Wilson, one of the Rands' servants. Referring to the elevator, Chance says, "I've never been in one of these." Thinking that Chance is talking about the wheelchair, Wilson explains that "It's one of Mr. Rand's. Since he's been ill...." When Chance wonders if the elevator has television, Wilson—still thinking their conversation is about the wheelchair—laughs and responds, "No—but Mr. Rand does have one with an electric motor." When Chance asks, in his continuing curiosity about the elevator, "How long do we stay in here?" Wilson replies, "I don't know; see what the doctor says...."

Later, when he and Wilson are again in the elevator, Chance remarks literally, "This is a very small room"; Wilson laughs and takes Chance's words as a joke. "Yes sir, I guess that's true—smallest room in the house." Wilson, in fact, is so impressed by what he presumes is Chance's wit that the next time they are on the elevator together, he breaks out laughing in anticipation of Chance's forthcoming jest.

In another scene, when the doctor tells him to stay off his leg for a while so that it has an opportunity to heal, Chance complies fully with the order. (See Figure 14.) He raises his injured limb and stands, in a ludicrous stork-like posture, on his good leg. Later, when Chance is able to walk around the estate, he wanders to the entrance of the house. A servant, Lewis, asks him if he would like a car. Chance takes Lewis's question literally; he pauses a moment and replies, "Yes, I would like a car." Lewis assumes Chance wishes him to arrange a chauffeur to bring one of the Rands' vehicles around for his use. The car pulls up to the front steps; Lewis announces, "Your limousine, sir"; Chance says "Oh, thank you," and then, without looking at Lewis or the limo, returns to the house with the doctor. Another time, Chance—ever literal—tells the President he "looks much smaller on television."

Figure 14. An injured Chance (Peter Sellers) is treated by Ben Rand's physician (Richard Dysart). Copyright © 1979 by United Artists.

There are also numerous visual gags, as when Chance shakes hands and addresses the Chief Executive by his first name, the way Ben did, or again when Chance does a childish hopscotch step down the hall of the Rand estate. And the parallel images of Chauncey and Ben, in their wheelchairs in the billiard room or in their adjoining beds in the converted medical area of the Rand estate, suggest (as Kosinski does in the novel) that the two are metaphysical twins—both dependent upon machines for their survival[2]—and that Ben is grooming Chance to take his place.

Yet the film portrays even more vividly than did the book the limitations of Chance's knowledge of the world. Since to him the real world outside the walls of his former home is a novelty, Chance does not know how to react to it and relates according to the few behaviors which are familiar to him. And because he has never been rebuffed, it never occurs to him that he might be (Hatch 92); he has no fear of failing because he has no appreciation of achievement or any awareness of failure. Immediately after leaving the Old Man's house, for instance, he sees a middle-aged black woman on the street, carrying a bag of groceries. Associating her with Louise, he approaches her and says, "I'm very hungry now. Would you please bring me my lunch?" The woman is understandably terrified by this bizarre request and ducks into the nearest doorway, that of an adult bookstore, just to escape him.

Once at the Rand home, Chance is treated for his injury by several physicians. Chance stares at Billings, the X-ray technician who is attending Ben, for a moment and then asks, "Do you know Raphael?...I have a message for him." He assumes that since Billings is black, he must know—or even be—Raphael. Chance is indeed like a traveller lost in space, as implied by the use of the music from *Also Sprach Zarathustra*, the familiar theme from the film *2001*.

While much of the script of *Being There* is faithful to the novel, some other changes were made in bringing the book to the screen. In addition to the shift in locale from New York to Washington, a few characters were modified—though none significantly. Chance, for example, is older (to accommodate Sellers in the role); as mentioned above, EE becomes simply "Eve" (to emphasize Chance's Adamic and biblical dimension); and a few minor characters are more fully fleshed out (the party guest who alleges on the basis of what he has heard that Chance is multi-lingual and multi-credentialed is given a suitable moniker: "Senator Slipshod"). The President, played by Jack Warden, becomes part of a running gag in the film; sensing that his renomination is in jeopardy and feeling stress and distress over his agencies' inability to turn up any information about Chauncey Gardiner, he is unable to respond sexually to his libidinous wife. Dr. Allenby, Ben's suspicious doctor, also has a dimension not explored in the novel. Carefully investigating his new patient at the Rand home, the doctor soon realizes that Chance "really is a gardener"; he is then content to keep this information to himself. No comparable character in the book is able to see Chance for what he really is. And Louise is given a small scene (not in the novel) with which she almost steals the movie. Shocked at seeing Chance elevated to superstardom on national television, she screams: "Goobledegook! All the time he talked goobledegook!...hell, I raised that boy since he was the size of a pissant an' I'll say right now he never learned to read an' write—no sir! Had no brains at all, was stuffed with rice puddin' between the ears! Short-changed by the Lord and dumb as a jackass." Her conclusion that "it's for sure a white man's world in America" brings hilarity as well as a certain topicality to the movie (Kosinski and Jones 72).

The greatest change, however, from novel to film is the ending. In the book, Chance leaves the blur of the ballroom to find momentary peace in the garden. Whether he will return to society or remain in the garden is unclear; like so many of Kosinski's works, *Being There* ends on a note of deliberate ambiguity. In the film, however, there is no such ambivalence. Rand dies (another departure from the novel, though in the book his death is imminent), and at his funeral Chance becomes the only heir to Ben's legacy. As Ben's coffin is about to be placed in the Rand family crypt (which is topped by an emblem which very fittingly resembles the image on a dollar bill), he leaves the service to wander around the estate grounds. (See Figure 15.) Stopping to examine a sapling, he then walks towards a pond. In the closing scene, he walks into the pond and on to the water. So the viewer does not mistake the fact that Chance is performing a rather miraculous act, the film shows Gardiner checking the pond's depth by dipping his umbrella several feet down and then walking on the water without sinking or getting wet himself. What is merely implied in the novel is made clear in the film: Chance is the new social messiah.

The ending is a weak moment in an otherwise fine and sustained handling of Kosinski's fable, and it has been universally criticized by reviewers. The *Los Angeles Times* wrote that "the last image in the film, which does not exist in the book, suggests that no one so innocent and so guileless, speaking in parables and making those about him feel better, could exist without the endorsement of an even Higher Power than television. The book does not so much end as stop. The film does solve the problem of an ending, although...the implications are not very helpful. The choices include that it takes a heavenly patience to put up with that much television, that you have to be crazy to be nice, or that a later Gabriel will blow his SONY instead of his horn, and we had better be listening" (Champlin 1). *The Nation's* reviewer concluded: "It must have been hard to find a way to end this fantasy, but...[this one] spoils the not at all innocent fun of watching Washington drink from the fountainhead of folly" (Hatch 92). And *Commonweal* observed that in the closing scene, "Hal Ashby's worst instincts" begin to get the best of him; the whole mood gets "ominously allegorical"; and only Sellers' underacting the miracle defuses "the annoying allusion to Christ" (Westerbeck 119).

Figure 15. Chance wanders away from Ben's funeral service. Copyright © 1979 by United Artists.

Despite the criticism of the ending, Kosinski, it seems, was pleased with the finished film. Referring to the "many people [who] listen to your story on the big screen," he noted that through the medium of film "you literally open on a street corner," which he contends is "one of the original ambitions of a story teller" (Kakutani 30). Delighted with Ashby's direction and Sellers' performance as Chance, he even considered filming other of his works and began a screenplay of *Passion Play*.

And indeed Ashby's film retained much of the fun as well as the bite of Kosinski's novel. Moreover, excepting the momentary lapse at the end, it offered essentially the same warning as the book did: that as Americans continue to give precedence to the medium over the message, they invite collectivization and usurpation of their selves. They move from "being here" to "being there," and ultimately to the most passive response of all, just "seeing there." And while Kosinski's cautionary tale allows the reader to imagine that danger, the film allows the viewer—quite appropriately—to see it for himself.

NOTES

[1]Westerbrook (118) observes that "'McFeely' sounds like a cutesy way to say feeling, as if emotions were, like excrement, something you have to make up euphemisms for. 'McFeelies' are what Chance has instead of feelings. He has about him that same inane sweetness that Mr. Rogers has. He offers to the world the sort of instant-on affection that Mr. Rogers offers to children. At the death of the Old Man whose garden he has tended all his life, Chance shows no grief. But when the industrialist (Melvyn Douglas) who has taken him in for a few days dies, Chance's eyes are moist. Only the 'chance' relationship, the brief acquaintance such as one might have with a character on a soap opera, can move him. The software of the emotional life is all that's available to him."

[2]As Robert F. Willson, Jr., notes (in "Being There at the End," *Literature/Film Quarterly* 9.1 [1981]: 60): "Most devastating of all the film's ironic truths is that despite the apparent differences in economic, social, and intellectual standing between Chance and Rand, they are twins locked up in a world of illusion and dependent on machines for their survival."

WORKS CITED

Aldridge, John W. "The Fabrication of a Culture Hero." *Saturday Review* 24 April 1971: 26.

Arlen, Gary H. "From the TV Viewer's Perspective." *WATCH Magazine* March 1980: 57.

Broeske, Pat H. *"Being There," Magill's Survey of Cinema.* English Language Films. First Series. Vol 1. Ed. Frank N. Magill. Englewood Cliffs, NJ: Salem Press, 1986.

Champlin, Charles. "A Best Role for Peter Sellers." *Los Angeles Times* 28 December 1979, Sect. 4: 1.

DeSalvo, Louise. *Being There: An Introduction.* n.p., n.d. 1.

Fosburgh, Lacey. "Why More Top Novelists Don't Go Hollywood." *The New York Times* 21 November 1976, Sect. 2: 13.

Harmetz, Aljean. "Book by Kosinski, Film by Ashby." *The New York Times* 23 December 1979, Sect. 3: 19.

Hatch, Robert. "Films," *The Nation* 26 January 1980: 92.

Kakutani, Michiko. "The New Hollywood Writer Vs. Hollywood." *The New York Times* 25 April 1982, Sect. 2: 30.

Kennedy, Adrienne. Letters Column. *The New York Times Magazine* 13 October 1970: 20.

Kennedy, William. "Who Here Doesn't Know How Good Koskinski Is?" *Look* 20 April 1971: 12.

Koskinski, Jerzy. *Being There.* New York: Bantam, 1972.

Kosinski, Jerzy and Robert C. Jones. Screenplay of *Being There.* 10 January 1979: 103.

Lavers, Norman. *Jerzy Kosinski.* Boston: Twayne, 1982.

Lewis, R. W. B. *The American Adam: Innocence, Tragedy, and Tradition in the Nineteenth Century.* Chicago: University of Chicago/Phoenix Books, 1967.

"Press Panels: Movies—and the Unexplained." *Publishers Weekly* 23 June 1975: 49.

Rich, Frank. "Gravity Defied." *Time* 14 January 1980: 70.

Sayre, Nora. "Films." *The Nation* 2 February 1980.

Schickel, Richard. "Sellers Strikes Again." *Time* 3 March 1980: 64.

Tucker, Martin. "Being There." *Commonweal* 7 May 1971: 222.

Westerbeck, Colin L. "Going Nowhere: The Software of Emotional Life." *Commonweal* 29 February 1980: 118.

Bruce Bawer

No film of recent years has received a smaller proportion of the attention and admiration it deserves, whether from critics or the viewing public, than George Roy Hill's *The World According to Garp*. This amazing film, which is about nothing less than what it means to be human, had the misfortune of being released in a year when everyone in America seems to have forgotten what it means to be human. *Time* named the Computer the "Man of the Year"; the movie public fell in love not with Garp, but with E.T. That humans can be as fascinating as hardware is fast becoming an outdated notion.

The film, scripted by Steve Tesich, is of course based on John Irving's novel about the struggles of T. S. Garp—writer, wrestler, husband, and father—against the brutal destructive forces of life. Garp, in Irving's book, is an all-too-mortal Everyman, at war with the Undertoad, the symbolic embodiment of the omnipotent supernatural entity that lies in wait to crush us all. The book has many funny, happy moments, but as it progresses, things become bleaker and bleaker, and a profound pessimism asserts itself, until by the end there is an overpowering sense of doom. "Life can be sublime," the book tells us, "but it is also unpredictable and cruel." Readers loved the novel for its humor, for its offbeat characters and witty dialogue, for its picturesque format and its quixotic protagonist. Garp, the tilter against windmills, became a cult hero.

Hill's film retains the thematic materials of Irving's book, but goes around and looks at them from the other side. If Irving's theme is, "Life can be sublime, but it is also unpredictable and cruel," Hill's theme is, "Life can be unpredictable and cruel, but it is also sublime." The reversal makes all the difference. Whereas Irving gives us Garp *vs.* Life, Hill gives us Garp *qua* Life. Or, if you prefer, Garp *in* Life, the way some people are in love. If the novel is cynical, the film is sentimental. But it is a sentiment tied to a comprehensive view of things, and a creative faculty which knows exactly how to mold the materials of *Garp* to the needs of its own somewhat different intentions. Hill, unlike Irving, refuses to see the good and bad aspects of existence as attributes of different entities. The happiness and sadness in life, his film tells us, are intimately connected. They are part of the

77

same whole. Everything is part of everything else; we are all part of each other. Frank Capra's *It's a Wonderful Life* has the same theme, and Hill's film resembles it in many particulars.

Both versions of *Garp* have been interpreted as political statements. Such readings, particularly in the case of the film, miss the point. For Hill's film, even more than Irving's novel, is meant to remind us that we are not mere sociological statistics or partisans of particular ideologies, but people—confused, complicated, here to make the best we can of ourselves, of this world, and of each other between the time we are born and the time we die. The only political statement the film makes is that political statements are limited, that to make a political ideal the center of your life is to deny life. The film tells us that people do not become heroes by dedicating themselves to pure, deathless, precisely formulated ideals, like John Reed or Gandhi. They become heroes by dedicating themselves to Life itself—a Life which is not simply one of evil and destruction, but which is the essence of contradiction: cursed by mortality, yes, but also much blessed, in particular by the human power of creation.

Though it may seem foolish to think of Hill's film in connection with *Ulysses*, perhaps the twentieth century's single greatest work about what it means to be human, about Life, the sublime and the contradictory, I propose to put them together for a while. The film itself seems to suggest this connection. *Ulysses*, in its Modern Library edition, is the book Helen Holm (Mary Beth Hurt), Garp's future wife, is reading when she meets Garp (Robin Williams). Like *Ulysses*, Hill's *Garp* contains elaborate patterns of signification which punctuate this theme of Life as the essence of contradiction. Some of these patterns are borrowed from the novel, and some are not; all, however, are successfully translated into cinematic terms and are intensified in accordance with Hill's thematic intentions.

One of these patterns we may call the *creation* pattern. It is, to be sure, important in the novel. Sexual reproduction and writing, in Irving's book, are both forms of creation, ways by which human beings may hope to achieve a sort of immortality. At the end of the novel, however, the ultimate power of death is affirmed; Irving's last sentence is, "In the world according to Garp, we are all terminal cases." As I have said, Hill turns things around. In the last scene of the film, the helicopter carrying the mortally wounded Garp rises out of the last shot (as Redford's plane rises out of the last shot of *The Great Waldo Pepper*, suggesting his death), and a moment later the baby Garp (with whom the picture began, and about whom more presently) rises into the frame and freezes in mid-air. The sky is bright blue, just as bright and blue as in the film's joyous opening shot; the tone is not defeated but uplifting, the implication not one of extinction but of endurance. In some way, the film suggests, Garp lives on—that baby remains pasted in the sky, gurgling and grinning. We may be mortal in one sense, the film tells us, but we endure, in various ways, nonetheless. We live on in what we leave behind—our writings, our children. Garp, author and father, will survive. (See Figure 16.) Like Joyce, Hill offers us comfort in cycles.

The film is full of comforting reminders of this cyclicality, some from the book, most original with the filmmakers. For example, in the film as in the novel, Garp is named after his dead father—the opening lines of the film make a big point of the identification of one with the other—and his baby daughter is named after her grandmother Jenny Fields (Glenn Close). Toward the end of both film and novel, Garp takes over the coaching job once held by his father-in-law, and, as his mother once did for him, checks out classes for his son Duncan (Nathan Babcock).

The film does more than borrow from the book, however. Some of Hill's additions can be classified as "nice touches": for example, a silly joke never heard in the novel is told by several generations of young males in the film: "Why can't basketball players become fathers? Because they dribble when they shoot." In the most gentle way, this recurring line tells us that there will always be young people, there will always be sexual awakening. And there will always be children, learning to talk: Garp's childhood malapropism, "Long Ranger," found nowhere in the novel, foreshadows those of his son Walt (Ian MacGregor), which do come from the novel.

The connection between writing and sexual reproduction as human acts of creation is made in the book and strengthened greatly in the film. In both the novel and the film, as the male is traditionally the "active" partner in sex, the female passive, so Garp is a writer, Helen a "reader," as she puts it. Jenny Fields, who violates the customary role by being the active partner in Garp's conception, is also a writer.

It is only in the film, however, that Garp and Helen look in on their sleeping sons, and he says: "I'll never write anything that lovely." And it is only in the film that, when the physical and emotional wounds brought on by the death of Walt begin to heal, two things happen: Garp begins writing again, and Helen gives birth to Jenny. Both are events of creation, and signs of a kind of psychological rebirth within the family. Unlike the film, the novel does not bring the Garp family all the way back from despair—and, on Garp's part, the paranoia—brought on by the accident. Garp's return to writing, in Irving's novel, is, accordingly, not linked with the birth of Jenny; and what comes out of his typewriter is a dark, paranoid work called *The World According to Bensenhaver*. This clearly would not belong in Hill's version of the story; Hill's Garp returns to writing not with *Bensenhaver* but with *Ellen*, an angry but sane book, which demonstrates not Garp's abandonment of faith in Life but his dedication to the good in it. It is as positive, as constructive, as hopeful an event as the birth of Jenny Garp.

Thus, *in the film*, when Garp returns to writing, it is a *cause célèbre*. Duncan, hearing Daddy's typewriter upstairs, smiles: "Is Daddy writing again?" Helen is overjoyed. The script (though not the final print) has her saying: "Can spring be far behind?" (A *perfect* reaction, Helen being an

Figure 16. Garp (Robin Williams) with the women in his life: wife Helen, daughter Jenny, and mother Jenny. Copyright © by Warner Bros.

English professor.) Appropriately, the return to writing takes place, in the film, around Christmastime—the sound of Garp's typing, in fact, filters downstairs while the family is trimming the Christmas tree. The suggestion of a seasonal cyclicality in human existence could hardly be more firmly—or powerfully, or beautifully, for that matter—set forth. Nor could the parallel between writing and the act of reproduction, the two ways of achieving immortality, be so solidly established.

The film's insistence on the imperishability of man explains, perhaps, why the film, unlike the book, begins just after Garp's birth and ends just before his death. For, in a sense, in the world of this film, whose boundaries lie just short of the boundaries of his life, *Garp never dies*—he always exists. Throughout the picture, he lives. The novel, on the other hand, begins with Jenny Fields' life before Garp's conception and ends with a long epilogue about "Life After Garp," detailing the ways by which Garp's survivors meander to their separate ends. Thus, while the film plays down Garp's mortality, the novel emphasizes it; in the novel, Garp is only a fact in time.

Likewise, the film's insistence on the transcendence of human creative powers is expressed unforgettably in one brilliant opening image, that of the baby Garp—who is, like any baby, a manifestation of those powers—flying through the air, smiling. On the soundtrack, the Beatles sing "When I'm Sixty-Four"—a very appropriate choice, because its wedding of a bouncy rhythm and jaunty tone to the twin themes of time and love is shared by the film. ("There Will Never Be Another You," the closing song, also deals with these two themes.) The sequence is arresting and beautiful, simultaneously funny and touching, and at once both establishes the focus—the film is about Garp, his life from infancy to death—and sets the proper tone: a baby-fresh fascination with the sheer wonder of life.

Moreover, the opening shot tells us that the film is about Life, about what it means to be human. For the shot deliberately shows us nothing but baby and sky—no clothes, no cars, no Coke machines or deciduous trees or telephone poles. This baby could be anyone, anytime, anywhere. To be sure, he is a *boy*, and the proof of that is deliberately not hidden from us: for this film is about the miracle of human life, and sexuality is at the center of that miracle.

It is one of the best beginnings a film has ever had. Rarely has a director managed so quickly to win his audience over, to make it laugh and cry, and to place it into the proper frame of mind. Rarely, too, has a director of a film adapted from a novel served notice so stunningly that he has made the material his own. For the scene is aggressively cinematic and establishes the buoyant tone that identifies Hill's vision as utterly different from Irving's.

The seashore of Hill's opening sequence is not accidental. Beaches are traditionally symbolic of the boundaries of life. As in the novel, the water which here heralds the beginning of life will later herald the end of it when little Walt dies in the automobile accident in the rain. In the film, though not in the novel, yet another form of precipitation presages Walt's death: in bed with Garp, Helen reads a story by Michael Milton (Mark Soper) with the oxymoronically foreboding title "Black Snow." Moreover, the association of precipitation with the accident that kills Walt continues, in the film, after the event itself: in the Christmas-tree decorating scene, Duncan, who lost his right eye in the accident, says he'd like to have a glass eye containing snowflakes. (Thus we have another echo of James Joyce: for the Irishman's story "The Dead" is famous for its closing metaphor of snow as death.)

What happens after the baby Garp stops bouncing in the air? Jenny carries her baby into her family house—a house which, being just above the beach, stands on the border between the known and the unknown. It is the womb, and Jenny is the earth mother, who will one day (in the film, though not in the novel), tell Walt that she is "as old as the hills." Pulling her baby out of the sky, she carries him from the beach into the house and then out into the world. Later in the film, as in the novel, lost and broken women will come to the house for Jenny's maternal love, comfort, and guidance. ("She was our mother, and now we are motherless," Sally Devlin says—*in the film*—at Jenny's funeral. "She was our home, and now we are homeless.") Garp will return, too, when his love for Helen seems decimated, his life destroyed. (See Figure 17.) Jenny will also—in the film—*toujours le film*—tell young Garp (James McCall) about death here, as the two of them stare out to sea.

As Jenny is the earth mother, so Technical Sergeant Garp, now (as in life) a denizen of the heavens, is the sky father, who has sent his son down to earth and set him into his mother's hands. (In the novel, he appears as a living character, and so can never be the supernal figure he is in the film.) This schema will be pointed up further on in the film when young Garp pouts: "I don't have a father and I can't fly." Jenny replies: "But you have a mother and you can walk."

The imagery can be read in a Christian as well as a pagan sense. Clearly a naked babe, the son of a heavenly father, sailing slowly and mysteriously through the heavens, and then falling into the arms of his almost-virgin mother, evokes Christ and the Madonna. Garp is certainly godlike in his creative power. In his fiction he makes a world of his own, thus the title *The World According to Garp*. Indeed, as the title indicates, the equation between the characters and gods originates in the novel. But it is a notion that is introduced tenuously, only so that it can be undercut by the book's ultimate negativism. In the film, however, Garp's creative powers *are* godlike: while he is putting the story "Magic Gloves" (original with Hill and Tesich) together in his mind, for instance, we see the action of the story on screen without the usual variation in camera technique or dissolves at beginning and end to separate the fictive events of the story from the "real" events of *Garp*. The result of this lack of boundaries between the two levels of action is to suggest that Garp's creations are as "real," in some sense, as the events of the film

Figure 17. Jenny Fields' beach house provides comfort and solace to Garp, as to many others in the film.

(which, of course, they are)—and thus, in turn, to strengthen the sense that such creations promise a kind of immortality.

And of course, that is the whole purpose of setting up an identity between the characters of the film and divinities: it gives the characters dimension, substance, eternality. It makes them transcendental heroes to match Irving's existential heroes.

To be sure, the film, like the novel, sets up this identity only to qualify it. We can be like gods, the film says, echoing the novel, but only for a time. We are gods that will die, gods that can get hurt. Physical mutilation, often as a representation of psychological mutilation, is ubiquitous in the film, as it is in the novel. Michael Milton loses his penis; Duncan loses an eye; Roberta has been emasculated; the young Garp loses an earlobe to the Percys' dog Bonkers (and, grown up, bites off Bonkers' ear in revenge); Ellen James and the Ellen Jamesians are missing their tongues. All of this comes right out of the novel. So do Duncan's words as he peers through a telescope at the streets of Manhattan from the office of John Wolf (Peter Michael Goetz). "I see a man with one leg," Duncan says. "I see a man with one eye." Broken human beings are all around. "Everyone here is wounded and maimed," Roberta tells Garp at the seaside house (in the film). But—*in the film*—the possibility of injury and the certainty of death do not mean that life is pointless, or that death is the only ultimate reality. "The thing," Jenny tells young Garp after his grandfather's funeral, "is to have a life before we die. It can be a real adventure...having a life." This line appears only in the film; there is nothing resembling it in the book.

To live, in Hill's film, is to fly. To be sure, the flying motif is borrowed from the novel, where it symbolizes the sublime parts of life which are undercut by the Undertoad; it becomes much more prominent in the film, however, in which the sublimeness of life is the essence of life. Whereas the mutilation motif—suggestive of mortality—is the more prominent of the two motifs in the novel, the flying motif—suggestive of immortality—predominates in the film. Hill and Tesich make the young Garp obsessed with airplanes, and with his dead father. There is no suggestion of either of these preoccupations in the novel. Although Jenny has told Garp that his father was a tail gunner (in the novel, a ball turret gunner), he insists, "My father was a flier," and argues just as defiantly that his father may yet be alive. This is never at issue in the novel. Years later, the manuscript of Garp's first story scatters to the winds—flies!—when he jumps out of the way of a car (a symbol of ungovernable danger throughout the film): a suggestion that art—stories, books, films—preserves the experience of life, symbolized by flight, even in the midst of one's exposure to its harshest perils. (The final freeze-frame of the film would seem to suggest the same thing.) This scene is, of course, original with the film; so is a single line of dialogue near the end of the film, when Helen, in a supremely happy moment, asks Garp what he will do with his time in the near future. His grinning reply: he will take up hang gliding. These occurrences of the flight motif are positive ones; another—a negative one—is, not surprisingly, taken from the novel. Garp and Helen are looking over their future house when a plane smashes into it. The event is so preposterous that we laugh. But it is also a reminder that the sublimeness of life—symbolized by flying—can be interrupted at any time, under the most unusual circumstances. And indeed, Walt, Jenny, and Garp all die unusual deaths.

Yet death, in this film, is no existential horror. It is an integral part of a sublime life. The end of the film, which I have already mentioned, is original with Hill and Tesich. Mortally wounded, Garp flies above the Steering School in a rescue helicopter. "I'm flying—ta-ra! Ta-ra!" he tells Helen, apparently joyfully, remembering his childhood fantasies about his father the flier. Like his character Stephen, in the story "Magic Gloves," Garp "feels life as he flies into the arms of death." (This is what Walt feels too, as he "flies" up the driveway—"Ta-ra, ta-ra!"—toward his fate.) Nowhere in his book does Irving even come close to looking upon death so benignly.

Nowhere in the book, either, does Irving suggest the symbolic events of the "dream"—an animated sequence—that young Garp has in the film. In this dream, Garp's father, in a godlike act, bestows the power of flight upon his son (quite appropriately, since flight equals life, and he certainly did give his son that). Then, machine gun in hand, he shoots down a skeleton symbolizing death (yet another godlike act: the subjugation of death). Later, Duncan will wear a skeleton costume similar to the one in the dream. The animated sequence and the live-action scene preceding it are, interestingly, full of phallic imagery, from Garp's drawings of airplanes and machine guns to his reference to the "Long Ranger." (In addition, the script had death, in the animated sequence, rendered as a snake.) This pattern can at least partly be explained by an Oedipal conflict. For Garp's longing for his late father is to a great extent not a desire for his physical presence as a third member of their small family, but a desire for the adult manhood he represents. Garp does not want *him* so much as he wants to *be* him. He wants to fly as his father flew—to experience life, joy, godhead, that is, as his father experienced it. In short, to sleep with his mother.

The Oedipal theme is explored further in the scenes of Garp's childhood. (See Figure 18.) The boy is attracted to wrestling because the school's wrestlers wear the same kind of helmet he imagines his father to have worn. (In the novel, on the other hand, it is Jenny's idea for Garp to become a wrestler.) One night, playing pilot on the Steering infirmary roof, Garp slips and saves himself by catching hold of a rain gutter. Jenny, hearing him call for her, steps out of a window onto a fire escape, grabs his leg, and tells him to let go of the gutter. He does so, and with a superhuman (godlike?) act of strength she holds onto him and saves his life. The gutter snaps off and falls to the ground—actually on top of Dean Bodger (George Ede). It is hard (especially considering that Garp has been playing the part of his father) to avoid

Figure 18. Garp with his future wife, Helen Holm (Mary Beth Hurt), who reminds him of his unusual mother.

interpreting the loose rain gutter as a phallic symbol, and the rescue by his mother, who hugs him and carries him back into the window of the infirmary (like the seaside house, a womb, a place of refuge) as an Oedipal-type scene. One might argue that Garp's Oedipal fixation is carried out to its logical conclusion: he marries a photostat of his mother. Helen resembles Jenny; when she meets Garp she is dressed as sexlessly as Jenny; her last name is a homonym for "home"—a fact upon which Garp comments more than once (and of which the film makes much more than the book). In marrying Helen, Garp perhaps attempts to return to the womb.

Sex plays a key role in *Garp*. It is what binds man and woman together, as wrestling binds man and man, and games on the lawn bind father and child. (Perhaps Garp and Roberta hug so much because their relationship does not fit easily into any one of these categories.) Near the end of the film—never in the novel—Garp says to Helen, "It's really nice, you know. To be able to look back and see the arc of your life...that it's all connected...and see how you got from there to here...to see the line, you know...." In *Garp*, the curve of life is plotted against an axis one end of which points toward joy and the other toward tragedy. The line swoops up, but will eventually swoop down, one never knows when. (The difference between the novel and the film is that in the novel, the line is mostly below the horizontal axis; in the film it is above.) The role of sex in *Garp* is best understood in the context of this flux. Sex is a catalyst, capable of directing the arc of one's life sharply downward or upward. The determining factor is Jenny Fields' bugaboo: lust. Sex as function of lust is dangerous—Helen's lust for Michael Milton leads to the accident that kills one of her sons and gouges out the other's right eye. But sex as a function of love is a good thing, the best possible way of people being close and knowing each other. Sex with love produces life; sex without love destroys it. A sexual motive is behind nearly everything, good and bad, that happens in the movie.

We see the results of sex with love in the scene in which Helen tells Garp she is pregnant. This sequence, completely original with the film, evokes similar sequences in dozens of vintage American movies. One is reminded in particular of *It's a Wonderful Life*, in which Donna Reed (who, like Helen, is in bed) tells James Stewart (who, like Garp, is not) that she is expecting. But the scenes deviate from there on. "George Bailey lassoes stork!" Donna Reed cried in Capra's film. But in Hill's film, there is no talk of storks, or of the baby being in heaven. Hill shows us where the baby is. Garp pulls the sheets down, and we see Helen's belly in closeup. "He's in there, eh?" Garp says. "Boy, oh boy. It's nice in there. I know." He draws the baby's face on Helen's belly, and kisses it. It is a very effective sentimental sequence, in the manner of a movie of forty years ago, yet at the same time refuses to ignore the clinical aspect of the situation the way an American director of forty years ago would have had to do. The sequence, besides establishing Helen's pregnancy and making an intimate moment of it, draws a strong, clear connection between sex and intimacy and reproduction, and thus dramatizes the fact that sexual contact, when tied to love, can lead to wonderful things.

Lust, however, is a different story. To be sure, the filmmakers go to great pains to establish the notion that, although lust may be destructive, it is also natural. In the first episode set at Steering, some boys are drooling over a girlie magazine (one of them, prefiguring Roberta, says, "I wish I was a girl. If I was a girl I'd take off my clothes and stand in front of a mirror and look at myself for hours.") In the same sequence, Jenny has to help one of the boys, who has been playing with himself, free his penis from his zipper. "Leave it alone for a while," she advises. Finally, one of the Steering boys puts the girlie magazines in Garp's crib. "Sick!" Jenny cries, telling the baby Garp to let go of the magazine (as she will later ask the young Garp to let go of the rain gutter). "Even when they're healthy they're sick with lust!" But she seems to accept the fact of lust years later, when she gives Garp money for a whore (Swoosie Kurtz), telling him to do "what you want to do, or what you *have* to do." (See Figure 19.)

Natural or not, however, loveless intercourse leads only to ruin in *Garp*. Helen's affair with Michael leads to the accident in which Walt dies. Garp's youthful adventures with Cushie lead to his murder by her sister, Pooh. "No glove"—i.e., condom—"no love," says Cushie in the film; but her definition of love is different from the film's. Condoms prevent pregnancy and, like the gloves worn by Stephen in Garp's story "Magic Gloves," blunt sensation. What Cushie gives Garp is not love but sex *sans* love—lust; Garp can only experience real love, real life, real joy, with Helen—gloveless, producing babies. Anything else is lust. And it is because of that lust that Garp's world is (as Donald Spoto says of Hitchcock's world) one "permeated with chaos-at-the-ready."

The film's chief symbol of chaos-at-the-ready is the car. This is appropriate, because the climactic accident of the film involves two cars. I have already mentioned the car (in the script, a hearse) that almost hits Garp when he is chasing after Helen with his first story. There is also the pickup that speeds dangerously through Garp's neighborhood. There is Garp's car, which, pulled over to the side of the road to allow Garp to play around with the babysitter (Sabrina Lee Moore) looms in the darkness like—can it be?—an Undertoad (Walt's malapropism for "undertow," which, as I have explained, signifies that unseen power that draws people suddenly and unexpectedly into the maelstrom of tragedy). Later, Garp, in bed with Helen, suggests that they move away because there are "crazy drivers everywhere." Ironically, the crazy driver who will be partly to blame for his family tragedy is Garp himself, whose unorthodox way of entering a driveway makes possible the accident that kills Walt. Of course, cars make possible Michael's seduction of Helen: he fixes her car so it won't start, then offers her a ride in his. (Perhaps, indeed, the school where Garp will die is called Steering because that word reminds us of cars, the instruments of death.)

Figure 19. Jenny Fields (Glenn Close) introduces her son to sex by paying for a prostitute (Swoosie Kurtz).

Each of these symbolic patterns—the motifs of flight and of cars, of love and of lust—is borrowed from Irving's novel, but in every case Hill and Tesich build an imposing and impressive metaphoric structure to serve their own altered thematic purpose. So expertly do they do this that sometimes a line from the novel, transplanted into the film, is given much greater import by virtue of the filmmakers' having added something of their own to the mix. For instance, when the climactic accident is about to happen, Duncan says, "It's like being underwater." Walt adds, "It's like a dream." Both lines are from the novel. But Duncan's comment is far more significant in the film, which has emphasized the thematic equivalence of water with the Great Beyond. And Walt's line, like Duncan's skeleton costume, seen hanging on the back of the boys' door in an earlier scene, hearkens ironically back to the young Garp's dream, in which Garp's father fights and defeats death. The accident demonstrates, as if any demonstration were necessary, that fathers cannot save their sons from death.

A symbolic pattern that seems to be original with Hill and Tesich involves the American flag. I did not notice this until my fourth viewing of the film, and I would not mention it except that it illustrates the fact that nearly every detail in Hill's film seems to be there for a good reason. There is a flag on the flagpole in front of Jenny's seaside house; there is one on a shelf in the living room of the family quarters at Steering, and in the animated dream that young Garp has in that room; there is one on a mysterious boat which Roberta notices in the harbor, shortly before the assassination of Jenny (the Ship of Death, coming across the waters of the Great Beyond to collect her?); and Duncan, decorating the Christmas tree, even suggests getting a glass eye with a picture of the flag on it. The final occurrence of the flag image is the one that all the other occurrences are leading up to: when Jenny is assassinated on the speakers' platform with the New Hampshire gubernatorial candidate, she is surrounded by flags. And when we first see all these flags, a little voice in our subconscious, which has noticed every detail, tells us that something is going to happen here.

Hill's *Garp* is, in short, that paradox of paradoxes. It is at once an adaptation as faithful as any adaptation from one medium to another can be expected to be, or *should* be, and an impeccably crafted personal vision. It is (one cannot avoid the temptation to say it) an inspired and inspiring film.

"You know," Garp says at one point, in a speech that appears only in the film, and which, perhaps, best summarizes the difference between the novel and the film, "Sometimes you can have a whole lifetime in a day and not even notice that this is as beautiful as life gets. I had a beautiful life today." One is tempted to read this line as a coy reference by the director to his film. For, in less than a day, the viewer does live a whole lifetime—Garp's—and, after experiencing that life, may well be inclined to subscribe to a somewhat altered version of that statement: this is as beautiful as film gets.

Sophie's Choice, Pakula's Choices

Barbara Tepa Lupack

Published in 1979, *Sophie's Choice* was selected by the Book-of-the-Month Club, spent over forty weeks on *The New York Times* bestseller list, and won the National Book Award for fiction. The praise it received from many important critics was effusive. Paul Fussell (*Washington Post Book World*) deemed it an "American masterpiece...in the mainstream of the American novel," which "offers splendid comedy, too." Stephen Becker (*Chicago Sun Times*) called *Sophie's Choice* a triumph: "A compelling drama of our age's central horrors.... A dazzling, gripping book of the highest intelligence, heart and style."[1] And John Gardner, in a front-page review in *The New York Times Book Review*, described it as a passionate and courageous book, "a thriller of the highest order, all the more thrilling for the fact that the dark, gloomy secrets we are unearthing one by one...may be the authentic secrets of history and our own human nature" (16).

Yet, like Styron's third novel, *The Confessions of Nat Turner* (1967), which also explored the evil of slavery and the nature of redemption, *Sophie's Choice* generated almost as much immediate controversy as it did critical acclaim. Some readers and critics, male and female alike, saw in Sophie's victimization a portrait of what they alleged was Styron's own misogyny and in the narrative voice of Stingo (the aspiring young novelist whom Styron closely modeled upon himself) Styron's narcissistic appropriation of Sophie's tragedy. Other criticism of *Sophie's Choice* was leveled by several Holocaust scholars, most notably Elie Wiesel, who took umbrage at Styron's very use of the Holocaust as the stuff of popular fiction. Wiesel argued that any writer, but particularly a non-survivor, profanes the sacred memory of the camps by attempting to capture their experience in mere words.[2]

Styron was hardly surprised by such reactions, especially in light of similar criticism about *Nat Turner*. But he defended both *Sophie's Choice* itself and his approach to the work. One of the key virtues "of the literary method, of literary art," he contended, "is its ability, its impetus, to go for broke, for a man to write like a woman, to jump racial barriers, to jump sex and sexual barriers. The idea that I would have to be a victim of the

91

Holocaust to write about it is as absurd as its corollary about fictionalizing it" (Sirlin 103). And, in fact, *Sophie's Choice* succeeds because it is essentially an honest work, not just because Styron based his heroine on a real character in his life, "a beautiful, but ravaged" girl[3] who was a Catholic survivor of Auschwitz and who lived on the floor above him in a Brooklyn boarding house one summer after the war. It is honest because it addresses very real issues of enslavement by racism and sexual politics and of the erosion of individuals' self-worth by abusive social institutions.

As the title suggests, the novel focuses largely on Sophie Zawistowska. Like so many other characters in contemporary literature, from Ken Kesey's Chief Bromden to Kurt Vonnegut's Billy Pilgrim, Sophie struggles to forge a healthy identity from the fragments of an existence shattered by circumstance. But instead of finding liberation, she merely moves from one form of bondage to another—from the tyranny of her father and her husband in Cracow to the horror of Auschwitz to untold violence in the new world of postwar Brooklyn, where her lover Nathan Landau, who suffers from his own measure of dislocation and of madness, manages to manipulate and ultimately to undo her in a way that even Höss and the other Nazis at the camp could not. The past she tries to bury in order to survive keeps resurrecting itself, and she keeps reenacting the same scenarios of abuse and pain. She feels a great kinship with her priapic young neighbor Stingo. Both are strangers in Brooklyn (Gentiles in a "Kingdom of the Jews");[4] both are nominal Christians who have lost their faith; both are infatuated with the same man; both share a certain culpability over their country's genocidal past and must confront the ethnic stereotypes which limit their vision (Sirlin 110); and both are haunted by a survivor's guilt—as well as an Oedipal fixation[5] related to a beloved opposite-sex parent. Still, even he fails to deliver her from her sorrows; and, ironically, by forcing her to confront the very truths she has tried to suppress, he precipitates her suicide.

The novel focuses not only on the horrible choice which Sophie must make on the platform of Auschwitz but on all of her choices, which are inherently similar. Lacking confidence and self-esteem, Sophie has no strong sense of her own self. In fact, her whole identity is relational:[6] she tends to define herself by means of others, especially by the men in her life—her father Professor Bieganski; her husband Kazik, the Professor's disciple; the chiropractor Dr. Blackstock who employs Sophie in Brooklyn; her schizophrenic lover Nathan; her immature but devoted admirer Stingo. Undoubtedly, most of them are "monsters," and all of them treat her with condescension, if not outright disdain, thus exacerbating her passivity and victimization. As Styron observed in an interview with *Psychology Today,* "I don't know of a woman in modern literature who has suffered so much at the hands of men as Sophie has" (Ellison 27). Her victimization finds its fullest expression in her self-hatred, a hatred which should more appropriately be directed at her oppressors (Sirlin 33). Instead, violence becomes the metaphor not only of Sophie's daily existence but of her dreams and sexual fantasies as well. And violence in particular becomes the metaphor of Sophie's life—and death—with Nathan, whose madness and guilt so closely mirror her own.

Though the novel *Sophie's Choice* was replete with cinematic images, Styron's Sophie—a complex, secretive woman of tragic proportions— portended to be a difficult character to cinematize. To filmgoers it therefore came as little surprise that the role went to Meryl Streep, who made it so fully her own that her performance earned an Academy Award.[7] What is surprising, however, is that Streep was not first choice for the part. Director Alan J. Pakula initially felt that Sophie should be played by Liv Ullmann or some other foreign actress. But various casting problems arose; delays occurred; and Pakula, who had earlier been advised by renowned Polish director Andrzej Wajda that Streep would be ideal, reconsidered his decision. By then much of Hollywood—including actresses as diverse as Marthe Keller and Barbra Streisand—was lobbying for the coveted role which Streep eventually won (Maychick 133-34).[8]

With characteristic singlemindedness, Streep studied Polish and German to help herself get a handle on the character; and, to hone her accent, she spoke Polish both on and off the set—reportedly at times scaring her baby with her strange, guttural sounds.

Streep's determination paid off: she virtually transformed herself into Sophie by assuming the character's physical mannerisms, from breathless, giggly amusement to the haunting, haunted, darkly ruminative reflectiveness over the former life she tries both to confront and to conceal. Streep even adopted the casual and reflexive flirtatiousness of the European, so diametrically opposed to the postwar American sexual repression which masqueraded as liberalism (typified in the novel by Leslie Lapidus and her circle). Simply by twiddling with her feathery boa or playing with her hair to push back curls from her face, Streep displayed a frank, easy sexuality. And her halting, Polish-accented speech convincingly imitated the cadences of a non-English speaker. Even her malapropisms, both those borrowed from the text ("Stingo...you're wearing your cocksucker, you look so nice" [233]) and those original to the film ("You want to come up and have a night hat with me?"), were memorable.

But brilliant as Streep's portrayal of Sophie was, the film itself—while compelling—was far from flawless. Its problems were rooted largely in Pakula's desire to remain as faithful as possible to Styron's text. Pakula, who not only directed but also wrote the screenplay for the film, maintained that there are two kinds of books, one "that has an interesting idea, but you feel the book itself is not a film, so you change it until it becomes one. The other is a book that must in some way be translated. If you translate successfully, the movie will have the life and soul of the book.... People will think they're seeing the book on the screen" (Maslin 1). For him, *Sophie's Choice* was obviously the latter. Yet, as Pakula soon discovered, adapting such a rich, long novel was not easy; many of the details and intricacies of Styron's plot had to be stripped away, and other aspects of the story had to be reworked.

In the process of adaptation, Pakula wisely chose to retain from the novel certain motifs and images. One such motif was the use of photographs as a way of evoking powerful, often repressed, emotions. In the book, Sophie recalled that her father was "a very talented photographer"; she collected some of his pictures in an album (since lost to her) which showed "how it was in Cracow before the war." Now, she tells Stingo, "just the memory" of those photographs is symbolic: "For me, a symbol for what was and could have been and now cannot be" (171). Earlier at Auschwitz, the Commandant's young daughter had shown Sophie a photo album full of pictures of herself at swim competitions at Dachau ("*Das bin ich...und das bin ich*" [487], Emmi Höss repeated with obvious pride); and Sophie had felt the graphic contrast between Emmi's egocentricity and her own lack of identity in the camps. And, even after her arrival in Brooklyn after the war, a *Look* magazine photo of Rudolf Höss taken just before his execution so upsets Sophie that she wanders for a few hours before showing up at work. "So disturbed by this obscene encroachment on her memory" (178-79), she cannot banish the picture from her mind for several days.

In the film, Pakula uses photographs in an equally interesting and symbolic way. The film ends with a haunting shot of Sophie's face, superimposed on the scene of Stingo's crossing the Brooklyn Bridge (itself an important symbol for Pakula) a final time; the shot, fading rapidly to white like an old photograph or a forgotten memory, contrasts past with future, Sophie's lost hopes with Stingo's limitless possibilities. An effective final image, it also suggests Sophie's ethereal but continuing presence and reconfirms the importance of her role in Stingo's life and story. As Benjamin Dunlap notes, in the original screenplay, Pakula had planned several other shots to extend the meaning of that closing image. E.g., the opening scene of his earlier script began with Sophie's face fading in from a white haze, like a photo in developing fluid, much like the Snowden episodes of Nichols' *Catch-22*. And in the original voice-over, which Pakula eventually revised to conform more closely to the novel's opening, Stingo began: "The landscape and the living figures of that summer, as in some umber-smeared snapshot found in the brittle black pages of an old album(,) have become dirty and distant as time unspools with negligent haste into my own middle-age; yet that summer's agony still cries out for explanation" (Dunlap 114).

Sophie's is not the only haunting visage in the film. An old photograph of Bieganski, seated behind a desk and typewriter with a young Sophie on his lap, opens the first flashback sequence. Sophie, by that time a married woman but still—as ever—the Professor's obedient child, sits below his image transcribing his remarks from an Ediphone near his desk. Though Bieganski never appears, his presence is unmistakable, and his disembodied voice pronouncing "extermination" for the Jews seems all the more ominous in the absence of him as an actual character to mitigate the cruelty of his words. When Sophie interrupts her work to visit the Cracow ghetto and sees firsthand the people for whom he was proposing such a horrible fate, her delay keeps her from proofreading the speech, which Bieganski delivers with all of its errors.[9] Afterwards, as in the novel, Bieganski berates her for her stupidity. The film's flashback ends with a close-up of Sophie's face, registering the deep pain and emotion absent in Bieganski's authoritarian, stony-countenanced portrait. (Nestor Almendros, whose excellent camera work caught the close-up of Streep and created subtle nuances of her character through his lighting, achieved other similar special effects. The brown, grainy texture of the Auschwitz scene, for instance, accomplished through color desaturation, suggested not only the bleakness of the death camp but also the fading of memory [Dunlap 541].)

Similarly, Pakula eliminated from the final cut a scene in which Sophie watches her father and her husband being removed by the Nazis from the University in Cracow. "The scene turns into a still," says the original script. "The camera moves in until the father's face fills the scene.... It is as if this nightmare face is staring not just at Sophie in the past but Sophie in the present" (Dunlap 538).

Sophie is not the only one to be haunted by such images from the past. Nathan, too, is obsessed: in his study, he preserves and pores over the still photos of Holocaust horrors. His obsession is no coincidence, for in his brutality towards Sophie he commits acts much like the Nazi atrocities. (Even the cyanide poisoning by which the lovers die, notes Styron, reenacts the method by which millions of victims perished in the camps.) In the film, Pakula tries to provide visual links between Nathan's evil and the evil of the camps: he allows the camera to pause on the photographs on Nathan's walls, in the same way that he creates corresponding freeze frames at other critical points in the film (e.g., Eva's face at the moment of selection).

Another motif which Pakula carries over, largely successfully, from Styron is the significance of music, a means for Sophie of establishing and maintaining identity. In the novel, classical music was Sophie's attempt at preserving her own precarious sense of self and her link with those whom she loved; Styron himself noted that the book is filled with music, "and people who fail to understand that may well fail to grasp the book on one of its most important levels" (Morris 59).[10] And in the film, though somewhat downplayed, the motif of music remains pervasive. Pakula makes clear to the viewer that music is one of Nathan's greatest gifts to Sophie: classical works as well as more popular songs emanate from their phonograph, and even while picnicking at Prospect Park they dance to the radio's waltzing sounds. Moreover, for her birthday, Nathan surprises Sophie with a piano. Although she says she no longer plays the way she used to, Sophie gazes adoringly in return at Nathan, who serenades her, and she tells Stingo of how the instrument brings back memories from her childhood—especially of her beloved mother practicing beautiful melodies. (In a particularly poignant scene, Pakula shoots Sophie and Nathan seated at the piano playing a song together—a moment which corresponds with Sophie's recollection, in the novel, of playing music for four hands with her mother.) Even Stingo appreciates Sophie's fondness for music; he promises that after settling into his Virginia farm they will "drive over to Richmond, get a good phonograph, maybe get some records."

Sophie, it is later revealed, instilled a similar love of music in her daughter, who clutched her beloved flute even as she was being led to slaughter at Auschwitz. The faint notes of Eva's flute music become a sort of haunting, haunted, tragic chorus throughout the film: they are heard at the beginning, as the credits roll; during the flashback sequence, as Sophie's children play in the courtyard in Warsaw, and later as the train approaches the concentration camp; and again, near the end, as Stingo follows Sophie back to Brooklyn to witness her final, fateful choice.

And, in a scene original to the film, Stingo and Sophie return from the movies one evening to find Nathan conducting an invisible orchestra in a stirring rendition of Beethoven's Ninth Symphony. Nathan's effort, at one level comic, is also painful to watch: sinking into madness, he seems to be trying to exorcise his demons with the baton. But, mirrored in three of the glass panels of Sophie's bay window at Yetta's Pink Palace, his reflection betrays the multiple selves that he ultimately is unable to conceal. The split images of Nathan, like his distorted face in the mirror of the Coney Island funhouse, suggest the fragmentation of his personality, which even Sophie cannot heal.

Pakula's choice to be faithful to Styron's text, however, is not always as successful as in some of the aforementioned scenes. At times he relies so much on specifics from the novel that his film becomes overrich with details or allusions, which often are lost on the viewers. For example, a picture of Höss's favorite stallion hangs on the wall of his office. But whereas in the book Styron turned the horse into a symbol (galloping freely in a pasture at the death camp, it provided a graphic contrast to the inmates' captivity and represented the freedom for which even Höss himself longed), Pakula does not attempt to imply any connection with the characters' plight; the picture is therefore mere decoration. And, near the movie's end, when Stingo and Sophie check into a Washington hotel, the bellboy acknowledges Stingo's tip by saying, "Thank you, Reverend." But, since the whole episode involving Stingo's disguise as the Reverend Entwhistle—a manifestation of the struggle which he, like Sophie, experiences with regard to faith—was eliminated from the film, that detail too seems inconsequential or irrelevant. Apparently, though, Pakula deliberately seeded the film with numerous such details. "It is terribly important," he once said, "to give an audience a lot of things they may not get as well as those they will" (Dunlap 531).

Yet, despite the amount of details which Pakula included in the final cut, ultimately many deletions had to be made—and some of Pakula's choices of material and ideas to be cut were less than prudent. Even Styron commented on the fact that "There were so many vast areas of the book that were not even suggested" (Lewis 261). For instance, the anonymous digital rape which Sophie experienced on the subway car in Brooklyn is entirely absent from the film. That rape, however, is necessary to understanding and appreciating Sophie's mental state because it extends her victimization to postwar America and foreshadows Nathan's sexual and psychological brutality, including the usurpation of the new life she has so tenuously reconstructed. Sophie's sense of doom, her sense of inability to escape the horror and violation of her past, even in her new world, makes her accept more readily the doom and horror which in the end is Nathan's only real legacy to her. Pakula also omitted from the film the various dream sequences—of Sophie's lust for her father's guest, the young industrialist Walter Dürrfeld, whom she meets again in Auschwitz (and who, as Höss's colleague, becomes, as her father did, an agent for her destruction); of Bieganski's cruel betrayal of her and of his denial of her need for music (which, by then, is her sole measure of identity); of Stingo's mixed feelings of love and longing for his late mother (whose cancerous face he momentarily associates with Sophie's). These and other critical dream scenes revealed much about both Sophie's and Stingo's guilts and served to link the two characters to each other as well as to other prominent characters in the story.

But perhaps the most glaring omission in Pakula's adaptation occurs with respect to the character of Nathan Landau. His Nathan (played by then-newcomer Kevin Kline) is simply not as ominous—and ultimately therefore not as credible—as Styron's Nathan, who is morbidly fascinated by the Holocaust, particularly by the tortures committed in the concentration camps. In both novel and film, Nathan's bullying behavior toward Sophie is due in part to the fact that she is a survivor of those camps; he punishes her to compensate for his own survival guilt. An American-born Jew personally untouched by the Holocaust, he tries to understand his own guilty, troubled conscience by compulsively questioning her for details about why she lives while millions perished.

Nathan's almost rabid interest in the Nazi behavior which parallels his own brutality is, of course, symbolic of his instability. But in the film Nathan's sickness never fully comes through. He is reduced to menacing smiles, lunatic stares, and anguished sweat because, as Benjamin Dunlap observes, "to read about a man who abuses women is one thing, but to watch him do it is another." So, as Dunlap contends, the worst of Nathan's harassment in the film consists of his wrongly accusing Sophie of infidelity and dousing the watch she buys for him in a glass of champagne Pakula furnishes just for that purpose. "So mild," writes Dunlap, "is the onscreen Nathan that he rescues Sophie in the library without even berating the obnoxious librarian. 'I ought to break your fucking skull,' Nathan rages in the earlier script (a line lifted directly from a scene in the novel that Nathan himself describes as 'cinematic'). In the movie, Nathan simply ignores the jerk and concentrates on helping Sophie" (Dunlap 540).

Although he curses and yells (and, at one point, badgers her so unrelentingly that she begins whimpering "no, no" in Polish, the only time other than the flashback sequences that she uses her native language), the film's Nathan commits no real abuse. He never strikes Sophie; never forces her to perform degrading sexual acts (like swallowing his urine after beating her and making her perform fellatio while kneeling on the ground before him); never calls her by the hated name Irma Griese (an allusion to the notoriously beautiful but traitorous blonde in the camps); never terrorizes her on their weekend trip to Connecticut by forcing cyanide capsules on her. Nor does he, as a result, create the sense of erotic rapture which caused Jack Kroll to dub the novel's lovers "the Tristan and Isolde of the Age of Genocide" (Kroll 87). Sheila Benson commented likewise that, instead of real scenes of love, the film gives "sort of television-commercial montages of nuzzling, of movie clichés of a day at Coney Island" (Benson 1). It is possible, albeit unlikely, that such artificiality was deliberate, a way in which Pakula felt he could imitate what Styron suggests is the cinematic nature of Sophie and Nathan's relationship in the novel. But even Styron, who found much to praise although he elected to stay utterly uninvolved in bringing his work to the screen, felt that the absence of the sadomasochistic eroticism which existed between the lovers was a real flaw in the film. "Sophie and Nathan were possessed by some sort of demons that caused them to devour each other, and that involved a great deal of erotic lunacy.... The death wish and the procreative wish have often been so closely connected you can't separate them. That was essential to me, and to the relationship between Sophie and Nathan." Yet it was "totally lost in the movie." Pakula's timidity in touching on that important area of the relationship, Styron believed, "vitiated the whole ending, because there is no premonition, as you get in the book, of why and how they're going to die together, by mutual suicide, by poisoning, not even a hint of that in the movie" (Lewis 262-63).

Similarly downplayed in the film is the importance of Stingo (Peter MacNicol). Hardly an equal in the charmed life in Brooklyn during the summer of 1947, he seems a voyeur of sorts, a receptive audience for Nathan and Sophie's theatrically flamboyant, exhibitionistic antics. (Stanley Kauffmann called him a confidant posing as a protagonist, "[occupying] space without dramatic justification" [Kauffmann 114]). Although in the book Stingo was as essential a character as Sophie, whose search for identity parallels his quest to become a great American novelist, in the film he becomes an adoring puppy—even down to his puppy face—who follows closely at her heel. Almost as helpless around Nathan as he is around Sophie, Stingo is virtually swept along by the force of their personalities. He stares, at first uncomfortably and later empathetically, at the lovers and acts as witness to the evolution—and rapid devolution—of their romance. (See Figure 20.) But his crucial function of interpreter and of narrative link is essentially lost in the film: the viewer sees what Stingo sees (and often more, given Stingo's naiveté). Stingo's presence is therefore not only less necessary than in the book but even superfluous, except to provide a frame for the story within his story.

Nor does Pakula translate very fully the important connections which Stingo and Sophie share in the novel, from the guilt over the slavery in their pasts, their own occasional bigotry, and their professed lapses of faith to their perversely erotic, death-haunted dreams and their enduring, though radically different, attachments to their fathers. In fact, Pakula provides Stingo with little significant past. The film audience is never told of his service in the Marines, and no reference is made to his publishing job, which establishes a motif of bureaucratic oppression and conformity in the novel. Stingo arrives directly in Brooklyn, "the Sodom of the North," and lands immediately at Yetta Zimmerman's without ever passing through the halls of McGraw-Hill, an experience whose description constitutes much of Styron's first chapter.

Pakula also ignores the vital issue of Stingo's inheritance, the money from the sale, many years earlier, of his family slave Artiste, which affords him the opportunity to embark on his career as a writer (a latter-day "artist"). Although Stingo at one point sits at his desk counting his stash of cash and at another point buys an entire case of Spam (which indicates—though somewhat elusively to the younger viewer—that his diet is dictated by penury [Dunlap 535]), in the film his stipend is not explicitly, or even implicitly, linked to the profits of slavery. It is that same slavery which causes him to feel moral recriminations and which links him further to Sophie, who feels a similar guilt over her father's legacy of enslavement (both Bieganski's proposed slavery of the Jews and his desire for her indentured servitude to him). Actually, other than Stingo's awkward Southern diction, the passing mention of the peanut farm bequeathed to him, and the extravagant Rhett Butler-Scarlett O'Hara costumery which Sophie and Nathan don on his behalf (in a scene original to the film, though consistent with the motif of masquerades in the novel), there is comparatively little to link Stingo with the South he so recently left and which, in the book, proves as critical to his development as Sophie's Polish experience does to hers.

Moreover, in Styron's novel, Stingo is working on his own novel, based upon his first love, a tormented young woman named Maria Hunt (who, in Pakula's version, is wholly absent as a character). Like Peyton Loftis, the heroine of Styron's first novel *Lie Down in Darkness* (1951), Maria took her own life and thus anticipated Sophie's tragic end and Stingo's obsessive need to understand her motives. In the film, Stingo writes not of Maria but of his mother, specifically of his mother's death, which occurred when he was twelve years old. When Sophie observes that he must have loved his mother

Figure 20. On the roof of the Pink Palace, Stingo (Peter MacNicol) observes the love between Sophie and Nathan. Copyright © 1982 by Universal City Studios.

a great deal in order to make her his subject, Stingo responds only, "I could have loved her more." Cutting from Stingo to Sophie, Pakula then uses the revelation not as a way of developing Stingo's character but as a deft segue into Sophie's searing memories of her father.

Nor does Pakula ever link, as Styron so ably does, Stingo's sexual obsession, especially his quest to lose his virginity, with his quest to become a successful author. Even Stingo's attempted seduction in the film of wealthy, Sarah Lawrence-educated Leslie Lapidus (a scene memorable mostly for its irrelevance) provides few clues to his character. By contrast, in Styron's novel, Leslie serves as a foil for Sophie; Leslie's seemingly liberal sexual attitudes (e.g., her ability to pepper her speech with explicitly sexual language) prove false and contrast sharply with Sophie's real sensuality and honest passion. Leslie can talk about sexual acts in which she ultimately cannot engage, whereas Sophie, despite being restricted by language, possesses a sexuality Leslie will never be able to articulate much less match. (Nevertheless, as Carolyn Durham observes, Stingo takes it upon himself to make History—and his story—out of *her* story.)

Just as he cut or abridged critical details and scenes with Leslie and with other of the women (like the aptly named "Whack-off artist" [429], Mary Ann Grimball) after whom the perpetually horny Stingo lusts, Pakula avoided some of the other interesting ambiguities which made Styron's novel so rich. For instance, although the novel's Bieganski is an ambivalent figure, hateful in his anti-Semitism but also a product of his time, in Pakula's version he is depicted entirely as a monster, as if to show that anti-Semitism can only be symptomatic of undiluted wickedness.[11] Accordingly, Pakula portrays Sophie's professed hatred of Jews to Höss as a temporary insanity, the act of a desperate and otherwise powerless victim. Styron, however, recognized the ambiguity of Sophie's "role playing" in assuming the pose of an anti-Semite with Höss and thus showed her engaging in other overtly anti-Semitic remarks or behaviors, particularly outbursts of anti-Semitism against Nathan when he rejects her.

Styron, through Stingo, also offered mild (if not altogether credible) explanations for Höss's and Auschwitz officer von Niemand's conduct: the former was an ex-Catholic who had perverted his religious inclinations in the worship of a false God, the Führer; the latter was a failed believer seeking redemption who still "kept a sense of Good and Evil" and for whom "the only way of making God real in a world He has deserted is to commit the most horrible sin imaginable." Pakula, on the other hand, for the most part shunned ambiguity and, in a movie already long at two and a half hours, was often reluctant to invoke or explore such ambivalences in character. He shows Sophie's lover, a brave Resistance fighter in Warsaw, for instance, and has Sophie recite the sad fact of his death, but Pakula never mentions Jozef's function as an assassin for the underground, since such ambiguity would only complicate the already complex cinematic narrative. And rather than refuting directly, if controversially—as Styron did—the notion of the exclusivity (e.g., the uniquely Jewish nature) of the Holocaust, Pakula makes non-Jewish suffering largely a matter of the film's texture (e.g., background figures crossing themselves as the train approaches the death camps). Similarly, Pakula censors Sophie's final statement of negation and despair, in which she curses God—who, she feels, like all of the male authority figures in her life, only brutalizes and abandons her—and "all his Handë Werk...and Life too" (607). Although intact in an earlier version of the film, in the final cut Sophie's words disappointingly become little more than an affirmation of Stingo's masculinity ("You're such a beautiful lover.... You are a great lover, Stingo").

Though Pakula's adaptation and handling of some scenes in the film can be faulted, the film's flashback scenes deserve special praise. They are handled quite effectively; and while the Auschwitz sequence is fairly long, it flows coherently from the cinematic narrative. Equally effective is Pakula's establishing of parallel scenes which comment on each other. Nathan, for instance, returns to the Pink Palace after his big fight with Sophie and tells her, "Sophie...we...are...dying" (92). In a later scene, but one which occurs chronologically earlier in their relationship, as Nathan revives Sophie from her faint, she tells him, "I think I'm going to die" (126). Moreover, Nathan's rescue of her is filmed with an angle shot from Sophie's perspective—lying on the floor and looking up—just as the scene of Emmi Höss resuscitating Sophie with the smelling salts is. (The similarities in shooting are quite deliberate: Emmi, like Nathan, is simultaneously Sophie's deliverer and tormentor.) And Nathan, on his first evening with Sophie after her ordeal in the Brooklyn College Library, fills her room with flowers and candles. It is a gesture romantic yet funereal, which foreshadows their eventual suicide on Sophie's bed in a comparably surreal setting.

The bed, in fact, becomes a pivotal visual image for Pakula in defining the relationship between the lovers: it shakes the ceiling so forcefully that it becomes one of Stingo's first impressions of them; its prominence in the room and in some of the scenes (e.g., Sophie and Nathan nuzzling at the piano, the bed in the background) alludes to their almost compulsive sexuality; and it implies the interrelatedness of that sexuality, as a life force, with the death force of their mutual suicide. (See Figure 21.) The bed also serves obliquely as their epitaph. In the novel Stingo, who feels compelled to compensate for the insipidly saccharine remarks the minister makes at the service, recites Dickinson's poem, "Ample make this bed," at the gravesite. Pakula, however, gives the poem even greater emphasis: he refers to it twice, in parallel scenes. In the film, only hours after they have met, Nathan gives Sophie the book of Dickinson's verse from his library, then sits on the bed and reads the poem aloud to her. The camera pulls back and then fades on their tender image, seen now from the outside of the room's rain-streaked window, as if in misty memory. Later, after Stingo returns to Yetta's to find Sophie and Nathan dead, he picks up the same book and reads aloud again

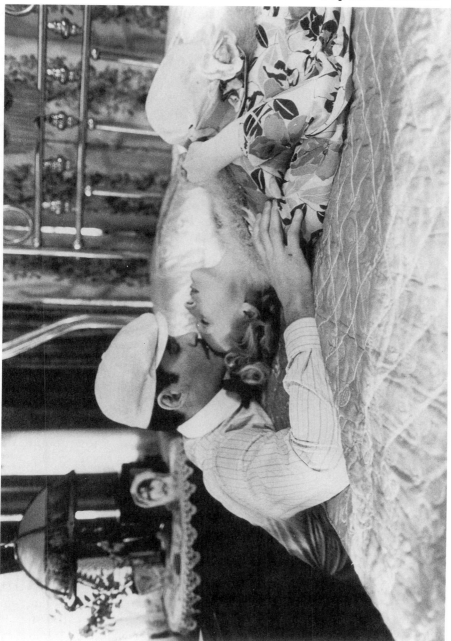

Figure 21. Sophie (Meryl Streep) and Nathan (Kevin Kline) on their bed, a central image in *Sophie's Choice*. Copyright © 1982 by Universal City Studios.

the poem from the foot of their bed, offering it as both benediction and eulogy.

Pakula uses windows, too, in a clever way throughout the film, much as Milos Forman did in *One Flew Over the Cuckoo's Nest*, where the windows kept the inmates apart from the world of nature—the real world—beyond Nurse Ratched's ward. For Pakula, as for Forman, windows suggest a physical and symbolic separation from all that is outside. In the opening scene of *Sophie's Choice*, Stingo is travelling by train to New York; the unfamiliar sights of the Northern waste land are reflected in the train's window, as is the embracing couple seated next to him. (The implication is that all Stingo knows of life and love comes from watching, not doing.) When he is finally together with Sophie in the room of their Washington hotel—at last a participant, no longer a spectator—he, significantly, is unable to pry open the windows more than a crack. Their hotel room, after all, represents a sort of hermetically sealed chamber—of horrors, for Sophie, who is beating back death; of delights, for Stingo, who is at long last embracing the goddess of his dreams. It also serves as a window inwards, a confessional where Sophie reveals her darkest secret to her confessor only hours before she dies.

That Sophie is trapped by the weight of her memories is demonstrated by Pakula even in the manner in which she first tells her story to Stingo. She sits on the window bench in her room at Yetta's, gazing forlornly and a little drunkenly at the street below. The evening light casts an eerie whiteness on her beautiful face. As she speaks of all that she has lost—her parents, her children, her faith—the camera shoots her image in regular close-up and then again in close-up from the outside of the window, as if to convey her entrapment. (The camera shots parallel those of the scene of her first evening with Nathan.) As morning approaches, Stingo, who has beseeched Sophie to live for him now, tries to shield her from the harsh glare of the morning sun, just as he tries to shield her from Nathan's violent temper; but he is unsuccessful. Sophie awakens, looks out the window, and runs to be reunited with Nathan, whom she sees sitting dejectedly on the curb below.

Sophie's windows, furthermore, become mirrors to the soul, reflecting not only Nathan's multiple selves but also Sophie's increasing inability to hide from the truth. When Stingo initially visits Sophie's room, it is decorated with her characteristic flair: matching fabrics line the tables and drape her windows, and green plants hang in front of the panels. But as Sophie's relationship with Nathan grows more acrimonious and both begin to move their belongings out, Sophie takes down her curtains and packs them away; her plants also disappear. The emptiness of the room, especially the translucency of the bare windows, symbolizes her emotional emptiness. Her pain is inescapable: no curtain, no lie can conceal it anymore. Though Sophie and Nathan's reconciliation includes a festive restoration of the things each removed, the redecorated room loses its comfortable familiarity and takes on an air of unreality—a sort of movie-set look. And that is just what it becomes, when the two dress in their period garb and swallow cyanide capsules, thus bringing an end to their sad romance.

Like Sophie, Nathan has much to hide. His duplicity is made evident in a scene original to the film in which he explains to Stingo why he and Sophie love to dress up. It is, he says, because the world is "so boring." He repeats the word "boring" several times, turning to the open window and shouting it out, almost cathartically. But, recognizing a neighbor who is standing below, Nathan immediately catches himself and transforms "you're boring" into "good morning!" His quick wit helps him to recover, just as it helps him to maintain so successfully and for so long his masquerade of sanity.

And, of course, it is through the window that Sophie and Nathan first enter Stingo's room, to "make up" and to invite him to join them at Coney Island (and ultimately in their fantastic lives), and through the same window that Nathan escapes with Stingo's manuscript. And Stingo peers out of his window to catch glimpses of Sophie, whom he can never fully possess, as she returns home with groceries or as she kisses Nathan goodbye in the morning—all part of the illusion of happiness which dissipates so quickly.

Even at Auschwitz, windows are symbolic: Emmi Höss's room, with its lace-curtained windows, is sweetly typical of any young girl's—except for the small swastikas embroidered on the curtains' fabric. And Sophie's dark basement room, with its tiny window, lets in as little joy as it does light: as she sits on her cot eating her meager ration of food, she overhears Höss discussing the high mortality rate in the children's camp and realizes that Jan, her son, may already be dead, despite her attempts to save him.

Circles, like windows, also assume a symbolic function in the film. Like Mike Nichols, who made circles the central image of his *Catch-22*, Pakula employs them to represent the circularity of human action and the inevitability of fate. Sophie survives the Nazi brutality of the camps only to arrive in Brooklyn, where Nathan duplicates the Nazi horror and brings her full circle to her death. The unbroken circle of evil is graphically depicted by the round mosaic in the floor of the Brooklyn College Library, where Sophie encounters the self-important, Nazi-like librarian who mocks her ignorance. Stingo too comes full circle, from innocence to experience, just as he makes a geographic circle in his travels from Virginia to New York, south again with Sophie, back to Brooklyn without her, and finally away from Brooklyn altogether. And Nathan is caught quite literally in a circle of madness he cannot escape. His plight is conveyed by the twister (see Figure 22) and the "Round-Up" he rides with Sophie at Coney Island, which represents their world, spinning out of control around them, and by the slowly rotating "tunnel of fun" in the amusement park. While Sophie and Stingo leap out of the tunnel, Nathan lingers inside it long enough to be turned upside down. Though neither Sophie nor Stingo is aware of it yet, Nathan is indeed upside down, psychologically out of sync with reality.

Figure 22. Unaware of the fact that their world is spinning out of control, Nathan, Sophie, and Stingo spend a day of fun at Coney Island.

But Pakula's finest work in *Sophie's Choice* involves those scenes which deal with the unspeakable madness of the Holocaust; and what makes his handling of those scenes so outstanding is his avoidance of trivialization. There are no graphic or realistic portrayals of the gas chambers, the beatings, the tortures, the medical experiments. Pakula focuses instead on the psychological horror of one woman, who loses everything, including her sense of self. Rather than shocking the viewer with the trappings of the camps, he forces the viewer (as Styron forced Stingo and his readers) to imagine the unimaginable.

Most horrific of all is the very matter-of-factness of the Nazi operation. When Sophie, for instance, is taken from her barracks to serve as Höss's secretary, she is led across a muddy field. Her escort is a stern, hefty female guard; Sophie, pale and gaunt, swoons as she walks, her legs too weak to maneuver the deep mud. On her way she passes the temporary barracks of the newly arrived prisoners marked for routine extermination. Though Sophie, in a voice-over, says that they were naked, thirsty, and confused, all the viewer sees is their hands—an ocean of hundreds of hands—thrashing and reaching out blindly from behind the barred windows. The disembodied hands bear witness to the depersonalization which the Nazis imposed in the camps: stripped of identification, people became numbers, anonymous masses slated for heavy labor or instant death, hands without bodies or minds.

Arguably the single most moving scene in the film—the moment of Sophie's tragic choice—could, with lesser direction, have been the most maudlin. Having left the train, Sophie is herded into one of several groups of new arrivals, virtually indistinguishable from each other in the dark. The camera pulls back to pan the platform, widening its shot to show the doomed, who seem to keep coming, line after line, group after group. The enormity of their numbers helps to explain the capriciousness of the Nazi selections: with so much potential slave labor readily available to the Reich, choices about who dies sooner and who dies later become both arbitrary and redundant. The prisoners, exhausted and broken in body and spirit, follow their captors' commands like obedient children. Incapable of resistance or protest, they remain fearfully silent and move only when instructed.

Pakula's guards, though, contrary to Hollywood-Nazi tradition, are almost interchangeable with the doomed, with the exception of the unnamed doctor (called von Niemand in the book) who confronts Sophie. As he approaches, his face is truly the incarnation of pure evil. When he makes his lewd remark to Sophie, who conspicuously tries to avoid his gaze, and when he mockingly deflates her expression of nationality and faith, he is nothing short of the consummate villain—a contemporary Satan presiding over an earthly hell. Most vivid is not his passion for his diabolical responsibilities but his dispassion, his bloodlessness within what Hannah Arendt called the ordinariness of the horror: Sophie is, for him, merely the object of brief amusement (as she was for Höss). By contrast, Sophie's face—like the face of her little girl—is a study in pain as archetypal as Abraham's for Isaac at the instant of his sacrifice. Pakula masterfully captures the moment at which Sophie grasps the fact that she may lose both of her children if she fails to respond: amidst blurred movements, confused and confusing actions, there is a dark tangle of uniforms, bodies, arms, and then a shot of Eva being led away crying, followed by the audience's realization of the implications of Sophie's horrible choice.

In the novel, Sophie is so blinded by her tears that she is spared this final heartbreaking vision; in the film, her agony is all the greater, for she must witness the consequences of her decision. She opens her mouth to scream, but all sound fails her; Eva's wailing, however, seems an echo of the lamentation which springs from Sophie's soul. Her face, virtually frozen in pain, recalls the freeze frame of Eva, juxtaposed against the black smoke rising from the crematorium chimneys, which ended the previous flashback sequence. (Earlier in the film, just before Sophie speaks for the first time to Stingo about her children, she glances down at the street outside her window and sees several neighborhood youngsters running toward the ice cream vendor's familiar cart. The very normalcy of that picture provides a strong counterpoint to the atrocities Sophie then begins describing. Like the boys and girls whom Sophie recalls playing ball in the Höss garden on the day she entered the Commandant's employ, the Brooklyn children seem to be in a world much different from that of Eva and the helpless young people who perished at Auschwitz.)

Pakula's choices, as director as well as screenwriter, were often difficult; and, in the end, his film of *Sophie's Choice* was compelling but imperfect. Critics, generally praising Streep's performance, found the film itself lacking. Stanley Kauffmann, who felt the film was "better than the book... [primarily] because we are spared almost all of Styron's grandiose prose" and "gummy rhetoric," concluded nevertheless that "in other ways the film is just as unsatisfactory" (40). Jack Kroll thought it captured much of the "scarifying heat" of the novel but, "in registering so much of Styron's potent rhetoric...[gave] a literary flavor to the film that sometimes makes it seem more like an illustrated novel than an explosively dramatic movie" (87). Sheila Benson observed similarly that "the film feels claustrophobic, prolix and airless to the point of stupefaction.... It's sad that in faithfulness to the weight of the book, the film has lost speed and urgency" (14). And Pauline Kael called it "an unusually faithful adaptation of William Styron's Holocaust Gothic...[but] an infuriatingly bad movie" (68).

Perhaps the best assessment—a judgment excellent and fair—of Pakula's *Sophie's Choice* was Styron's. Noting his "feeling of deeply qualified approval," Styron commented: "I think the great virtue of the film is that it extracted the essence of the book, the central story. The message of the book was retained. Of course, it could not contain any of the purely philosophical points that were made, but I thought it did an awfully good job of capturing the basic outline" (Lewis 261).

NOTES

[1]Reviews as cited in the Bantam paperback edition of *Sophie's Choice* (New York, 1980).

[2]Gloria Steinem, in "Night Thoughts of a Media Watcher," *MS.* Nov. 1981, contended that Styron brought his "liberal chutzpah and [an] infuriating bias" to the portrayal of his title character. Although Sophie had survived years of atrocities in a concentration camp, including the deaths of her children, and had vowed to outlive Höss, the hated Commandant so that he would not triumph, Styron—according to Steinem—depicts her freely loving "a sexual fascist in New York" and then fulfilling the adolescent fantasies of another chauvinistic lover, who ultimately usurps her experience. Such a portrayal, Steinem claims, demonstrates Styron's galloping sexism, which condones criminally insane behavior as a normal male mating style and takes for granted "female self-hatred, egolessness, and obsessions with pleasing men." (Steinem's comments are cited in Rhoda Sirlin, *William Styron's Sophie's Choice: Crime and Punishment* (Ann Arbor: UMI Research Press, 1990) 27-28.

Carolyn Durham, in an important article "William Styron's *Sophie's Choice*: The Structure of Oppression," *Twentieth Century Literature* 30 (Winter 1984): 4, also examines *Sophie's Choice* from a feminist perspective but takes issue with some of Steinem's arguments. She writes that Styron's novels "are not oppressive but about oppression, not racist but about racism, not anti-Semitic but about anti-Semitism, and...not sexist although, in the instance of *Sophie's Choice*, [they] are persistently about sexism" (449).

Among those to criticize Styron for trivializing the Holocaust in his novel are the following: Elie Wiesel, in "Art and the Holocaust: Trivializing Memory," *The New York Times* 11 June 1989; Alvin H. Rosenfeld, in *A Double Dying: Reflections on Holocaust Literature* (Bloomington: Indiana University Press, 1980); Alan L. Berger, in *Crisis and Covenant: The Holocaust in American Jewish Fiction* (Albany: SUNY Press, 1985); and Cynthia Ozick, in "A Liberal's Auschwitz," *The Pushcart Prize: Best of the Small Presses*, ed. Bill Henderson (New York: Pushcart Book Press, 1976). Wiesel's comments were typical; he argued that any writer, but particularly a non-survivor, profanes the memory of the camps by attempting to capture their experience in mere words. Since Auschwitz is beyond description, he urged silence (a curious appeal for a man who himself has spent a lifetime writing about the Nazi terror). "Only those who lived [the truth of Auschwitz]," he concluded, "can possibly hope to transform their experience into knowledge. Others,"—and Wiesel singled out Styron—"despite their best intentions, can never do so."

[3]Styron says the book "was suggested by a mere germ of experience. I had been living in a boarding house in Brooklyn one summer after the war and such a girl lived on the floor above me; she was beautiful, but ravaged. I never got to know

her very well, but I was moved by her plight. Then, about five years ago, I awoke one morning with a remembrance of this girl; a vivid dream haunted my mind. I suddenly sensed that I had been given a mandate to abandon the novel I had been at work on and write her story" ("About the Author," opposite p. 626 in the Bantam paperback edition of *Sophie's Choice*).

[4]The first edition of *Sophie's Choice* was published by Random House in 1979. The reference here is to page one of the paperback edition published by Bantam the following year. All subsequent references will be to the paperback edition and will be given by page number in the text.

[5]The Oedipal fixations are discussed in "Dreams and the Two Plots in Styron's *Sophie's Choice*," an unpublished paper by Daniel W. Ross, as cited by Samuel Coale, "Hawthorne's Guilt, Poe's Palaces," *Papers on Language & Literature* 23.4 (Fall 1987): 520.

[6]Carolyn Durham uses this approach (of Sophie's identity being "relational") to define her relationships; other critics follow Durham's lead.

[7]Though her first Academy Award as Best Actress, the Oscar was actually the second which Streep had received. Her first, for Best Supporting Actress, was given for her performance as Joanna in *Kramer vs. Kramer*.

[8]Maychick, in Chapter 21, "*Sophie's Choice*," gives an extended description of the casting and filming of *Sophie's Choice*.

[9]In the novel, it is not a speech but rather an essay which Sophie is preparing for the printer. The repercussions of Sophie's haste, however, are the same.

[10]Not only, as Styron says, is music crucial to a full understanding of the book; it is also one more way in which Nathan manipulates and terrorizes Sophie. Every time they fight, he demands the return of the records he has purchased for her. He knows that she has defined her identity, at least in part, by the music which she loves; and each time he withdraws that music from her, he asserts his very powerful role in shaping her identity as well as her destiny.

[11]Dunlap (539) observes that it is understandable that "monsters like Höss can love their monstrous children." Far more complex is "how good and bad get inextricably intermixed, how victims are haunted by guilt and villains by convictions of their innocence. Or how monsters themselves become pathetic with nooses about their necks, and their victims vindictive when they get their retribution."

WORKS CITED

Benson, Sheila. "Streep Shines Through 'Sophie's' Drawbacks." *Los Angeles Times* 10 December 1982, Calendar, Part IV: 1, 14.

Dunlap, Banjamin. "Pakula's Choices." *Papers on Language & Literature* 23.4 (Fall 1987): 114-541.

Ellison, James. "William Styron: An Interview." *Psychology Today* January 1983: 27.

Gardner, John. "A Novel of Evil." *The New York Times Book Review* 27 May 1979: 16.

Kael, Pauline. "Tootsie, Gandhi and Sophie." *New Yorker* 27 December 1982: 68.

Kauffmann, Stanley. "Pakula's Choice." *The New Republic* 10, 17 January 1983: 40, 114.

Kroll, Jack. "The Sorrow and the Evil." Rev. of the film *Sophie's Choice. Newsweek* 20 December 1982: 87.

Lewis, Stephen. "William Styron." *Conversations with William Styron.* Ed. James L. W. West, III. Athens: University of Georgia Press, 1981. 261-63.

Maslin, Janet. "Bringing 'Sophie's Choice' to the Screen." *The New York Times* 9 May 1982: 1.

Maychick, Diana. *Meryl Streep.* New York: St. Martin's, 1984. 133-34.

Morris, Robert K. "Interviews with William Styron." *The Achievement of William Styron.* 2nd ed. Ed. Robert K. Morris with Irving Malin. Athens: University of Georgia Press, 1981. 59.

Sirlin, Rhoda. "A Conversation with William Styron." *William Styron's Sophie's Choice: Crime and Punishment.* Ann Arbor: UMI Research Press, 1990. 27-110.

Adapting *The Color Purple*:
When Folk Goes Pop

John Peacock

The rage—positive among white audiences, negative among black (especially black male) critics and reviewers—over Steven Spielberg's adaptation of *The Color Purple* has subsided since the film came out in 1985, and the movie has gone on to become a staple of the home video business.[1] Perhaps it is time, not to rehash the film's controversy, but to understand its popularity. A clue might be found in Walker's 1973 short story "Everyday Use," which satirizes a radically chic character who puts the functional quilts she once despised on her walls, framing them as popular culture art objects, which she now finds beautiful.[2] By analogy, we might ask, what happened to Alice Walker's depiction in *The Color Purple* of quilting and two other African and African-American folkways—face scarring and the verbal repartee known in the African-American community as "signifying"— when reframed in a popular film? As we shall see, depending on the particular instance, the film either deleted these practices altogether or radically altered their meaning.

To begin with a definition of "signifying": in *The Psychology of Black Language*, Jim Haskins and Hugh F. Butts write that African-Americans generally understand that "to signify upon" someone means "to berate [or] degrade" him or her. "Signifying" can also refer to "a more humane form of verbal bantering" (Haskins and Butts 86, 51). As Henry Louis Gates, Jr., has pointed out in his study of signifying, this second meaning is sometimes confused with the first by people outside the African-American speech community (81).

Steven Spielberg may be one such outsider. Berating or degrading is always the whole point of signifying in his adaptation, but only initially the point in Walker's novel. In the film, characters signify upon one another and then separate as a means for keeping their verbal aggression from getting out of hand. In the novel, the same words eventually lead characters to patch up differences verbally and then, as if to symbolize this in a different medium than words, to quilt or sew together. Spielberg deletes these sewing scenes, perhaps because, given his restricted notion of signifying, he cannot understand how it could lead to anything other than characters separating to avoid further conflict. When these characters do come back together in the film, their differences seem resolved for no apparent reason rather than worked through in the way Walker shows.

This is not to say that characters in the novel never berate, only that they become reconciled through real human interactions. Both novel and film show main character Celie (Whoopi Goldberg) signifying upon her abusive husband Albert (Danny Glover) after Shug Avery (Margaret Avery) tells him that Celie is leaving him to go to Memphis with her. "[O]ver my dead body," he responds, "I thought you was finally happy.... What wrong now?" Celie answers in a classic instance of the first kind of signifying defined above: "You a lowdown dog is what's wrong, I say. It's time to leave you and enter into the Creation. And your dead body just the welcome mat I need" (207).

One desired effect of berating is to get the better of someone, and Albert's reaction shows that Celie has succeeded: "Say what? he ast. Shock...Mr. _____ start to sputter. ButButButButBut. Sound like some kind of motor.... Hold on, say Harpo" (207), Albert's son (Willard Pugh), tryies to intervene, but Celie turns her signifying powers on him as well: "Oh, hold on hell.... You was all rotten children, I say. You made my life a hell on earth. And your daddy here ain't dead horse shit" (207).

Henry Louis Gates, Jr., describes this speech as Celie's "signifying declaration of independence" (252), and at this stage in Celie's relationship to her husband and stepchildren that is exactly what it is. On the other hand, she is never more like Albert than at this moment, as is shown by his delayed reaction when he finally does find his voice and signifies upon Celie in return:

> Mr. _____ try to act like he don't care I'm going. You'll be back, he say. Nothing up North for nobody like you. Shug got talent, he say. She can sing. She got spunk, he say. She can talk to anybody. Shug got looks, he say. She can stand up and be notice. But what you got? You ugly. You skinny. You shape funny. You too scared to open your mouth to people. All you fit to do in Memphis is be Shug's maid. Take out her slop-jar and maybe cook her food. You not that good a cook either.... And this house ain't been clean since my first wife died. And nobody crazy or backward enough to want to marry you, neither. Look at you. You black, you pore, you ugly, you a woman. Goddam, he say, you nothing at all. (212-13)

Albert's speech typifies what Gates calls signifying's often "phallocentric orientation" (65). In her declaration Celie, while keeping the overall tone of abuse, seems only to have reversed the roles of who generally abuses whom in her marriage.

Celie will not really be independent from Albert until she can disentangle her voice from his and learn to speak even to him in a way that is neither as submissive as she once was nor as vindictive as she is in her declaration. Talking with her relative Sofia in a conversation which we will examine shortly, Celie develops a version of signifying that black women use with each other to achieve more conciliatory ends than getting the better of someone. Though Celie's means are rhetorical, the ends she achieves are developmental, resembling those described in psychologist Carol Gilligan's book *In a Different Voice: Psychological Theory and Women's Development.*[3]

Not just her oral conversations but also the letters Celie writes in this epistolary novel typify Gilligan's finding that "a young woman's account of her crisis of identity...centers on her struggle to disentangle her voice from the voices of others and to find a language that represents her experience of relationships and her sense of herself" (51). The novel's very first line—"You [Celie] better never tell nobody but God [about having been sexually abused by your father]. It'd kill your mammy" (1)—supports Gilligan's finding that "The secrets of the female adolescent pertain to the silencing of her own voice, a silencing enforced by the wish not to hurt others but also by the fear that, in speaking, her voice will not be heard" (51).

Because she fears both hurting her mother and not being heard, Celie starts writing to God. Her first letter begins by stating that she is an adolescent: "I am fourteen years old. ~~I am~~ I have always been a good girl" (1). The struck-out present tense suggests that already Celie is moving beyond and reflecting back on the stage in her life when, as Gilligan puts it, "the good is equated with caring for others" (74). Celie cared for her own sister Nettie by allowing herself rather than Nettie to be sexually abused by the man they mistook for their father. In the same way, Celie shielded Nettie from Celie's own husband, Albert. She also took care of Albert's children by a previous wife.

Gilligan describes the first big change from this stage in women's development as follows: "[W]hen only others are legitimized as the recipients of the woman's care, the exclusion of herself gives rise to problems in relationships" (74). Such a problem arises when Celie, despite having tried to be good to Sofia by making curtains for her wedding, resents her because Sofia demands to be treated better by her husband, Harpo, than Celie is by Albert. Celie acts out her resentment by telling Harpo to beat Sofia when he complains about his wife's having a mind of her own.

When Sofia finds out about what Celie told Harpo, she brings back the curtains and throws them down at Celie's feet. "Just want you to know I looked to you for help" (42), Sofia angrily tells Celie. Part of the rest of their conversation follows:

Ain't I been helpful? I ast....
You told Harpo to beat me, she said.
No I didn't, I said.
Don't lie, she said.
I didn't mean it, I said.
Then what you say it for? she ast....
I say it cause I'm a fool, I say. I say it cause I'm jealous of you.
I say it cause you do what I can't.
What that? she say.
Fight, I say. (42)

The very idea of fighting leads Celie to what Gilligan calls "a reconsideration of relationships in an effort to sort out the confusion between self-sacrifice and care inherent in the conventions of feminine goodness" (74). Instead of physically fighting, the two women signify upon one another. Sofia begins with what superficially appears to be the signifier's standard citing of her credentials as a fighter, only the context is not street fighting (as it sometimes is in black male signifying), but domestic abuse at the hands of males:

All my life I had to fight. I had to fight my daddy. I had to fight my brothers. I had to fight my cousins and my uncles. A girl child ain't safe in a family of men.... Now you want a dead son-in-law you just keep on advising him like you doing. (42)

The next sentence—one that Spielberg deletes—concludes Sofia's rather direct statement on an oddly indirect note: "She put her hand on her hip. I used to hunt game with a bow and arrow, she say" (42). This is a perfect instance of the "introduction of the semantically or logically unexpected" that linguist Geneva Smitherman says is one of the defining characteristics of signifying (118). Its effect is to cut the angry tension and provide an opportunity for reconciliation that Spielberg omits but that Celie immediately takes, recounting: "I stop the little trembling that started when I saw her coming. I'm *so* shame of myself, I say" (42). Picking up on and modifying Sofia's drift, Celie herself introduces the next trope for what will become two-way signifying: "And the Lord he done whip me a little too" (42).

Now the women engage in some indirect putting of each other down:

The Lord don't like ugly, [Sofia] say.
And he ain't stuck on pretty [says Celie]. (42)

Spielberg ignores the different direction of Celie's next thought—"This open the way for our talk to turn another way":

> I say, You feels sorry for me, don't you?
> [Sofia] think a minute. Yes ma'am, she say slow, I do. (43)

Then, as if reversing a classic "'yo mamma" insult—part of a variant of signifying called "playing the dozens" or "mother-rapping"—Sofia starts talking about her own mother: "To tell the truth, you remind me of my mama. She under my daddy thumb. Naw, she under my daddy foot" (43). In "'yo mamma" insults, one of the things classically bandied about is the particular (sexual) way "'yo mamma" is under a man. Sofia radically modifies this form of put-down, turning its degradation into regret about how her father treated her mother:

> Anything he say, goes. She never say nothing back. She never stand up for herself. Try to make a little half stand sometime for the children but that always backfire. More she stand up for us, the harder time he give her. (43)

What Sofia is getting at indirectly is a sympathetic criticism of Celie: the same kind of unvitiated self-sacrifice for the sake of others that made Sofia's mother tolerate her husband's abuse also made Celie tolerate her father's and husband's. By contrast, Sofia's own attitude—"I loves Harpo, she say. God knows I do. But I'll kill him dead before I let him beat me" (42)—is an example of what Gilligan calls "the morality of rights that dissolves 'natural bonds' [like marriage] in support of individual claims" (132). (Sofia eventually leaves Harpo.)

Spielberg retains Sofia's tough talk but out of context, so that it becomes a way Sofia (Oprah Winfrey), instead of encouraging Celie, can assert her own moral superiority to her. Thus Spielberg reverses the point of the whole exchange as far as its influence on Celie is concerned. In the novel, Sofia's morality of rights does conflict with Celie's morality of goodness and self-sacrifice, but it is a conflict not just between the two women but within Celie's own mind. Sofia helps her resolve it. In her relationship with Sofia, Celie has reached the point at which, in Gilligan's words, "[w]omen begin to notice their own exclusion of themselves [and] consider it moral to care not only for others but for themselves" (149). For the first time in her life evidently, Celie is questioning being so good to others, though not in a very self-reflecting way in the beginning.

In the novel, Sofia concludes her signifying by remarking that her father "hated where children come from." With a characteristic trace of signifying humor she adds: "Tho from all the children he got you'd never know it" (42-43). Next the women's talk turns to exchanging information about the size of their families of origin, Sofia specifically asking about the number of girls in Celie's family and telling how the girls in her own family stuck together in family fights. Sofia then gets to the root of Celie's acting out by asking Celie when she last got mad. Celie responds: "I can't even remember the last time I felt mad. I used to git mad at my mammy cause she put a lot of work on me. Then I see how sick she is. Couldn't stay mad at her" (43). Evidently at this earlier point in her life, Celie felt it would not have been fair to get mad at a sick woman. From interviews with women over a period of ten years of research, Gilligan postulated a stage in many women's development when fairness to others and self-sacrifice on their behalf so overwhelms any consideration of the woman's own needs that, in Celie's words, "after while every time I got mad, or start to feel mad, I got sick. Felt like throwing up. Terrible feeling. Then I start to feel nothing at all" (44). Celie invokes the conventional morality of "Bible say, Honor father and mother no matter what" (44). The God of this moral universe is the one to whom Celie first confides in her letters. Her signifying discourse with Sofia obviously has another, more human dimension.

When Celie tells Sofia that instead of ever even feeling mad, she feels nothing at all, "Sofia frown. Nothing at all?"

> Well, [Celie responds], sometime Mr. _____ get on me pretty hard. I have to talk to Old Maker. But he my husband. I shrug my shoulders. This life soon be over, I say. Heaven last all ways. (44)

Sofia punctures this rationale in a way that is "teachy but not preachy"— another of Geneva Smitherman's defining characteristics of signifying (121): "You ought to bash Mr. _____ head open, she say. Think about heaven later" (44). Celie does not take this suggestion literally, but just fantasizing with another woman about reversing the power relationship between husband and wife is cathartic: "Not much funny to me. That funny. I laugh. She laugh. Then us both laugh so hard us flop down on the step" (44).

Such fantasies and such catharsis are other defining aspects of signifying (Gates 59, Kochman 257). Laughter is the desired result. The scenes from Ralph Ellison and other black male writers that Henry Louis Gates, Jr., quotes in his study of signifying all end up with people howling in laughter. But what is different here is that neither woman ends up having one-upped the other (as in all the incidents Gates quotes). Instead Celie and Sofia end their verbal sparring by making a Sister's Choice quilt:

> Let's make quilt pieces out of these messed up curtains, [Sofia] say.
> And I run git my pattern book.
> I sleeps like a baby now [an allusion to the sleepless nights Celie had had after telling Harpo to beat Sofia]. (44)

This resolution is omitted entirely from Spielberg's adaptation.

H. Rap Brown once said that "signifying allowed you a choice—you could either make a cat feel good or bad. If you had just destroyed someone or if they were down already, signifying could help them over" (quoted in Gates 44).[4] In choosing to make Celie feel good rather than bad, Sofia is opting for a kind of signifying that Gates says (mostly white) linguists, anthropologists and (we might add) filmmakers sometimes misconstrue. In the film, Sofia's advice to Celie to "bash Mr. _____'s head" is spoken and taken entirely seriously. Moreover, Celie is left looking ashamed for her part in bringing abuse on Sofia, and the scene ends with the still smoldering Sofia restraining her anger by withdrawing through the corn field whence she came.[5]

In the novel, Sofia shows Celie that there are less dangerous ways to assert herself than to act out as Celie did when she originally told Harpo to beat Sofia. According to Gilligan, "when assertion no longer seems dangerous, the concept of relationships changes from a bond of continuing dependence to a dynamic of interdependence" (149). In the novel the two women signal that interdependence by quilting together.

Thus, before Celie ever signifies upon Albert in the declaration that comes later in the book, she learns an important lesson about the possibilities and limits of self-assertion when she acts out inappropriately against another, more successful survivor of spouse abuse. Sofia does not remain angry in response when she finds out why Celie told Harpo to beat her: "[Sofia] stand there a long time, like what I said took the wind out her jaws. She mad before, sad now" (42). Gilligan would say that Sofia's softening to Celie at this point rather than acting out in kind is a result of her having already learned to be more honest than Celie about her own needs. Thus, writes Gilligan: "Judgment becomes more tolerant and less absolute" (149).

Unfortunately, in other contexts of her own life Sofia is not able to practice all that she teaches Celie. In another scene of the movie, for example, Squeak (Rae Dawn Chong), Harpo's mistress, slaps Sofia for dancing with her own husband. To concentrate viewers' attention on the intense look Sofia gives Squeak in response, the camera shoots Sofia close up turning her head in slow motion. We feel exactly as Squeak must feel looking into Sofia's enraged eyes. Then the action speeds up in a round-house punch as Sofia decks Squeak and a fight breaks out in the juke joint.

This scene accurately adapts a scene in the book. Nevertheless, it is not completely accurate to conclude as feminist film critic Andrea Stuart does that in general "the casting and performance of Oprah Winfrey as Sofia... captures Walker's meaning perfectly [in that] the Sofia of the film...survive[s] disaster with a glint in her eye" (72). It is true that, not just in the confrontation with Celie but in Sofia's exchanges with other characters such as Squeak, the film conveys Sofia's strength through the powerful looks she gives people in anticipation of or in reaction to angry confrontations.

The problem is that a glint in Sofia's eye is of survival value only in confrontations with other blacks, not when it comes to the white powers-that-be with whom she shares neither equality of power nor a means through signifying for mitigating anger. Though Sofia helped Celie move to the stage of mutual care in their own relationship, Sofia herself comes to grief over whether she will "take care" of the mayor's children when his wife, seeing how well Sofia takes care of her own, offers her a job as maid. (See Figure 23.) Sofia says "Hell, no," and the mayor strikes her. Again the action slows and the camera focuses on Sofia's powerful glance, this time looking up at the unyielding white mayor. Sofia decks him just as she had Squeak. Greater violence again erupts, but this time a white deputy sheriff holding a pistol comes and pokes its butt right in one of Sofia's powerful eyes. This eye will remain closed and blinded for almost the rest of the movie until Sofia, broken by prison, opens it again years later when she witnesses Celie—a different woman herself now—signifying upon Albert at the dinner table in the declaration of independence we have already examined.

While this sequence in Spielberg's film shows racism's general injustice, Walker's novel is much more specific in clarifying that white supremacists refuse to let black women get to a point (of asserting their rights) that could ever be integrated with an ethic of care. They expect them to be totally self-sacrificing in the manner, for example, of William Faulkner's "Mammy" Caroline Barr, to whom he dedicated *Go Down, Moses* with the words "[she] gave to my family a fidelity without stint or calculation of recompense and to my childhood an immeasurable devotion and love." Celie typifies the anger and dishonesty on the part of oppressed black women to which this often idealized self-sacrifice may lead when not integrated with any notion of reciprocal rights. Thus, while racism is the overall culprit, Walker holds African-American women themselves responsible for its internalized legacy in the form of acting out against each other, just as she holds African-American men responsible for having internalized racism when they abuse black women.[6]

Through Sofia's character, Walker also shows the limits of blindly asserting rights. Sofia exemplifies how, as Martin Luther King once put it, insisting on an eye for eye, a tooth for tooth, so often only leaves blacks blind and toothless. She survives racism not with a glint in her eye but through care provided by family, friends, even former rivals. (Squeak, her husband's lover, is raped by Sofia's warden when she tries to get Sofia out of jail. After Squeak's efforts end so disastrously, Sofia's relatives, fearful that she will die in prison, manipulate the warden by lying to him, saying that Sofia doesn't mind jail as much as being the mayor's maid, which she is then released from prison to become.)

Because Sofia's own development was stunted by racism, she is succeeded by Shug Avery in the novel as the woman who completes Celie's moral education. Shug keeps Celie from killing Albert when Celie finds out he has been stealing Nettie's letters to her. Enraged as well at his beatings,

Figure 23. An angry Sofia (Oprah Winfrey) rejects the mayor's offer to become his maid. Copyright © 1985 by

Celie thinks on one occasion of cutting his throat while she shaves him. In the movie Spielberg cross-cuts this scene with another scene in Africa in which Adam (Celie's long-lost son) and Tashi (a young girl his age) are getting their faces ritually scarified. Celie strops Albert's razor; the camera cuts back to an African musician playing a scraping instrument during the scarification ritual. A shaman approaches the defenseless children from behind; the camera cuts back to Celie approaching Albert from behind. Both Celie and the shaman are glaring at their victims, who do not notice this and whose sight lines the camera does not follow. The pace of these cross-cuts picks up; African drum music gets louder and is played over both visually equated scenes. Then, also in Georgia, off in a field near the front porch where Celie is stropping the razor, Shug Avery, painting her fingernails blood red, is told by some children that Celie is about to shave Albert. Shug runs to stop her, in effect increasing the tension of the cross-cutting.

Walker's novel does not connect face scarring with throat cutting in any way—including interior monologue or fantasy. While both shaving and face scarring scenes occur in the book, they are separated by 120 pages of text. Instead, face scarring has the following very different context: Tashi, a more mature African woman than the child Spielberg makes her out to be, reluctantly gets her face scarred as a gesture of tribal solidarity after her village has been destroyed by white colonial road builders. Adam—Tashi's fiancé and Celie's son, who has himself grown up in Africa—is initially shocked by this "barbaric" ritual. Tashi therefore refuses to marry Adam, who wants her to return with him to America: she is afraid she would soon be abandoned there without mother, country or tribe for an unscarred, light-skinned African-American woman. To convince her otherwise, as a gesture of support for Tashi, Adam allows his own face to be scarred.

The novel presents Tashi as, after some hesitation, ultimately choosing to have her face scarred. Between her own and Adam's changing response, face scarring is presented as a complex tradition of self-laceration to affirm commitments and compensate for the loss of community in contemporary Africa. Though Spielberg's film does show the Olinka village being destroyed by whites, never does it intimate that face scarring may be a kind of response. Like African-American signifying, African face scarring is a folkway that Walker may initially associate with characters' anger and destructiveness, but she gives it a different conclusion than Spielberg does.

Not just the means used to express and restrain aggression but the moral issue of aggression's consequences is framed differently in the novel and the film. In the film, Shug tells Celie that killing Albert isn't worth it. In the novel, she specifies that killing him would mean that the returning Nettie would find Celie in the same brutalized condition in jail as Sofia and that Shug herself would be deprived of both Celie and Albert as lovers. The upshot of Shug's reasoning is to teach Celie that nobody must be hurt, or, in Gilligan's words, that "just as...violence is in the end destructive to all, so the activity of care enhances both others and the self" (74). Later when Shug tells Celie she believes in God, she doesn't mean the same God Celie had used to rationalize away her anger but what Gilligan would call a "postconventional" deity who, in Shug's words, "ain't a he or she" and (in what might be taken ironically in light of Spielberg's adaptation) "ain't a picture show. It ain't something you can look at apart from anything [or anyone] else, including yourself" (202). This is exactly what Gilligan means by an ethic of care in which one takes care of oneself as part of being in any relationship. By contrast to this simultaneity and mutuality, the picture show Shug has in mind is watched by a passive observer, removed from direct involvement in the action. As feminist film critics have pointed out, most picture shows follow only one character's sight line at a time, implying at best an impartial ethic of equal, reciprocal points of view—each one treated fairly—and at worst a perspective on others as objects of the self, its needs, desires, and development. These two possibilities resemble the best and worst of the camera's point of view in many Hollywood films and, coincidentally, the best and worst of masculine perspective in general, according to Carol Gilligan. The reason for the coincidence is that the camera's eye in Hollywood movies so often represents a male point of view.[7]

As a result of the different voice Celie develops in her relations with Sofia and Shug, by the time Albert signifies upon Celie for leaving him, she doesn't signify in kind as she had in initially declaring her independence from him. Instead she simply concedes: "I'm pore, I'm black, I may be ugly and can't cook.... But I'm here" (214). Like Celie in this remark, some of Gilligan's women subjects also learned to "focus on the self in order to ensure survival" (74) in abusive relationships. For an informant named Sarah "a step in taking control is to end the relationship in which she has considered herself 'reduced to a nonentity,' but to do so in a responsible way.... [S]he seeks to act in a 'decent, human kind of way, one that leaves maybe a slightly shaken but not totally destroyed [other] person'" (95). Gilligan concludes that Sarah's new-won sense of a "power to destroy...formerly had impeded assertion" of her independence. In order to assert herself in a way consistent with the ethic of care, Sarah "considers the possibility for a new kind of action that leaves both self and other intact" (95).

How Celie considers this possibility vis-à-vis Albert is handled very differently in the novel and the film. Both depict Albert, after Celie has left him, drunk and filthy in his messy house—i.e., in a state similar to what Gilligan's subject Sarah was trying to avoid reducing her man to by leaving him "totally destroyed." Later, in the film, Albert sits brooding in a rocking chair on his porch, listening to the strains of the gospel song "God Trying to Tell You Something" wafting from a nearby church. This is the only clue as to why Albert helps Celie rejoin the same sister from whom he originally separated her. There is no face-to-face reconciliation that Celie and he achieve.

Spielberg visually narrates the steps Albert takes to reunite Celie and Nettie (Akosua Busia) in three scenes devoid of any dialogue between the estranged husband and wife: in the first Albert appears at the Immigration and Naturalization Office (presumably to aid in repatriating Nettie and Adam); in the second Celie sees or imagines she sees Albert through the window of her store (she looks down and when she looks up again, he is gone); in the third, Albert is neatly dressed and standing in a field far behind Celie's home-coming African relatives as Celie reunites with them. Close-ups of his face, cross-cut with Shug's returning his gaze from where she stands up on the porch with Celie, suggest that Shug realizes Albert had a part in bringing Celie and her family back together. The point of all these scenes is that Albert has apparently been thinking of Celie and realizes he needs to mend his ways, concluding from his sad plight ever since Celie left that he mistreated her throughout their marriage.

Since Albert never talks to Celie during any of these scenes, she never knows his thoughts. The sequence of reaction shots grossly oversimplifies how Walker originally developed Albert's reconciliation with Celie: the estranged couple patch up their differences after Albert starts visiting Celie again in her new home where he finds her sewing pants. He remarks that he himself used to sew as a child until he was laughed at. "Nobody going to laugh at you here," Celie says. So Albert takes up sewing again, and this becomes the pretext for long talks with Celie, culminating in Albert's proposing they remarry, which Celie declines, saying that men without their pants remind her of frogs. But she thinks to herself that though she is no more attracted to Albert sexually than she ever was, he has become a person she can talk to. In the book, Albert is up on the porch sewing and talking with Celie and Shug when Nettie arrives from Africa with Celie's children. He is not gazing from far off in the fields.

What Spielberg leaves out is that Albert stops being abusive in part because Celie develops what Gilligan would call a mature ethic of care—including care of herself and honesty about her own needs along with an attitude that is neither as submissive nor as vindictive as she had at different times been toward him. This is a hard-won achievement in Celie's development. Her letters in part trace how she first learns to feel, then how she copes with wanting to kill Albert by being able to signify upon him verbally as he has upon her, and finally how she learns to temper her words so that she can talk to him even if she cannot love him. Celie's growth in her ability to handle Albert is predicated on her (1) having gone through a less charged version of the same growth with a female adversary and friend—Sofia—and on her (2) having learned from Shug no longer to live her life as if she were only the source of other people's care and/or the object of abuse in somebody else's picture show.

The conclusion of Celie's odyssey as Walker wrote it is quite a bit different from the "visual and emotional marginalisation of men" (74) that

Andrea Stuart admires at the end of Spielberg's film when she accurately describes the film's final scene: it "begins with a powerful shot of the three women emerging from Celie's house, where they all live, on to the balcony, down the steps, to welcome Nettie—their husbands all in the background, at the edges of the screen" (70).

Spielberg does do what Andrea Stuart wrongly says Walker does—puts men not only on the margin of the shot but on the margin of the process of women's development, making men objects of it rather than participants in it. This is, in fact, what men sometimes do to women in failing to see them as subjective participants in men's own development. Gilligan's research shows that men, in speaking of their lives, often foreground relations with members of their own sex—friendships and professional ties that could further their success—over relationships with the opposite sex. Women also may employ this strategy, says Gilligan, when they move out of the stage of self-sacrifice to the survivor mode. Some of Gilligan's female subjects even said they had considered adopting such an orientation after having observed how well it seemed to allow men to get what they wanted—an orientation that, however necessary as a step, the women often thought better of, or at least came to reconcile with an ethic of care.

Carol Gilligan's research confirms why at the end of the story told in her own voice Celie does not want to have grown at the expense of anybody, not even the man who hurt her. This is not some Pollyanna vision of women: indeed the self-sacrificing, do-gooder was one of Celie's early stages—followed by its male-imitating antithesis in woman's development. The mature ethic of care that Gilligan describes some women achieving is a synthesis that goes beyond opposed images of woman either as willing to sacrifice herself or as able to fight like a man (Celie describes Sofia and Harpo "fighting like two mens" [39]). Andrea Stuart's image of marginalization is interesting, however, because, according to Gilligan, women do tend to fantasize about being at the center of connection and consequently fear being too far out on the edge (as opposed to the fantasies of men of being alone at the top and consequently fearing that others will get too close). Walker's description of Celie shows her developing a mature ethic of care that leaves no one out on the edge. In Gilligan's words, "[e]veryone will be...included...no one will be left alone or hurt" (63). To replace phallocentrism with gynocentrism is not Walker's vision. Rather it is to portray women working through problematic relationships with each other and finding alternatives to marginalizing anybody.

In conclusion, signifying is the particular speech act for the differentiation and eventual accommodation of female and male black voices in *The Color Purple*—a means of working through differences in the novel, a means that Spielberg misinterprets in his adaptation. In Walker's novel, the signifying that Celie engages in with both Sofia and Albert ends with their sewing

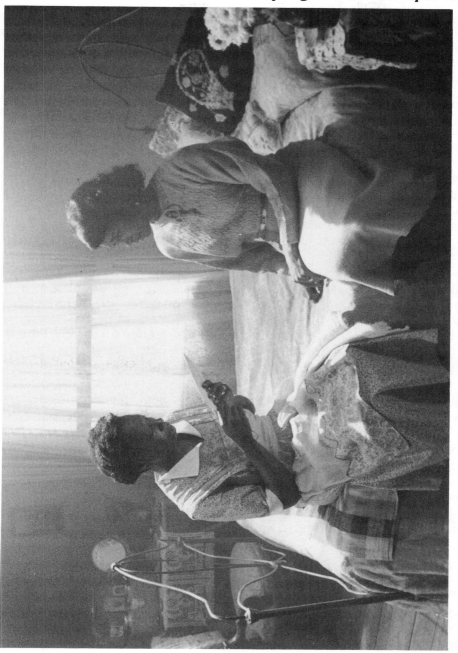

Figure 24. Celie (Whoopi Goldberg), with friend Shug Avery (Margaret Avery) beside her, reads letters from her beloved sister, Nettie. Copyright © 1985 by Warner Bros., Inc.

together, whereas Spielberg concludes both Sofia's confrontation with Celie and the throat-cutting scene between Celie and Albert with shots of them glaring intently at each other, full of emotions that are never resolved in the particular developmental directions Gilligan's research describes or in the particular rhetorical directions that Walker's fiction does. Spielberg especially misconstrues the signifying of African-American women to resemble the stereotypic one-upmanship of black male signifying (stereotypic because black males do not signify just to degrade and berate each other either). Walker, on the other hand, depicts signifying as what Henry Louis Gates, Jr., calls a ritual from which "the black person...derives[s]...a complex attitude toward attempts at domination" (77). Just as Gates points out that the aggressive verbal signifying young black men do on street corners may mature into the more productively competitive jazz "cutting sessions" in which soloists try to outdo one another, Walker shows how the affiliative signifying more characteristic of women may lead to their sewing or quilting together.

Spielberg, in other words, could not hear the different signifying voice that Celie disentangled from and then conversed in with Albert. Spielberg's announced goal for the project was to make an adult film that reflected a more mature side of himself than some of his previous projects. By Hollywood's standards, and in comparison to many of his other hits, he certainly succeeded; by Gilligan's standard of maturity—the integration into a male perspective of a different voice—he did not.[8] While Spielberg does show Celie, in first declaring her independence from Albert, signifying upon him in words as aggressive as he ever used on her, Spielberg never shows the corollary: Albert learning to signify in the gentler voice of sewing.

Like letter writers, people who sew together concentrate on the medium to which they both contribute without necessarily having to confront one another's gaze—the power dynamics which have been the subject of a long line of commentary from Hegel to Sartre to Lacan to recent feminist and psychoanalytic film critics. Sometimes quilters and letter writers do not even look at each other's contributions while they are working on their own: years pass before Celie and Nettie read each other's letters, to give an extreme example.

Spielberg is understandably following a film convention when he uses voice-over narration to convey the substance of the letters Celie and Nettie write. What seems unconsciously political, however, are his deletions or modifications of African-American folkways. If the film can invent static moments of Celie and Shug reading Nettie's letters (see Figure 24), there is no justification on the usual basis of concentrating on action scenes for the film to delete Celie's sewing with Sofia and Albert as part of a domestic ritual for patching up differences. These scenes could easily have been adapted as important transitional moments in the film, shot in mid-focus from neither character's point of view, thus objectifying what happens.

Instead, Spielberg deletes or distorts the solidarity-affirming aspects not only of quilting but of face scarring and signifying—traditions which Walker's oppressed Africans and African-Americans practice in order to reinforce threatened gender and tribal identities. The causes of oppression remain, but without these domestic, tribal, and rhetorical practices, blacks might turn against each other (as Celie initially did against Sofia) or provoke a backlash from whites (as Sofia did from the mayor). The symbolic point of quilting, face scarring, and signifying is that they are all both social and self-directed ways to cope with overwhelming external aggression and its internalized legacy within oppressed individuals and groups.

Spielberg did not get beyond his own popular culture when he projected images of an angry woman contemplating cutting her husband's throat onto an African scarification ritual and when he made expressing anger the whole point of signifying. In adapting an African-American feminist novel, Spielberg failed to translate the very different folk traditions of that genre and ended up perpetuating Anglo-American stereotypes about blacks. When folk went pop—at least in the case of *The Color Purple* adaptation—important African-American cultural resources got left on the cutting room floor.[9]

NOTES

[1]In 1991, when a much shorter version of this essay, entitled "When Folk Goes Pop: Consuming *The Color Purple*," was published in *Literature/Film Quarterly* (19.3: 176-80), I cited a *Video Marketing Newsletter* ranking *The Color Purple* among the top hundred all-time best-selling videos (figures for home-rentals were not included). (This list was reprinted in *The Washington Post T.V. Week* for 29 January-4 February 1989 [7].) *The Color Purple*, having sold 365,000 copies, placed 95th (just after *Donald in Mathmagic Land*). While far behind the number one and two best-sellers up until then—*E.T. The Extra-Terrestrial*, another Spielberg production (12.5 million sold), and *Cinderella* (7.2 million)—*The Color Purple* had the distinction of being the only video in the top hundred all-time best-sellers to date that was concerned with black feminist issues. Because of a new policy by Warner Brothers not to release sales figures, I was unable to update these statistics, but industry sources at Philips Publishing International, which puts out *Video Marketing Newsletter*, informed me that a half million units sold would be a conservative estimate.

[2]For a discussion of the cultural history of African-American quilting as reflected in Walker's short story, see Houston A. Baker, Jr. and Charlotte Pierce-Baker, "Patches: Quilts and Community in Alice Walker's 'Everyday Use.'" Barbara Christian writes about quilting as a metaphor for Walker's own craft in *Black Feminist Criticism* (85-89). Walker describes how she quilted while writing *The Color Purple* in *In Search of Our Mothers' Gardens* (358-60).

[3]Using Gilligan's study to understand an African-American woman's development may strike some readers as problematic since her research has been criticized for being based mostly on white middle class women and men. In "The Culture of Gender: Women and Men of Color," for example, Carol B. Stack argues for "an African-American model of moral development" in which "women's and men's voices [are] in unison with one another" unlike the tension between them that Gilligan found. Stack studied black return migrants from the urban Northeast to the rural South and found

> that under conditions of economic deprivation there is a convergence between women and men in their construction of themselves in relationship to others, and that these conditions produce a convergence also in women's and men's vocabulary of rights, morality, and the social good. I view black women's and men's contextualization of morality and the meaning of social ties as a cultural alternative to Gilligan's model of moral development, with a different configuration of gender differences and similarities. (109)

My essay argues that while Celie's and Albert's voices will eventually come into the kind of unison Stack has in mind, this is not a given but an achievement won largely by Celie's learning to speak in a different voice (following Gilligan in principle but taking the particular form of a different type of signifying than Albert's initially degrading signifying—a voice that over time Albert himself will learn to respond to in kind).

[4]Scholars of the subject agree; Haskins and Butts in *The Psychology of Black Language* write that signifying can be used either for "putting down" another person, or alternatively for "making another person feel better" (Haskins and Butts 51).

[5]Gilligan identifies healing as a priority that women place above one-upping each other. One of Gilligan's female subjects said that "responsibility...connotes an act of care rather than [just] the restraint of aggression" (38). By contrast, Gilligan's male informants mentioned restraining aggression more often than taking care of someone as a responsible act (38). Spielberg turns Walker's depiction of healing into a scene in which Sofia restrains anger by withdrawing. The reason men are generally more comfortable with separation than women, according to Gilligan, is that they often construe separation as an effective means for restraining aggression, whereas women tend to construe separation negatively as jeopardizing relationships. Why women and men construe separation differently in the first place gets back to the different ways they develop their gender identities very early in life: boys by separating from their mothers and identifying with male models; girls by elaborating their early bond with mother into more complex connections with her and other female models. This distinction between male and female ways of developing gender identity was first articulated by Nancy Chodorow and later incorporated by Carol Gilligan into her theory of the different voices women and men use in speaking about how they resolve moral issues.

[6]Black feminist critic Barbara Christian says Walker defines "nigger" as "a black person who believes he or she is incapable of being responsible for his or her actions, who claims that the white folks are to blame for everything, including his or her behavior" (84). Christian quotes Grange Copeland in Walker's *The Third Life of Grange Copeland*: "...when they get you to thinking they're to blame for everything they have you thinking they're some kind of gods.... Shit, nobody's as powerful as we make them out to be. We got our own souls, don't we?" (207).

[7]Laura Mulvey's essay "Visual Pleasure and Narrative Cinema" explains the dynamics of sexual power in the filmed gaze. For a useful summary of where feminist film criticism has gone since Mulvey's now classic essay, see Judith Mayne, "Feminist Film Theory and Women at the Movies." Mulvey herself does not talk much about films like *The Color Purple* with women as protagonists. For a striking case of one of those, see Pam Cook and Claire Johnston's study of *The Revolt of Mamie Stover*.

[8]Gilligan believes that gender differences, while culturally conditioned in a patriarchal society, are not immutable and that maturity for either sex includes developing sensitivity to the "voice" of the opposite sex.

[9]The tension I have been describing between African-American "folk" and Anglo-American "popular" cultures is an instance of what in another context Henry Louis Gates, Jr., has described as

> the (political, semantic) confrontation between two parallel discursive universes: the black American linguistic circle and the white. We see here the most subtle and perhaps the most profound trace of an extended engagement between two separate and distinct yet profoundly—even inextricably—related orders of meaning. (45)

WORKS CITED

Andrews, Malachi and Paul T. Owens. *Black Language*. West Los Angeles: Seymour-Smith, 1973.

Baker, Houston A. and Charlotte Pierce-Baker. "Patches: Quilts and Community in Alice Walker's 'Everyday Use.'" *Southern Review* 21.3 (1985): 706-20.

Chodorow, Nancy. *The Reproduction of Mothering*. Berkeley: University of California Press, 1978.

Christian, Barbara. *Black Feminist Criticism: Perspectives on Black Women Writers*. New York: Pergamon Press, 1985.

Cook, Pam and Claire Johnston. "The Revolt of Mamie Stover." In *Raoul Walsh*. Ed. Phil Harvey. Edinburgh: Edinburgh Film Festival Publication, 1974.

Faulkner, William. *Go Down, Moses*. New York: Random, 1940.

Gates, Henry Louis, Jr. *The Signifying Monkey: A Theory of African-American Literary Criticism*. New York: Oxford University Press, 1988.

Gilligan, Carol. *In a Different Voice: Psychological Theory and Women's Development.* Cambridge: Harvard University Press, 1982.

Haskins, Jim and Hugh F. Butts. *The Psychology of Black Language.* New York: Barnes and Noble, 1973.

Kochman, Thomas. "Toward an Ethnography of Black American Speech Behavior." *Rappin' and Stylin' Out: Communication in Urban Black America.* Urbana: University of Illinois Press, 1972.

Mayne, Judith. "Feminist Film Theory and Women at the Movies." *Profession* (1987): 14-19.

Mulvey, Laura. "Visual Pleasure and Narrative Cinema." *Screen* 16.3 (1975): 6-18.

Smitherman, Geneva. *Talkin and Testifyin: The Language of Black America.* Boston: Houghton Mifflin, 1977.

Stack, Carol B. "The Culture of Gender: Women and Men of Color." *An Ethic of Care: Feminist and Interdisciplinary Perspectives.* Ed. Mary Jeanne Larrabee. New York: Routledge, 1993. 108-11.

Stuart, Andrea. "*The Color Purple*: In Defense of Happy Endings." *The Female Gaze: Women as Viewers of Popular Culture.* Ed. Lorraine Gamman and Margaret Marshment. Seattle: Real Comet Press, 1989. 60-75.

Walker, Alice. *The Color Purple.* New York: Simon & Schuster, 1982.

_____. "Everyday Use." *In Love & Trouble, Stories of Black Women.* New York: Harcourt Brace Jovanovich, 1973.

_____. *The Third Life of Grange Copeland.* New York: Harcourt Brace Jovanovich, 1970.

_____. "Writing *The Color Purple*." *In Search of Our Mothers' Gardens.* New York: Harcourt Brace, 1983. 358-60.

Ironweed and the Snows of Reduction

Benedict Giamo

> The power that perceives the course of time
> is not the power that captures all the mind;
> the former has no force—the latter binds.
>
> Dante, *Purgatorio*

Cycle and Form

Ironweed, William Kennedy's fourth novel, was published in January 1983 to widespread critical acclaim and won both the Pulitzer Prize and the National Book Critics Circle Award the next year. A MacArthur "genius" award coincided with the release of the novel; and Kennedy used part of the largesse to establish the Albany Writer's Institute (later named the New York State Writer's Institute). An academic promotion followed, along with honorary doctorates, movie deals, public recognition, and an overriding sense of personal vindication: yes, without question, Kennedy had finally "beat[en] the bastards."[1]

The novel had been turned down by thirteen publishing houses before Saul Bellow, acting on his own initiative, contacted Viking Press and persuaded them to come around. That it took so long for the novel to land is astounding, especially considering its literary merits and Kennedy's record as a writer of fiction. But Kennedy was used to laboring in relative obscurity. He had, after all, spent sixteen years writing in both apprenticeship and journeyman stages before publishing his first novel, *The Ink Truck* (1969). Thirteen more years of diligence, productivity, yet lack of recognition (for works like *Legs* [1975] and *Billy Phelan's Greatest Game* [1978]) followed before he achieved his literary success.

Ironweed also brought Kennedy popular success—ironically, though, not so much as a result of the novel itself, so rich in its complexity, but rather by its reduction to a Hollywood movie. Adapted to the screen in 1987, *Ironweed* went through a predictable cultural cycle: from novel to film to world premiere. The movie was directed by Hector Babenco, the Argentinian director (*Pixote* and *Kiss of the Spider Woman*), and it starred Jack Nicholson as Francis Phelan and Meryl Streep as Helen Archer. Kennedy himself wrote the screenplay.

131

The film premiered in December 1987 at the Palace Theater in Albany, New York, Kennedy's hometown and the vital setting for both novel and film. About 2,500 premiere-goers, mostly celebs and politicos, all bedecked and bejeweled, paid $125 per ticket to attend. They arrived in stretch limos, Rolls Royces, vintage autos, and even horse-drawn carriages to see the film whose meaning the *Knickerbocker News* codified as the "story of hoboes, a hometown and redemption of a wayward soul" (Sheffer).[2]

To accommodate the magnitude of the event, the Palace was equipped with thirty-seven speakers and two special 35mm projectors (fitted with 45,000 watt bulbs) to cast images onto a 45-foot screen 176 feet away. After the movie, the audience was shuttled over to the Hilton Hotel for a grand celebration (the planning of which was compared to D-Day by the Hilton's food and beverage director), including 50,000 to 60,000 hors d'oeuvres, fourteen well-stocked bars, several bands, ice sculptures, canvas backdrops, and general hoopla and high fashion (Sheffer).

Although billed as a homecoming and a kind of redemption for a heretofore unrewarded talent so long in ascending, the premiere made some feel left out in the cold. Local extras complained that the ticket price was prohibitive. As one put it, "I can't afford it, with all my kids and my husband [a city maintenance worker] out with a back disability" (Grondahl). Local organized labor reps protested against the headquarters of the production company, Colonie's Turf Inn, because its workers were nonunionized. And, of course, to nobody's surprise, the homeless outcasts were entirely unaware of the events taking place that night: they were in the shadows and, if not in the weeds, in shelters, missions, or park bathhouses (Sheffer). Though central to the design of both novel and film, the "brotherhood of the desolate" and the "wayward souls"—the very individuals from the depths of society represented so faithfully in the novel—were excluded from the cultural homecoming, their plight appropriated by Hollywood for its own benefit and profit.

The adaptation of *Ironweed* into film, in fact, entailed much reduction of the novel. While the film incorporated all of the significant elements of the novel's narrative structure, it ultimately diminished the value of the book by restricting its powerful thematic depth and eclectic stylistic range. This demotion was not unlike Francis's own feeling of being downgraded and forgotten—erased—by the "snows of reduction" until only the traces remained. So eloquently conveyed in the novel, the characters' richly developed interiors and abstractions, and the complex reconstructions of their lives, flicker only vaguely on the screen. In the novel, wherein Kennedy is the sole medium, the subjective presence affords an authentic expanse of time, place, dramatic action, and consciousness; but that is missing in the film *qua* film, which by contrast is eminently objective, concrete and visible.

Kennedy was highly aware of what the process of adapting novel to film involved. Relating his experience in writing the screenplay for *Billy Phelan's*

Greatest Game, which preceded his involvement with the *Ironweed* film project, he noted: "I see my own work there and I'm juggling it. I'm taking essences out of it and reducing.... It's an enormous cut-back, but still you can find the nugget.... You know, chop and change.... You get the boom-boom-boom" (Thompson 56). Odd words coming from a writer who put Albany on the literary map of the world, akin to Joyce's Dublin and Faulkner's Yoknapatawpha. But Kennedy certainly had reason for his arguments.

Although Kennedy acknowledged Bergman, who advised against making films from novels on the basis that the latter were often "untranslatable" into the visual medium, he accepted the reduction as a matter of course. "The novel," Kennedy asserted, "as receptacle of the entire spectrum of the imaginative...can only be duplicated...in its own mirror image, not in any other medium" ("Re-creating" 21).[3] Ultimately, though, Kennedy did not heed Bergman's conceptual distinction between the two mediums. Being pragmatic, he worked on translating those elements of the novel that did lend themselves to the peculiar medium of film, i.e., the "boom-boom-boom." Kennedy admitted, however, that the novelist within the screenwriter does not come away from such work unscathed. He believed the adaptation of one's own novel into film is tantamount to "self-amputative surgery":

> You eventually pose in front of the mirror without a left ear, a right thumb, with a thigh partly sliced away, the left leg dangling at the ankle, and then you decide that you're ready for the premiere. Just comb the hair a little to the left, wear gloves, bulky trousers, and a high shoe, and who'll notice? You may even set a new style. (22)

The real pose here is Kennedy's good-natured optimism. The writer, and the movie itself, still function despite their missing or detached parts, their reduction of being.

Of course, there have been works of high cinematic art that were based on novels or stories. In some cases, the medium of film has realized and even thematically deepened the full potential of the novel (as in Kosinski's *Being There* [Hal Ashby] or James M. Cain's *The Postman Always Rings Twice* [Luchino Visconti's *Ossessione*]). But generally the accomplishments of adapted films have fallen short of the novels on which they were based.

In the case of *Ironweed*, the subjective and surrealistic essences of the novel were mostly unfilmable. The very idea of making a movie true to its many levels, voices, and visions was much like the conviction expressed by the narrator when he conjured the dead infant Gerald, who "was beyond capture by visual or verbal artistry. He was...an ineffably fabulous presence whose like was not to be found anywhere" (Kennedy, *Ironweed* 17-18).

In the novel, Kennedy's rich and varied novelistic style ranged from the quotidian and slapstick to the lyrical and surrealistic; it combined the prosaic and poetic, the past and present, and the natural and supernatural into a vision of "total reality." In the film, total reality became Babenco's own purchase on the whole, and a very idiomatic way of adapting the notion of magical realism to the States (Farrelly 26).[4] Rather than seeing the novel's fictive world as composed of rigidly rationalized dichotomies (real vs. surreal, substantial vs. insubstantial, living vs. dead), Babenco perceived it *in toto*. Consequently, as director, his ultimate challenge was to capture the seamless totality of the novel's reality on film.

But achieving "total reality" through a process of reduction is, to say the least, paradoxical. This is especially true considering Kennedy's narrative style, a voice often detached and empathic, floating along somewhere on an exquisite plane between writer and character:

> I thought my third person voice was me at first, but the more I wrote, the more I realized that the third person voice was this ineffable level of Francis Phelan's life, a level he would never get to consciously, but which was there somehow. And that became the style of the telling of the story; and the language became as good as I could make it whenever I felt it was time for those flights of rhetoric up from the sidewalk, out of the gutter. (Allen and Simpson 50-51)

This "ineffable level" says the unsayable for both Francis and Gerald Phelan as well as for other characters in the novel who are among the living and the dead. Since the film cannot retain this complex narrative voice, this spokesman for the ineffable, it loses the very genesis and composition of "total reality." At best, the film can only suggest its presence.

Ironweed, as a result, flattens out on the screen, its total reality totaled by critical omissions and superficial treatments of the supernatural, the phantasmic haunts that hound Francis, and the main characters' compelling reveries. Although some of Babenco's cinematic techniques and graphic representations are strong and convincing in advancing the story and conveying thematic depth and dramatic action, overall there is no real sense of inventiveness in the film to match the literary innovations of the novel. Rather than exploiting the possibilities of filming in high contrast black and white (interrupted with color to show the impact of those phantasmic haunts and vivid memories), or forming a collage of film, still frames (especially to evoke sense of place), voice-over with narrative commentary, and subjective camera angles, Babenco and Kennedy stayed the course, more true to the accepted standards of Hollywood than to the experimental vigor of the novel.

Nevertheless, despite the lack of magic on the screen, the film does work, if only on the surface, to suggest the three overlapping dimensions of the novel: the landscape of death (both real and symbolic); the preoccupation with memory; and the primary movement of flight. In addition, the excellent casting of leads as well as supporting actors/actresses helps to animate the otherwise inert context of the movie, whose presence derives not from the atmosphere of setting or time period or social texture but from several of the characters themselves. The performances of Nicholson, Streep, Tom Waits (as Rudy), Hy Anzell (as Rosskam the ragman), and Diane Venora (as Peg) are particularly strong.

A thematic and stylistic comparison of novel and film should help to reveal some of the problems of reduction. In addition, those moments of the film that exist, perhaps not as "total reality" but as luminous and legitimate remainders, will be discussed as well.

Among the Dead

True to the epigraph from Dante's *Purgatorio*, the novel opens within the neighborhood of the dead. On the bum for twenty-two years, Francis Phelan (a man who has truly journeyed over "a sea so cruel") takes on some day labor at St. Agnes Cemetery. It is 1938, All Hallow's Eve, and Francis is working to pay off a debt to Marcus Gorman, an Albany lawyer who got him off on a technicality for registering twenty-one times to vote. More important than this political pretext for being back in his hometown, however, is the real and symbolic landscape of the dead that confronts him.

In the cemetery, death is at once physical and social, mimicking the hierarchical organization of humankind. Arthur T. Grogan's simulated Parthenon depicts the prestigious dead, while monuments and cenotaphs mark off the next level, of privileged ones. Francis, glancing over such finery, eventually locates his kith and kin among the undistinguished masses whose modest headstones and crosses define their backgrounds.

From underground, we glimpse the dead at various stages of rest and unrest. Francis's father is packing his pipe with pulverized root essence, while his mother weaves crosses from weeds only to eat them with utter and compulsive disgust. The point of view of the dead, in fact, comically juxtaposed with Fran's and his friend Rudy's vaudevillian banter and gallows humor, predominates throughout the opening chapter.

As Francis fills in the hollows of the newly dead, the dust of the ancient dead comes to mind. Daddy Big Dugan, one-time Albany pool hustler, now among the freshly dead, advises him to avoid that which sent him down under: "Never inhale your own vomit" (Kennedy, *Ironweed* 5). Two brothers, both canalers killed and dumped into the Erie Canal around 1880, comment sympathetically on Francis's alcoholic desolation and outcast status. The "tenement grave" of Strawberry Bill, once a fellow traveler, contrasts with the rich and powerful Grogan and reminds Francis of his own plight.

Although still alive, Francis is as good as dead. Marked for life by his experience with violent death and homelessness, he bears the death taint:

"He knew...that he would be this decayed self he had been so long in becoming, through all the endless years of his death" (Kennedy, *Ironweed* 99). A special relationship to the past and to the otherworldly accompanies this stigmata, for it is through Francis, fallen and lowly man, that the dead— and old Albany, city of the dead—come to vibrant life again.

The dramatic core of Francis's experience among the resident dead surfaces when he confronts his infant son's grave for the very first time. Twenty-two years earlier Francis lost his grip on the baby's wet diaper and Gerald Michael Phelan fell to his death on the kitchen floor. From his grave and web-like hammock, which protects him from the natural processes of decay, Gerald, now a "genius...among the dead," watches his father approach. After listening to Francis openly and honestly unburden himself of his tremendous guilt, the dead infant urges him on toward greater acts of atonement and renewal:

> Gerald, through an act of silent will, imposed on his father the pressing obligation to perform his final acts of expiation for abandoning the family. You will not know, the child silently said, what these acts are until you have performed them all. And after you have performed them you will not understand that they were expiatory any more than you have understood all the other expiation that has kept you in such prolonged humiliation. Then, when these final acts are complete, you will stop trying to die because of me. (Kennedy, *Ironweed* 19)

Francis, the Late Repentant, belongs more precisely to Ante-Purgatory—the place for those who delayed repentance, especially for traitorous acts done to one's own kin—than to Purgatory itself. Yet, in keeping with Dante's grand medieval scheme, the exertions from Gerald's grave function like the very gates of the latter. The son offers his father a way out of guilt, pain, suffering and humiliation, if only Francis should choose to move through the gate by taking on his own "deadly sins."

For the time being, though, Francis turns his gaze toward the sky and sees, in the chapter's concluding image, a "vast stand of white fleece, brutally bright, [which] moved south to north in the eastern vault of the heavens" (Kennedy, *Ironweed* 20). The image reinforces the novel's expansive sense of spatial structure—the natural earth-bound (those on the ground); the supernatural underworld (those below ground); and the spiritual heavens (those over and above it all). That sense of space is complemented by a fluid, non-linear pattern of narration which situates Francis's dramatic predicament within a context that is at once deeply personal, eminently social, and magically cosmic.

Compared to the novel's beginning, the film's opening—which condenses time and place at the cost of weakening the development of critical themes and perspectives—is rather pedestrian. The film starts in more linear fashion, not in the cemetery but in an empty lot, with Francis rising from his covers of cardboard and newspaper set against a brick wall. The image of Francis as a fallen man, smack up against it all, captures his condition effectively, albeit from a purely naturalistic approach. He wakes up, staggers a bit, rounds the corner, walks to the mission where he hooks up with Rudy, and then the two of them move on to the cemetery for a day's labor.

Although in these early scenes the dialogue between Francis and Rudy is sharp and clever, it does not depart from the novel. Instead, it lifts fragments of black humor and repartee that essentialize the existential outlook of the homeless characters who are, individually and as a group, "inching toward death." While this perspective, by depicting obvious conditions, reinforces the "physical litany of the dead" and perhaps even hints at the notion of social death, it omits entirely the point of view of the dead and thus the surreal underworld of the supernatural so strikingly portrayed in the novel.

Once inside the cemetery, the film remains on the surface, earth-bound and grounded. With no dramatic depths underfoot and no ethereal flights overhead, no illusions of time and place, the multi-leveled spatial structure of the novel flattens to a horizontal plane. This flattening holds true for the construction of meaning as well. Without distinctive voice to manage the multiple shifts in perspective from living to dead, the thematic resonance thins out accordingly.

Yet, though there is no consciousness of the dead and although Gerald's eerie genius is conspicuously absent, the film's cemetery scene manages to retain some significant images and elements of the narrative. For instance, Francis is shown lying on a mound of dirt in the back of a flat-bed truck as the vehicle winds up the cemetery road—a brief but captivating image which establishes the presence not of the dead, but of the living dead. His membership in this underclass is further affirmed by his quick reference to the Parthenon of Grogan, who—though dead—has more clout than Francis alive.

The dramatic action heightens as the guilt-ridden Francis visits his unfortunate son's grave. Correspondingly, the camera shifts from a rear to a frontal view of him walking up to the plot, hat in hand. This shift in angle, while concentrating on the living, suggests the tension between them and the dead. As Francis addresses his infant son and recalls the events which led to the accident, he displays a mixture of contrition and restraint, grief and remorse. Caught in low angle, with his knees pitched forward, he palpably carries his burden of pain, humility, and sorrow. Thus, though we as viewers are not underground (as readers of the novel were), we are at least at ground level watching a man call forth to memory that which he had stubbornly forgotten for twenty-two years.

Like Nicholson, who moves in and out of this brief early scene of suffering rather gracefully, carefully avoiding both piety and sentimentality, the scene itself ends with comic relief when Francis tells Rudy he was paying his respects to a kid who died young after falling to the floor. "Hell," replies his sidekick, "I fall on the floor about twice a day and I ain't dead." "That's what you think," Francis retorts.[5] The timing of the exchange, played perfectly by Nicholson and Waits, brings the focus back to the social at the expense of the supernatural. Excising the novel's underlying meaning of expiation and foreshortening the allusion to Purgatory and the possibility of redemption, the film's burlesque at least offers some refuge.

The evocative juxtaposition of worldly and otherworldly realms is more evident in the early introductory frames of the film. The first image, seen as the credits roll, is a steam locomotive, still as an iron snake in the dead of night. Slowly, it begins to move along the tracks, which serve to keep the focus horizontal and suggest the delimitation of human existence. Meanwhile, the camera starts to trace the steam upward, as it climbs vertically to span the clouds, moon, and stars in the night sky. The transition is nicely handled: steam leads to clouds; night turns imperceptibly to the blue sky of daylight; geese fly overhead; and Francis wakes up down below. The camera's movement suggestively crosses the lines between the substantial and the insubstantial, between body and spirit, between dream and waking. The moment, however, soon gives way. When the viewer finds Francis "rising" with the dawn, the camera begins its sustained focus on the embodiment.

Memory…as Vivid as Eyesight

Though away from home for twenty-two years, Francis has assembled his own rich "household" while living in extremis. Of course, this household is not the privileged site of kinship obligation. Rather, as the novel makes clear, it is a free-floating collection of sacrificial victims, defining moments, fated events, and bitter consequences, all of which have shaped Francis's nomadic life and continue to inhabit (and haunt) his consciousness. The nature of this household is expansive, as if built to withstand the snows of reduction that threaten to erase time, memory, and being. "A bum is a bum," the ragman concludes after his day of work with Francis (Kennedy, *Ironweed* 150). But Francis is and is not a bum. Although down, he is not out—not yet. At various moments in the novel, he becomes storyteller, witness, historian, striker, labor hero, ballplayer, gift-giver, husband, father, lover, and warrior. In short, a complex and inscrutable individual who defies reduction, he exists in a mystery of time and place.

It is because of the conditions of flight and the vehicle of memory that Francis is not reduced but completed. The "fugitive thrust" first propelled Francis into movement after the Trolley Strike of 1901, when he killed the scab Harold Allen by throwing a brick at him. This was a movement he later reenacted symbolically every spring and summer while playing professional baseball. After Gerald's death in 1916, this motion finally became naturalized as a "quest for pure flight as a fulfilling mannerism of the spirit" (Kennedy, *Ironweed* 75). Over time, memory "as vivid as eyesight" coheres the various yet interconnected flights into a meaningful series of perceptual encounters.

In the novel, the dramatic center of Francis's household begins to take shape after he leaves Gerald's grave. Soon other relations (mainly those united by violent death) appear to Francis as antagonists. The novel treats these phantasms ambiguously, both as subjective projections of Francis' unconscious and as mystical elements in their own right, inexplicable forms from the Great Beyond. Haunts like Harold Allen, Rowdy Dick Doolan, Fiddler Quain, the haberdasher and the shopper expose the persistent pattern of Francis's life: death—flight—guilt—suffering. Having died violently as a direct or indirect result of his actions, these shades also express the whole tragic slope of Francis's many transgressions. Moreover, exerting a spiritual authority and a claim to truth, they force him into a searing dialectic of the soul. Individually and collectively, the phantasmic haunts evoke the troubled past and knit together the frayed strands of Francis's own present state of mind. In the face of this, Francis, "at war with himself," has no other choice: he must review, examine, and justify his life.

"I got arguments...I got arguments," Francis yells back to Harold Allen on the bus from the cemetery to the mission; it is an explosive response to Allen's accusation of cowardice and flight from responsibility, both ingredient to the pattern (Kennedy, *Ironweed* 26). From that moment on, the haunts appear willy-nilly, at times alone, at times in packs. Over the course of the novel, they naturally (and supernaturally) build to a culminating moment of transcendental insubstantiality. During Francis's homecoming, which the antagonists indirectly help to steer him toward, they give way to the memorable dead of Francis's youthful era. The spooks, once captured in a beer picnic photo of 1899, assemble on bleachers in Annie's backyard and, by candlelight, sing the *Dies Irae* (the aptly named "Day of Wrath"). Through the process of irritation, all of the supernatural figures in the novel not only provoke Francis into reconciling his past and present lives, but also push him forward toward his primary household and spur him on toward greater acts of completion, toward a greater synthesis of meaning and purpose.

Kennedy employs a variety of literary techniques to enhance the perceptual oscillation between natural and supernatural (or between past and present), such as development by association, stream of consciousness, and interior monologue. Never abrupt or intrusive, the occurrences of the phantasmic haunts or fanciful reveries are handled with remarkable control and facility. The transitions, in particular, are extremely well crafted and often imperceptible in the context of the whole.

Throughout the novel, Kennedy keeps this "total reality" alive and interesting through various, often unpredictable methods. On the one hand, as with the strike and Harold Allen, reverie prefaces an encounter with the otherworldly. On the other, as with Rowdy Dick, a phantasmic haunt intensifies the moment and is followed by a remembrance of the past. Sometimes Francis's vivid recollections are independent of the haunts, as when he invokes his former neighbor Katrina, his girlfriend Helen, and his mother and father while riding with Rosskam the ragman through the old neighborhoods of Albany. At other times, Kennedy pairs a rather prosaic telling of the past with a rhapsodic reverie of the same event, as with Aldo Campione, the horse thief whom Francis unsuccessfully tried to help jump a freight train. Or, similarly, the narrator depicts a sordid event (Rosskam and the hot lady of the house banging away atop some ash cans in their "cellar of passion") and matches it with Francis's exalted reveries of sexuality and love: "Love, you are my member rubbed raw. Love, you are an unstoppable fire. You burn me, love. I am singed, blackened. Love, I am ashes" (Kennedy, *Ironweed* 97). Such stylistic and technical combinations not only demonstrate Kennedy's imaginative range but also heighten his use of language by bringing lyrical qualities to the act of memory.

In the film, however, the phantasmic haunts of Francis's secondary household appear too objectified. They do not seem to be projected outward from Francis's unconscious, nor do they possess any immanent aura of mystical presence. The exposure of their horrific wounds notwithstanding, they are too much of this world to be credible antagonists. On the surface, the forms are bothersome and somewhat menacing to Francis; they evoke conflict, memory, bemusement, and anger. But their role as catalysts for Francis's odyssey of completion is acutely foreshortened. At best, the phantasmic haunts (who, in the movie, apparently all share the same tailor) offer the viewer only a glimpse of intersubjectivity.

Cinematically, the most extraordinary features of Francis' encounters with the ghosts of his past are the means of transition away from and back toward present reality. These transitions are effectively achieved through tight close-ups of Nicholson's face. Love, as Katrina's poet told her, may very well enter through the eyes; but so too the departure from the quotidian. Nicholson's eyes, so brilliantly spectral, so utterly elsewhere, indicate his altered state of perception and serve almost eerily to transport the scene from present to past. Unfortunately, such transitions are often far more engaging than the visual imagery and dramatic action which they bracket.

In order to stage the first of many such transitions in the film, Babenco and Kennedy utilize the time frame of Halloween. We see children running alongside the bus in which Francis rides; their masks capture his attention. Then, as if by enchantment, Francis has a flashback to the Trolley Strike of 1901: he recalls the masses of strikers and sympathizers running alongside and in front of the scab-driven and soldier-armed car. The flashback, generally true to the novel, ends with a shot of Francis, in the present, staring out the bus window.

In a kind of reality check, Francis peers cautiously over to Rudy, who is sitting across the seat from him; then, glancing a few seats up, he spots the dead scab Harold Allen. All the while, the camera successfully captures the workings of Francis's mind as it moves from the memory of the strike back to the present and then on to the phantasm which haunts him and evokes his guilt for past actions; it also conveys the unique way in which Francis transmutes the events of the world, past and current, around him.

The technique of tight-frame close-up, with a focus on Nicholson's intense eyes, becomes an almost shamanistic vehicle of transition which is successfully repeated throughout the film. It is particularly effective in the scene during which Francis finishes shaving in Jack's and Clara's bathroom. Looking into the mirror, another kind of window to the self, Francis sees Allen, Campione, and Doolan stylishly poised amid the fixtures. This encounter leads to the boxcar flashback, a major cinematic alteration, in which twenty-nine years of novelistic time is compressed into a single moment.

An equally memorable moment occurs when Nicholson, eyes flashing, harks back to his sexual awakening with Katrina, that "rare bird." Although the actual content of the film's flashback is rendered much too concisely, both the way in and out of this scene are poignant. It is Rosskam who abruptly ends the reverie by yet another variation of reduction; he shouts: "Hey bum. Come here." Transition and action again unite in Nicholson's excellent portrayal of Francis's rage when he confronts the assembly of spooks in Annie's backyard. This time not only Nicholson's eyes but his whole body bespeak his passion. "I'm the one puts you on the map," Nicholson yells, bringing a line from the novel sharply to the screen. As he disengages from the scene, Nicholson turns and walks back toward Annie in a rigid and vacant manner which conveys the form, look, and gait of a somewhat monstrous being just coming out of a deep spell. Later, inside Annie's house and before the reunited family sits down to their turkey dinner, he looks out from the kitchen window onto the backyard bleachers and the candlelit chorus. Reminiscent of the bus scene and the tight-frame close-up of Nicholson against the window, this image reveals his profound sense of loss and regret. His face is compressed against the kitchen window; his eyes—at first locked into a trance-like vision—gradually roll to the side as he responds to the gathering sounds of yet another present moment requiring his attention. In the film, the eyes signal all of the mysteries of time and place, of reality and unreality.

These transition shots, and the flashback technique in general, clearly emphasize the character's point of view in the film. But, in the process, the ambiguities that accompany the underlying dialectic of the soul are attenuated. So too is the dynamic role of memory and the phantasmic haunts in nudging Francis closer and closer toward home—the *axis mundi* of his journey.

The film does, however, foreshadow Francis's homecoming in a very evocative way—a way which, ironically, does not draw on spooks or reveries, or even on Nicholson's expressive eyes. This foreshadowing occurs in a strikingly graphic scene which is the only scene in the movie that has no literal reference in the novel.[6] Francis drops Helen off for the night in Finney's car to protect her from the elements and from raids; but before he himself goes down in the weeds to sleep, he takes a detour. It is late, and as he walks down an alleyway, he casts a Hopper-like shadow against a tall wooden fence. The looming shadow advances before the man, as if to proclaim the fundamental alienation of this tormented mortal in its tow. The "holy Phelan eaves" seem to be beckoning Francis; and soon he finds himself, along with his now elongated shadow, standing directly across from his former house, where his wife and children still reside. The camera moves from a horizontal, street-level view to a high-angle shot which encompasses the opposing elements of the scene and its tense, chiaroscuro-like atmosphere. Aside from presaging Francis's return, the overhead view depicts the pathos implicit in this contrast between home and homelessness. Also, because of its height, this shot reduces the physical scene, thus reinforcing the vulnerability of a man and his forsaken household, both transfixed in the wake of destiny.

The Fugitive Dance

Francis manages to still the maddening beat of his fugitive dance long enough to reenter his former home. "All there is is this visit," he tells Annie in the novel. "I don't want nothin' but the look of everybody. Just the look'll do me" (Kennedy, *Ironweed* 162). During his homecoming, Francis emerges once again as the Late Repentant as he expresses sorrow for fleeing the family, remorse for the long absence, and his abiding love for Annie and the children. He makes amends and—in a pardon which in both novel and film is too facile—is clearly forgiven by his family. Even his daughter Peg, who shows some degree of resentment and resistance, softens and comes around in the end. When Annie asks if he would like to come home on a permanent basis, Francis, true to his pattern, faithful to his own transgressions, turns her down. He is simply beyond the verge. The family's unconditional acceptance of Francis is probably best understood as a reflection of Dante's notion of the Infinite Goodness, which, despite Francis's sins, "has arms so wide that It accepts who ever would return" (Dante Alighieri 27).

Francis gives in momentarily to the possibilities that such an embrace affords. He asserts his status as gift-giver: to his wife Annie he brings a turkey; to his grandson Danny he offers a baseball signed by Ty Cobb (see Figure 25); to his son Billy he gives his old mitt from the "bigs"; and to his daughter Peg he reads a letter she wrote him years ago, in this way enabling Peg to touch her youthful innocence again. These exchanges of intimacy in the novel are poignant moments in which Francis's familial roles as husband,

Figure 25. Francis (Jack Nicholson), as gift-giver, offers his prized baseball to his grandson. Copyright © 1967 by Taft Entertainment Pictures/Keith Barish Productions.

father, and grandfather come to life. And when Francis ritualistically cleanses himself and dons his old gray herringbone suit from the trunk in the attic, he toys with the idea that he "is not yet ruined, except as an apparency in process." An old photo of a baseball caught yet arcing in flight evokes a meditative thought:

> What the camera had caught was two instants in one: time separated and unified, the ball in two places at once, an eventuation as inexplicable as the Trinity itself. Francis now took the picture to be a Trinitarian talisman (a hand, a glove, a ball) for achieving the impossible: for he had always believed it impossible for him, ravaged man, failed human, to reenter history under this roof. Yet here he was in this aerie of reconstitutable time, touching untouchable artifacts of a self that did not yet know it was ruined, just as the ball, in its inanimate ignorance, did not know yet that it was going nowhere, was caught. (Kennedy, *Ironweed* 169)

Does the ball still fly? Does Francis live on to play another day?[7] The ambiguity in the novel is quite deliberate. There is potential: he just might; then again, he might not.

Caught by the rhythm of the fugitive dance, Francis leaves his former home and moves on, to return to the vehicles that keep him in such perpetual motion: missions; booze; flophouses; hobo jungles; and trains. "What and who were again separating Francis from those people after he'd found them? It was a force whose name did not matter, if it had a name, but whose effect was devastating" (Kennedy, *Ironweed* 205). In a further act of completion, Francis comes to terms with this "fugitive thrust," its genesis, and the overall meaning inherent in the pattern of his life. Rejecting the role of labor hero in the Trolley Strike (a role advanced by Edward Daugherty in his play *The Car Barns*), Francis sees the events of that day as nothing more than chaos which impressed upon him and upon Harold Allen the need to survive. Over time, the primal need turns into a full-blown mission of survival, which gives meaning and significance to Francis's life on the road.

In an interesting reversal, Francis absolves Allen, who gave him the death taint and initiated his relentless cycle of violence, flight, and memory: "I forgive the son of a bitch" (Kennedy, *Ironweed* 207). But Francis does not forgive himself. Instead, he holds himself hostage to the past. His battle to survive against all odds transforms him into a "warrior," an embodiment of failure, guilt, suffering, and the enduring human spirit. He asserts this self-definition, the basis for identity, with the pride and wisdom of one who has a tortured though profound insight into the very essence of his nature:

> He had fled the folks because he was too profane a being to live among them.... [S]omehow it involved protecting saints from

sinners, protecting the living from the dead. And a warrior, he was certain, was not a victim. Never a victim.

In the deepest part of himself that could draw an unutterable conclusion, he told himself: My guilt is all that I have left. If I lose it, I have stood for nothing, done nothing, been nothing. (Kennedy, *Ironweed* 216)

Francis's intense attachment to his identity as profaned "other" demonstrates that, for all his running, he does not flee his own guilt. Rather, he carries it with him, and it becomes necessary to the life of his soul. The sentence is harsh, but the recognition honest. His guilt inextinguishable, Francis must continue to course through the underworld.

The film, by contrast, though it capably depicts Francis as Late Repentant and gift-giver and thus retains the obvious elements of the literary narrative during the homecoming scenes, fails to capture the meditative qualities that express the character's consciousness. So while the film suggests the course of time, it lacks the power to convey the reflections of Francis's mind. Absent is the complex perspective of the character and his search for meaning both during the reunion scenes and afterward. Absent also is the depth of subjective accounting: in the film, there are no confrontations with the fugitive dance, no insights into the importance of survival, and, most damning, no comprehension of Francis's completion as "warrior."

In visualizing the course of time, however, the film depicts the surface of dramatic action in a way that the novel simply cannot. Through the cinematic technique of cross-cutting, Babenco and Kennedy show related actions that occur at the same time. This alternation between scenes, sustained for almost half the film, condenses and relates three chapters of the novel. It also shows the thematic unity which connects Francis and Helen even as they go their separate ways during the second day of the story—All Saint's Day.

The cross-cutting, effectively paced and divided equally between Helen and Francis's spans fourteen scenes. Some brief, some of longer duration, together the scenes build toward the climactic interrelationship of Helen's end and Francis's homecoming and subsequent flight. The sense of a dynamic destiny is clear as Helen and Francis move along in their separate orbits. While Helen is shown making her way from St. Anthony's church to the diner, library, music store, and finally to a room at Palombo's Hotel, where she prepares to die, Francis is shown working for the ragman, lost in reverie, and returning home. Despite their separate paths, however, they manage to intersect occasionally, as good soul-mates often do, and to leave behind traces of significance. (See Figure 26.)

For instance, during one of the cross-cut transitions, Helen is shown vomiting on a sidewalk in front of a store display window while a reflection of the ragman's wagon (with Francis on board) moves across the glass behind

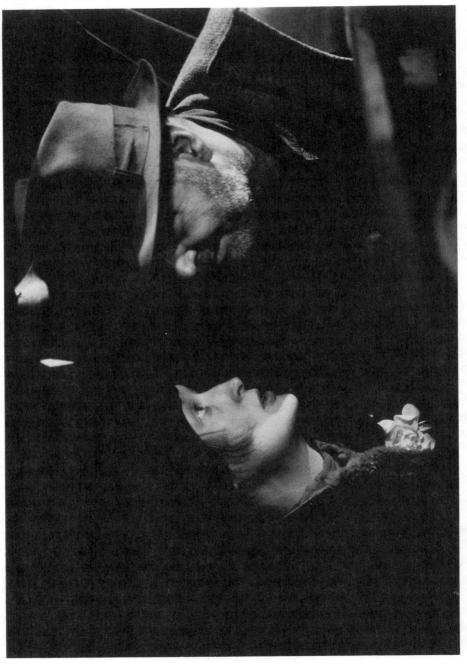

Figure 26. Soul-mates Helen (Meryl Streep) and Francis cross paths. Copyright © 1967 by Taft Entertainment Pictures/Keith Barish Productions.

her. They pass by unseen. Other examples of separation and connection involve the juxtaposition of scenes which reveal the following: the characters' special talents (Helen's music and Francis's ballplaying); a heightened sense of order and harmony in both the Phelan household and Helen's hotel room; ritualistic cleansing (Helen's at the hotel, Francis's at his former home); and peacemaking with the past (enhanced by the symbolic value of Francis's old trunk and Helen's reclaimed suitcases). By far, the best detail in the movie is when Helen, looking to beautify her room so she can die with dignity, nonchalantly picks up a shoelace from one of the suitcases and sets it out for Francis. (Throughout the entire film, he has gone without it.) Later, after leaving Rudy's body at the hospital only to find Helen sprawled dead on the floor, he pockets the shoelace. Only Helen knows just what Francis needs.

During the long cross-cut portion of the film, Nicholson and Streep demonstrate their complete mastery of their roles. Engaging in her internalization of the character, Streep credibly "acts out" Helen Archer's various moods and expresses intense pride, fury, nausea, exhaustion, serenity, and beauty. She also delivers the two best lines in the movie (taken from the novel). As she examines herself in the hotel room mirror, she quips: "What if I did drink too much wine? Who knows how much I didn't drink?" Her rhetorical question is at the same time a fine defense against the rank forces of condemnation. Nicholson, similarly outstanding in his role, strikes a number of effective postures as he moves (in his inimitable way) from contrite to bewildered to maddened to meek and conciliatory.

Although stylized and somewhat sentimentalized, the scenes framed by the cross-cuts, especially those which involve Francis's homecoming, are finely composed and well-crafted. In particular, the striking imagistic contrast between Francis's old trunk, which looks like a coffin with its lid up, and his grandson Danny's room, which "gets the morning light," works very effectively to foreground the dramatic struggle between death and life. For the moment, possibility is kept alive, as suggested by Annie's off-screen voice, which blends with the light of Danny's room. In addition, the match cuts which comprise the final scene of Francis's homecoming demonstrate a good sense of internal rhythm and enable the viewer to empathize with the emotional predicament of each character. The shifting camera angle and its distance from the actors intensifies the resistance and reconciliation between Francis and Peg. By the time the family has made peace, the camera finally levels out and no one is above or below the other. The scene ends with a long shot of the Phelan household, arranged tableau-like at the kitchen table. (See Figure 27.)

Hard Travelin': Conclusion Through Convergence

Both novel and film ultimately converge; the ending, set in motion by the Legionnaires' raid on the hobo jungle, encapsulates the whole cycle of violent death, crazed flight, and ardent memory. During the raid, Francis—

Figure 27. The Phelan household reconciled around the kitchen table. Copyright © 1967 by Taft Entertainment Pictures/Keith Barish Productions.

attired in his 1916 suit—is re-christened in venom, violence, and blood. One of the Legionnaires is most likely killed by Francis; Rudy dies; and Francis discovers Helen dead in her hotel room. He then hops a freight train, going south. In the end, as Francis travels farther from Albany on the train, we see that the wheels are still in spin. The themes converge. His torments grow.

In the novel, before he is visited in the train car by a vision of Strawberry Bill, Francis visualizes again the merger of his own female fates; just moments earlier in the novel, he realized that the course of his life had been shaped by several women (his mother, Katrina, Annie, Helen). And, in an image rich with mythic resonances, he originally recalled them, "...witnesses all to the whole fabric of Francis's life. His mother was crocheting a Home Sweet Home sampler while Katrina measured off a bolt of new cloth and Helen snipped the ragged edges. Then they all became Annie" (Kennedy, *Ironweed* 202). After the reappearance of his fates in the train car comes the "thought" of Annie's attic and Danny's room. Both the uprooted pattern of lived experience and the imagined setting of rootedness describe Francis's condition at the end.

In highlighting the contrast between a destined life on the road and the longing for the domestic harmonies of the Phelan household, Kennedy demonstrates the complexity of his character and the ambiguity of his situation in the final moment of the story (an ambiguity which some critics have misread). The novel concludes without the resolution of a happy ending. Daniel Murtaugh's incisive commentary on the novel for *Commonweal* explicates the irony of the conclusion and its challenge to interpretation:

> Everything that really happens is conveyed to us in conditional verbs. Everything that is merely a dream is conveyed with indicative verbs. What really happens is that Francis hops a freight out of town. What happens in a wishful dream—and in sentences whose very grammar tries to make the dream real—is that he returns to "the holy Phelan eaves" and the protective love of Annie.... Francis holds in his heart the hope of return. (302)[8]

In the film, there is no visit by Strawberry Bill; and only Annie, offering tea, appears to Francis in the freight car. Far more importantly, the trains in the film provide an effective frame for the entire story: their images and movements reinforce the cyclical nature of Francis's condition. Consistent with Kennedy's novelistic vision, Babenco, preferring to end the movie with Francis "on the road" rather than back with the family, allows him to keep going.[9] Furthermore, to his credit, in the film Babenco retains the incongruity between appearance and reality so crucial to the novel's ending. The visual irony of the film's ending is literally brought home by the final image on the screen—Danny's room, flooded with the morning light. Babenco begs the question: Is it a flash-back or a flash-forward? Consequently, the image works to integrate Francis Phelan's past and present, while it leads the viewer to further conjecture. The knowledge that Francis is moving farther and farther away from that for which he yearns reinforces the contrast between home and homeless, youth and age, light and darkness. Finally, the dramatic tension between these oppositions speaks directly to the dialectic of the soul and its alternation between the desire for redemption and the enactment of repetition.

The conclusions of novel and film converge on an essential observation: Francis Phelan is not redeemed; he is revealed. He does not release himself (nor do circumstances release him) from blame, harm, and distress. Although he makes amends with Annie and the family, he does not repair or restore self with household and community—at least not in deed. In fact, in both novel and film, the separation between thought and deed, combined with Francis's abiding fate as outcast, suggests that a classical Greek substructure undergirds the facile Christian notion of salvation. Francis's flashes of recognition amid his overriding sense of finitude suggest that he is caught in a web of inevitable suffering as fatalistic as that of any classical hero. He ends, therefore, not at the peak of Purgatory but in the depths of Hades, with only a vestigial thought of earthly paradise. The convergence of the film's ending with the novel's ending shows the hard traveling in store for him. For in both novel and film, Francis continues to pay the price, "inching toward death" in so many ways, not just because of Gerald, but because of the entire course of his life. Thus novel and film come together in their final moments and join in *expanding* upon Francis's journey through that "sea so cruel."

NOTES

[1] A reference both to the character of Francis Phelan in *Ironweed* (207) and his philosophy of survival and to Kennedy's own comment in an interview (Douglas R. Allen and Mona Simpson, "The Art of Fiction CXI: [Interview with] William Kennedy," *The Paris Review* 112 [Winter 1989]: 45). In the interview, Kennedy repeats the phrase "to beat the bastards" when discussing the long, solitary and arduous writing process.

[2] Proceeds from the premiere benefited local organizations serving the homeless and the classic film series at the State University at Albany.

[3] This essay also appears as the Introduction to *The Making of Ironweed*, photographs by Claudio Edinger (New York: Penguin Books, 1988).

[4] Babenco explains his approach to the film: "I never thought of two levels of reality [realistic and surrealistic]. Both of them were total reality for me."

[5] *Ironweed* [the movie], directed by Hector Babenco and screenplay by William Kennedy, Taft-Barish Productions (a Tri-Star Release), 1987. These lines in the film are taken verbatim from the novel.

⁶In the novel, Francis walks to North Albany and then on to the flats where the canal had been. He finds some shelter in the shell of "Welt the Tin's" barn, only 25 yards from his lost home where he dropped Gerald 22 years ago. Asleep in the barn, Francis has a dream of ascent: "Horns and mountains rose up out of the earth…. Francis recognized the song the trumpets played and he floated with its melody. Then…he ascended bodily into the exalted reaches of the world where the song had been composed so long ago" (90).

⁷I am paraphrasing Kennedy with these two questions. In the novel, there are two declarative sentences followed by an interrogative sentence: "The ball still flies. Francis still lives to play another day. Doesn't he?" (See 169.)

⁸In an interview, Kennedy remarks on the ending of the novel: "I did that [use of the conditional] not in order to make it hypothetical, that was not the intention. As far as I'm concerned that's real, everything that happens there is real…. It's a very complicated situation in which he [Francis] exists at the moment, and I think I'm representing the complexities, variously…. What those last two or three pages say is what Francis Phelan's condition is when we take leave of him." See Kay Bonetti, "An Interview with William Kennedy," *The Missouri Review* 8.2 (1985): 82-83.

For a sample of the happy ending interpretations, whereby Francis, in finding his family and earthly paradise, is "purged, reconstituted, and regenerated," see J. K. Van Dover, *Understanding William Kennedy* (Columbia: University of South Carolina Press, 1991) 94-97, and Edward C. Reilly, *William Kennedy* (Boston: Twayne, 1991) 76-77; 83-84. Also, see Reilly's "The Pigeons and Circular Flight in Kennedy's *Ironweed*" and "Dante's *Purgatorio* and Kennedy's *Ironweed*." Respectively, these articles are in *Notes on Contemporary Literature* 16.1 (March 1986): 8, and *Notes* 17.3 (May 1987): 5-8. I quote from Reilly, *William Kennedy* 84.

⁹Babenco clarifies his view of the film's ending: "I could have finished the movie with Francis coming home and having a turkey dinner with his family. We took the chance of doing a movie in which the main character keeps going, without really accepting the love values of the family. He preferred the road. That's a traditional American characteristic." Quoted in Robert Denerstein, "*Ironweed* Director Eases Up," *Arkansas Democrat* (6 March 1988): 7E.

WORKS CITED AND CONSULTED

Allen, Douglas R., and Mona Simpson. "The Art of Fiction CXI: William Kennedy." *The Paris Review* 112 (Winter 1989): 34-59.

Black, David. "The Fusion of Past and Present in William Kennedy's *Ironweed*." *Critique* 7.3 (Spring 1986): 177-84.

Bonetti, Kay. "William Kennedy: An Interview." *The Missouri Review* 8.2 (1985): 71-86.

Clarke, Peter P. "Classical Myth in William Kennedy's *Ironweed*." *Critique* 7.3 (Spring 1986): 167-76.

Croyden, Margaret. "The Sudden Fame of William Kennedy." *New York Times Magazine* 26 August 1984: 33-73.

Dante Alighieri. *Purgatorio. The Divine Comedy of Dante Alighieri.* Trans. and Introd. Allen Mandelbaum. New York: Bantam, 1982 Canto III, 27.

_____. *Inferno. The Divine Comedy of Dante Alighieri.* Trans. and Introd. Allen Mandelbaum. New York: Bantam, 1980.

Denerstein, Robert. "*Ironweed* Director Eases Up." *Arkansas Democrat* 6 March 1988: 7E.

Edinger, Claudio. *The Making of Ironweed.* New York: Penguin, 1988.

Farrelly, Patrick. "Francis Phelan Goes Hollywood." *Irish America* 51 (November 1987): 25-29, 51.

Grondahl, Paul. "At Last, *Ironweed* Plays the Palace."(Albany, New York) *Times Union* 18 December 1987: F8-9.

Ironweed [the movie]. Directed by Hector Babenco and Screenplay by William Kennedy. Taft-Barish Productions (a Tri-Star Release), 1987.

Kasindorf, Martin. "Down and Out In Albany." *Newsday* 18 December 1987: F11-12.

Kennedy, William. "Be Reasonable—Unless You're a Writer." *New York Times Book Review* 25 January 1987: 3.

_____. *Ironweed.* New York: Viking, 1983.

_____. "Re-creating *Ironweed.*" *American Film* 13.4 (January-February 1988): 18-25.

_____. "Why It Took So Long." *New York Times Book Review* 20 May 1990: 1, 32-35.

Kurp, Patrick. "*Ironweed*: Beautiful, Sad—and Dark." (Albany, New York) *Knickerbocker News* 18 December 1987: F14.

Murtaugh, Daniel M. "Fathers and Their Sons: William Kennedy's Hero-Transgressors." *Commonweal* 19 May 1989: 298-302.

Nichols, Loxley F. "William Kennedy Comes of Age." *National Review* 37 (9 August 1985): 46-48.

Ozer, Jerome S. *Film Review Annual, 1988.* Englewood, NJ: Film Review Publications, 1988.

Pritchard, William H. "The Spirits of Albany." *The New Republic* 14 February 1983: 37-38.

Quinn, Peter J. "William Kennedy: An Interview." *The Recorder: A Journal of the American Irish Historical Society* 1.1 (Winter 1985): 65-81.

Reilly, Edward C. "An Averill Park Afternoon with William Kennedy." *The South Carolina Review* 21.2 (Spring 1989): 11-24.

_____. "Dante's *Purgatorio* and Kennedy's *Ironweed*: Journeys to Redemption." *Notes on Contemporary Literature* 17.3 (May 1987): 5-8.

_____. "The Pigeons and Circular Flight in Kennedy's *Ironweed.*" *Notes on Contemporary Literature* 16.1 (March 1986): 8.

_____. *William Kennedy.* Boston: Twayne, 1991.

Robertson, Michael. "The Reporter as Novelist: The Case of William Kennedy." *Columbia Journalism Review* 24 (January-February 1986): 49-50, 52.

Ironweed and the Snows of Reduction **153**

Sayles, John. *Thinking in Pictures: The Making of The Movie Matewan.* Boston: Houghton Mifflin, 1987.

Sheffer, Gary. "World Premiere of *Ironweed*: Plenty of Hoopla and High Fashion." (Albany, New York) *Knickerbocker News* 18 December 1987: F2-3.

Thompson, David. "The Man Has Legs: William Kennedy Interviewed." *Film Comment* 21.2 (March-April 1985): 54-59.

Tierce, Michael. "William Kennedy's Odyssey: The Travels of Francis Phelan." *Classical and Modern Literature* 8 (1988): 247-63.

Van Dover, J. K. *Understanding William Kennedy.* Columbia: University of South Carolina Press, 1991.

Yetman, Michael G. "*Ironweed*: The Perils and Purgatories of Male Romanticism." *Papers on Language and Literature* 27.1 (Winter 1991): 84-104.

Tough Guy Goes Hollywood: Mailer and the Movies

Barry H. Leeds

Norman Mailer's relationship with the world of film has grown throughout his career from passive and distant to active and quite intimate.

The earliest adaptations of his work—the movie versions of *The Naked and the Dead* (1958) and *An American Dream* (1966)—are quite awful. While both films have many weaknesses, the primary failure in each case lies in the respective conclusions, which dramatically reverse Mailer's intended vision.

In *The Naked and the Dead* (1948), Mailer's celebrated first novel, the liberal, Harvard-educated Lieutenant Hearn struggles politically and metaphysically with the conservative General Cummings, while the malevolent Sergeant Croft plots to regain control of Hearn's platoon. One of Mailer's primary thematic messages in the novel involves the collusion of Croft with Martinez to withhold information which ultimately results in Hearn's death. Thus, on an allegorical level, Mailer forcefully suggests that postwar American liberalism will be destroyed by the uneasy alliance of the upper and lower classes in their affinity for reactionary political views. In the movie version of *The Naked and the Dead*, however, Sergeant Croft (played by Aldo Ray) is killed by Japanese fire, while Lieutenant Hearn (Cliff Robertson) is wounded, but carried safely back to headquarters by the enlisted men of his platoon, notably "a Baptist preacher and a wandering Jew," thus thwarting the tyrannical fascist General Cummings (Raymond Massey). In fact, in the screenplay by Denis and Terry Sanders, Robertson's Hearn triumphantly announces to Massey's Cummings, "There is a spirit in man that will survive...godlike, eternal, indestructible."

In Mailer's *An American Dream* (1965), the existential and ultimately hopeful vision of the novel is implicit in the fact that Stephen Richards Rojack survives the horrific American experience, aided by the sacrificial deaths of his lover Cherry and her ex-lover, the black jazz musician Shago Martin. In the movie (whose title in British release was *See You in Hell, Darling*), Rojack (Stuart Whitman) is killed by mobsters after being betrayed by Cherry (Janet Leigh), who thus saves herself. The last line in the movie is her solitary murmur: "What did you expect from a whore?" Shago (Paul Mantee) is present for only a brief moment. Thus, Mailer's indictment of the flaws and hypocrisies endemic in American society, coupled with existential hope and expressed so powerfully in the novel, is replaced in the film by a general sense of purposeless cynicism; and the novel's allegorical implication that what is potentially fine in the American character can best be realized by an alliance with downtrodden groups like blacks and women is completely lost on the screen.

During the late 1960s, Mailer's relationship with Hollywood took a new turn: he produced, directed and starred in three feature-length films: *Wild 90* (1967), the story of three gangsters in hiding; *Beyond the Law* (1968), set in a police station during a series of interrogations; and most notoriously, *Maidstone* (1970), a mystery involving an assassination attempt upon a presidential candidate/film director, Norman T. Kingsley (played by Norman Kingsley Mailer). Made with no script, no retakes, and no continuity ("Everything...is created as he cuts," noted Sally Beauman) (Mailer, *Maidstone* 9), these unconventional productions were critical and financial failures, though Mailer demonstrated a gathering understanding and control of cinematic technique with each one. When *Maidstone* was issued as a paperback book in 1971, Mailer added an essay on filmmaking (in which, among other things, he contemplated the difficulty of "transporting a novelist's vision of life over to a film" [143] and concluded that, since the coherence of the original novel is "cremated and strewn" by the process of adaptation, it is "no wonder great novels invariably make the most disappointing movies...and modest novels...sometimes make very good movies" [144]). A decade later, in 1981, he returned to Hollywood in yet another role: a cameo appearance as Stanford White in the movie version of E. L. Doctorow's *Ragtime.*

Also in 1981, Mailer wrote the screenplay for the 1982 NBC Television Network miniseries based on his 1979 "true life novel," *The Executioner's Song,* which was later shown on cable premium channels and seen in theaters in Europe. Mailer was nominated for an Emmy award for the screenplay, and Tommy Lee Jones won one (Outstanding Actor in a Drama Special) for his starring role as Gary Gilmore, the first man to be executed in America in ten years. So eager was Mailer to write this screenplay himself that he took the unusual step of writing on speculation. The fact that this was clearly a labor of love shows in the vitality of the production, which garnered generally strong reviews. Subsequently, Mailer explained: "I thought no one could do 'The Executioner's Song' as well as I could. Part of the problem is that it's a very long book with over 200 characters, and a job of digestion had to be done. I wrote that book, so I'd already done that digesting" (Harmetz).

But the most important film of Mailer's career to date is unquestionably *Tough Guys Don't Dance,* based on his 1984 novel of the same title, for which Mailer wrote the screenplay and also directed. (See Figure 28.) *Tough*

Figure 28. Mailer not only wrote the screenplay for *Tough Guys*, he also directed the film. Copyright © 1987 by Cannon Films.

Guys is the story of Tim Madden—ex-con, ex-amateur fighter, and unsuccessful writer—who wakes up with a hangover one morning to discover a new tattoo on his arm, a fresh blood stain on his car seat, and a severed head in his marijuana stash. Although Tim has only vague memories of his activities during the previous night, he begins to fear his complicity in the various murders which are soon revealed; and he tries to reconstruct the events so that he can prove his innocence, to himself and to others who suspect him.

For Mailer, the novel was like "an illegitimate baby. It was written in two months, therefore born out of wedlock" (Bowden 40-44). In fact, he was surprised by the fact that the event even took place, since—though he had been drawing an advance—he had not written a word for months. "[I]f I didn't write it," he remarked after *Tough Guys'* publication, "with all that I owed the IRS and my old publisher, I'd have to begin cheating Random House [publisher of *Tough Guys*] immediately" (40).[1]

Nevertheless, the form which Mailer adopted in the novel was one to which he had been drawn for some time. "I'd been thinking of doing [a murder mystery] for many years. And I've always loved Hammett and Chandler. Whenever I get tired of writing, I go and read them. I read them five times, eight times. Every one of their books. This is over many years, over 40 years. They're a tonic. So, I've always wanted to write a murder mystery and I've always been curious as to how it would turn out" (Bowden 44).

Tough Guys Don't Dance turned out to be a relatively insignificant novel, clearly overshadowed by Mailer's substantial body of work, particularly by *Ancient Evenings* (1983), which it most immediately follows, and *An American Dream* (1965), which it most closely resembles. But its similarities to the latter are particularly interesting. For, while *Tough Guys* suffers by comparison to the earlier novel, it does represent a return to themes and situations first developed in *An American Dream*, including many of the significant and symbolic preoccupations that have governed Mailer's work for decades: a highly personal vision of American existentialism, an obsessive preoccupation with cancer as a symbol of moral failure, and, above all, a Manichaean vision of the universe.

Moreover, many of the plot details in the two novels are similar. Again, an estranged wife is murdered, possibly by her husband, the first-person narrator. Again, the existential will of the protagonist is tested by the danger of falling from heights, by a hostile police investigator, and by various other adversaries from the demi-monde. Again, cancer figures prominently, supernatural omens abound, and potential salvation is offered through a regenerative heterosexual love. Even the circumstances of the composition of the novels were much the same: *American Dream* was written hurriedly against monthly deadlines for publication in *Esquire* (January through August, 1964); *Tough Guys* was completed in sixty days, and two long sections from it were published in *Vanity Fair*.

In *An American Dream*, two primary structural patterns lend coherence to Mailer's thematic preoccupations. One is the sense of a pilgrimage by Stephen Richards Rojack from imminent alcoholism, madness and damnation to sanity and salvation. In a modern analogue of *Pilgrim's Progress*, he confronts a series of adversaries, defeating them and the weaknesses in himself that they represent, and in the process absorbing their strengths. The second is a pattern of sexual connections among the characters, with Rojack at its hub. These structural patterns are replicated in both versions of *Tough Guys Don't Dance*.

In *Cannibals and Christians* (1966), Mailer writes of James Baldwin's *Another Country*:

> There is a chain of fornication which is all but complete…With the exception of Rufus Scott, who does not go to bed with his sister, everybody else in the book is connected by their skin to another character who is connected to still another…. All the sex in the book is displaced, whites with blacks, men with men, women with homosexuals; the sex is funky to suffocation, rich but claustrophobic, sensual but airless. Baldwin understands the existential abyss of love. In a world of Negroes and whites, nuclear fallout, marijuana, bennies, inversion, insomnia, and tapering off with beer at four in the morning, one no longer falls in love—one has to take a brave leap over the wall of one's impacted rage and cowardice. And nobody makes it, not quite…. They cannot find the juice to break out of their hatred into the other country of love. (114)

In *Tough Guys Don't Dance*, as in *An American Dream*, Mailer presents a series of characters as promiscuously connected to one another sexually as those who people Baldwin's book. But while the sexual world of Mailer's characters is as dark as Baldwin's, it is in the realm of sexual love that Mailer offers his statement of hope for salvation; for Tim Madden and Madeleine Falco (like Rojack and Cherry in *American Dream*) are ultimately able, in both versions of *Tough Guys*, to take the "brave leap over the wall of…impacted rage and cowardice." (See Figure 29.)

Ironically, *Tough Guys*, a far less ambitious novel than *American Dream*, becomes in Mailer's hands a far more artistically successful film. As both screenwriter and director, Mailer manages to translate to the screen much of the tonal ambience of the novel's fictive voice, as integral to his work as Fitzgerald's finely styled narrative is to *The Great Gatsby*. But whereas *Gatsby's* tonal resonance is lost and the awkwardness of the bald plot made prominent (despite Nick Carraway's verbatim voice-over in the third film adaptation), Mailer as director is able to evoke even more fully than he did in the novel the bleakness of his Provincetown winter; and while his adaptation

Figure 29. Tim (Ryan O'Neal) is reunited with his true love, Madeleine (Isabella Rossellini). Copyright © 1987 by Cannon Films.

of *Tough Guys* still highlights (as in the *Gatsby* films) the excesses of the murder mystery plot, they are ameliorated to some degree by a pervasive tone of black humor.

Mailer's protagonist in the film *Tough Guys Don't Dance*, the aspiring novelist Tim Madden (surprisingly well-evoked in his seedy alcoholism by Ryan O'Neal), lies at the center of a complex round of sexual connections. Just as Rojack in *American Dream* is linked to his satanic adversary, Barney Oswald Kelly, by the fact that each has had affairs with Deborah, Ruta and Cherry, Tim Madden in *Tough Guys* is connected to his former colleague, multimillionaire Meeks Wardley Hilby III (called Wardley Meeks III in the film and played by John Bedford Lloyd) through Tim's estranged wife Patty Lareine (Debra Sandlund), and to Meeks' associate, Lonnie Pangborn (R. Patrick Sullivan) through Jessica Pond (Frances Fisher), whom Tim meets— and sleeps with—on the fateful night he does not fully recall. But Madden's most significant connection is to Alvin Luther Regency (Wings Hauser), the Acting Chief of Police of Provincetown, who, like Madden, has been intimate with Patty Lareine and Jessica Pond and who is married to Tim's former lover, Madeleine Falco (Isabella Rossellini).

Wings Hauser is quite effective at portraying Regency's intense rectitude (echoed in his middle name, "Luther") as well as his criminal venality, his sexual rapacity and his borderline madness. (He sometimes looks as if he is about to rotate his head 360° and vomit pea soup.) In fact, he tells Tim and his father, Dougy, that he has two sides, "the enforcer and the maniac." In both novel and film, the primary antagonist and the police investigator become one, as Madden finds himself unwittingly participating in a wife-swap with Regency. Unlike the relatively simple, deceptively innocent swap twelve years earlier in which Madden met Patty Lareine (then married to her first husband, the football coach-preacher-chiropractor called "Big Stoop") and ultimately lost his real love, Madeleine, this one has life and death stakes.

These geometric sexual patterns in turn are part of a series of shifting criminal alliances and betrayals which lead in the book to five murders and two suicides (six and one in the film), and two postmortem beheadings, treated with a more disarming black humor in the film's conclusion than in the novel. Yet the most significant relationship in both versions is that between Tim and his forceful father Dougy (powerfully portrayed by Lawrence Tierney, an actor who in life had a history of drunken brawling similar to that of his character).[2] (See Figure 30.) It is Dougy who provides Tim with the veritable Zen koan which forms the book's title (although the boxing anecdote is omitted from the film); it is Dougy who, despite being ravaged by cancer, remains the tough guy (though—as he confesses—the spirits now hover around him at night and taunt him, telling him it is time for him to dance); and it is Dougy who performs the dirtier responsibilities, such as disposing of the severed heads, which Tim cannot. (In a nice symmetry at the end of the film, however, Dougy—made a little less tough by his illness—

Figure 30. Tim seeks advice from his father, Dougy (Lawrence Tierney). Copyright © 1987 by Cannon Films.

and Tim—made a little more tough by his recent experience—work together to clean up the week's terrible mess when they sail out at night and dispose of the bodies.) It is no wonder, then, that of the animal imagery so pervasive in the novel, the most positive has been reserved for Dougy. He has "tiger's balls" and is as "powerful as a Kodiak bear," descriptions which emphasize his massive size and courage and his large role as a moral paradigm for his son (Mailer, *Tough Guys* 254, 88). (Tim, by contrast, is more diminutive, feeling "like a cat trapped for six days in a tree" [99] when he cannot complete the climb up the Provincetown monument and "like a puppy in a new house" [75], soiled by panic in fear of his unseen adversaries.)[3]

In the film as in the book, no one and nothing is as it appears to be. Regency, the top police officer, is actually a criminal. Tim, the apparent murderer, is the only entirely innocent character. Patty Lareine, the "murdered" wife, is actually a murderess until she herself is murdered. Both homosexuals, Wardley and Pangborn, become temporarily heterosexual. The menacing Bolo Green (a.k.a. "Mr. Black"), Patty's chauffeur and lover, acts amicably toward Tim (who had been Patty's chauffeur and lover when she was married to Wardley). Even Tim's Black Labrador, Stunts (so named because he knows none), performs one surprising and heroic act by taking in his heart the knife intended for Tim.

A series of minor *Doppelgängers* populates both versions of *Tough Guys*, echoing the Tim/Regency connection. Patty and Jessica are so interchangeable as blonde sex objects that when Tim finds the first severed head in his marijuana stash he is confused as to whose head it actually is. (This confusion is somewhat deemphasized in the film.) Wardley and Pangborn have parallel anomalous sexual relationships with Patty and Jessica, respectively, in which they are replaced by Tim Madden, and ultimately in the book they shoot themselves with matching pistols. (In the movie, however, Pangborn is shot by Jessica, who wields the pistol he has handed over to her.)

Similarly, in the novel, Tim Madden is connected to a seemingly unlikely counterpart, the sordid and unsavory Hank "Spider" Nissen. Like Tim, Spider is an unsuccessful writer (Mailer, *Tough Guys* 102); like Tim, he is supported by the woman with whom he lives (though Spider and Beth's circumstances are more modest than Tim and Patty's); and, like Tim (who was kept from completing his climb by the overhang near the top), he made an abortive attempt to scale the Provincetown Monument. While Tim's attempt, made many years earlier, is beneficial to his soul and his nerve, Spider's attempt serves less purpose. Rather than any existential reserve, it merely provides Spider with a parallel which he happily emphasizes. "[Spider] would look at me," says Tim, "and give me a giggle as if we had both had a girl together, and each took turns sitting on her head" (101). (The parallels, however, are omitted from the movie; only the suggestion that Spider is supported by Beth remains.)

But if Spider, in his pinched venality, his vicious treachery, is an unlikely alter ego for Tim, Wardley is even more so. Wardley was, incredibly, a classmate of Tim's at Exeter. Both were expelled on the same day, for different reasons. They were, too, "classmates" at a school of harder knocks: a Florida penitentiary. Further, both have been married to Patty Lareine (Wardley being the rich man Patty marries after leaving "Big Stoop" and becoming a stewardess, an intention she announced to Tim the day after the wife-swap a decade earlier).

But as in *An American Dream*, the differences between these parallel lives are far more important than their similarities. Wardley is a homosexual by eager and early choice; Tim resists successfully even the enforced homosexuality of the prison power structure. ("They called me Iron Jaw" [Mailer, *Tough Guys* 254], he tells Dougy in the novel; in the film his declaration becomes, "I did three years in the slammer standing up. Nobody made a punk out of me.") And two instances of appearance masking reality serve finally to define these men. In the book, the one redemptive act of courage ever committed by Wardley, the daring creep along a ledge from one window to another of his father's house (though committed in the service of a venal blackmail scheme), has always elicited from Tim a certain admiration. Tim claims, in fact, that it was this image in his mind that stayed his hand when Patty Lareine asked him to kill Wardley (before she realized that divorce was almost as lucrative as murder). Near the book's conclusion, Wardley admits with glee that the story is pure fabrication. Again, where Tim suspects himself of being Patty's murderer, Wardley admits that *he* is responsible. Finally, while Tim goes on to a redemptive new life and love with Madeleine Falco Regency, Wardley shoots himself (after threatening to kill Tim and then dying in his arms). Meanwhile, Spider, the other dubious brother of the heights, is revealed as the other half of the Patty-head crime: after Wardley killed her, Spider beheaded her. (In both novel and film, Wardley in turn kills Spider and buries him near the two headless women.)

Many of the differences between the film and the novel versions of *Tough Guys Don't Dance* are implicit in the respective strengths and limitations of the two media. It is obvious that Mailer was obliged to telescope various events and limit or omit scenes or characters in order to fit the several hundred pages into two hours. Examples include the omission of minor characters like the eccentric local Harpo, nicknamed for his desire to "harpoon" women; in the novel Harpo does Tim's new tattoo, while in the movie that task falls to Spider's accomplice, Stoodie. Bolo Green (played by Clarence Williams III of *Mod Squad* infamy) disappears after the first scene, and the plot is altered so that his murder of Stoodie is committed by Wardley. The motives for most of the murders and beheadings are ascribed almost entirely to greed over a proposed cocaine deal, with dashes of lust and jealousy (notably in Patty Lareine's murder of Jessica Pond), whereas in the novel much of the plot involves a real estate scam.

While all of the aforementioned changes are explicable, even expected, there are two striking alterations—in point of view and in the film's conclusion—which profoundly alter the thematic message of the work. The loss of Tim Madden's first person narrative and his concomitant internal cerebrations weaken the film somewhat, since Tim's existential struggles with his own fears (as in the case of the climb up the Provincetown monument) are omitted or less effectively evoked. This is evident at its most awkward in the scene when Tim, confronted by Madeleine's note informing him that her husband Regency and Tim's wife Patty are having an affair, repeats the seemingly interminable litany, "Oh God, Oh man," as the sky wheels about him.

Mailer addressed the issue of point of view directly in an interview with Dinitia Smith for *New York* magazine:

> It's difficult not entering Madden's head. There's no offscreen narration. Narration in a film is a confession of weakness. Offscreen narration ruined *Sunset Boulevard* and *Apocalypse Now*. The more sardonic aspects of Madden's character can hardly be captured.

Mailer does, however, bring the illusion and flavor of the first person narrative into the early stages of the movie by the common and simple expedient of having Tim relate the story to date to his father: awakening on the twenty-eighth day of Patty's "decampment" to find Dougy seated at the table in his dining room, Tim recounts the strange happenings of the last week.

And Mailer does succeed in bringing some of the central novelistic themes into the film. In *An American Dream*, cancer (in Deborah, the mafioso Eddie Gannucci, and others) was perceived as a metaphor for moral failure. In *Tough Guys Don't Dance*, Patty Lareine speaks disdainfully of middle class kids "Trying to get vengeance on their folks for giving them cancer!" (Mailer, *Tough Guys* 106). More significantly, Dougy Madden presents a cohesive vision of life in which cancer is the eventual consequence of a major failure of will. Ultimately, he forces his own disease into remission through a crucial act of selfless courage on behalf of his son: sinking the severed heads of Patty and Jessica at sea. In a scene near the end of the film, which echoes a conversation occurring earlier in the novel, Dougy again remarks on the high (moral) cost of curing cancer.

In the film *Tough Guys* as in the novel, God and the devil are again embattled in a Manichaean struggle over the best and worst in the human soul.[4] Just as Rojack's journey through the New York night, and later through the artifice of Las Vegas, is seen as infernal, Tim's drive to his marijuana stash where the *heads* are secreted (Mailer may be punning here) smacks of a trip into hell and provokes an equivalent dread in him. His salvation ultimately must lie in overcoming his visceral terror. This internal struggle, though, is far less evident in the camera's eye than in Tim's narrative in the book.

But perhaps the greatest difference between the two versions of *Tough Guys*—and the greatest difference between *Tough Guys* and *American Dream*—is in the endings. The numerous murders and beheadings, for instance, when revealed in the novel, are reminiscent of Elizabethan blood tragedy. Stated in bald outline, they seem almost silly. The seven deaths and two postmortem decapitations, perpetrated by nine different culprits, suggest that Mailer is just having fun with the reader, toying with the genre. In *An American Dream*, Mailer took a cliché (as indicated by his title) and made of it a sophisticated allegorical indictment of American society. In *Tough Guys Don't Dance*, he takes a potentially serious popular form and, in a good-natured and unpretentious, if bloody manner, makes an ultimate cliché of it.

Yet whereas *An American Dream* ends on a sophisticated series of controlled ambiguities, with a resolution of Rojack's existential quest but no simple final solutions to the various mysteries presented in the course of it (nuances which are omitted in the film)—e.g., What was Jack Kennedy's true connection to Barney Oswald Kelly? Was Deborah really a spy, or even a double agent? What was the nature of the "work" Cherry did for Detective Roberts?—*Tough Guys* ends on a lengthy series of elaborate, often forced explanations of how the nine culprits and an additional supporting cast did away with the seven victims. There are solutions in abundance, but no true resolution.

Perhaps Tim's return to Madeleine, a pallid echo of Rojack's discovery of love with Cherry, may serve as a metaphor for Mailer's return to his old love for the mystery novel in an attempt to replicate his daring success in *An American Dream*. But as Mailer said of *Barbary Shore* (1951) in *Advertisements for Myself* (91-92), *Tough Guys Don't Dance* collapses in its last hundred pages, and never recovers (94).

In the novel, after a series of somewhat improbable resolutions (or simple solutions) to the involved plot, Tim and Madeleine move to Key West, living modestly both in terms of finances and hopes:

> Madeleine and I went out to Colorado for a while, and now we inhabit Key West. I try to write, and we live on the money that comes from her work as a hostess in a local restaurant and mine as a part-time bartender in a hole across the street from her place. Once in a while we wait for a knock on the door, but I am not so sure it will ever come. (Mailer, *Tough Guys* 367)

Thus, Tim and Madeleine find themselves in similar, if slightly more modest and certainly more satisfying, circumstances to those they lived in at the beginning of their affair years earlier.

In the screenplay, however, Madeleine surprises Tim with a house, presumably in Key West, purchased with the two million dollars from the aborted coke deal which precipitates most of the murders, money which she found in a briefcase in Regency's closet. Her final line—and the final line in the film—is, "Carry me across the threshold, you dummy." In terms of verisimilitude, it may be remarked that two people appearing so suddenly and acquiring their home so mysteriously would seem quite obtrusive. But Mailer's intent here may be part of the borderline parody and consequent black humor of the film's concluding messages, which makes the film's ending superior to the book's: we have just witnessed Dougy and Tim sinking six bodies at sea, while "Pomp and Circumstance" plays in the background and they discuss cancer and schizophrenia as mutual cures for each other. In the novel, Mailer writes, "Doubtless I am in danger of writing an Irish comedy, so I will not describe the gusto with which Dougy now made his preparations to take Alvin Luther to the watery rest..." (*Tough Guys* 367). In the movie, he makes us witnesses to the act itself. Perhaps because of this disarming shift to black humor, the film's excesses are more acceptable than those of the novel, since the audience's expectations of verisimilitude are lowered.

Mailer apparently enjoyed bringing his novel to the screen. He spent six months on the screenplay (compared to only two months for the writing of the book on which it is based); and, as he remarked to me and to other interviewers, he liked the excitement involved in directing, especially after decades of writing in isolation:

> I enjoyed it a lot. The trouble is, I like making movies more than writing now. I'm tired of writing. I've been doing it for forty years, and there's not much fun left. (Leeds 359-77)

Furthermore, in addition to directing the film, throughout the production he engaged himself personally in other ways: it is his Provincetown home— radically redecorated, with white lacquer and pastel colors in keeping with Patty Lareine's social aspirations—which serves as Tim and Patty's Provincetown residence; and Mailer even co-authored the lyrics to one of the film's songs, "You'll Come Back (You Always Do)." There was also a special kinship with some of the actors: Ryan O'Neal was an old sparring buddy, whose reputation for bellicosity rivals Mailer's. And Mailer's fifth wife, Carol Stevens, played the voice of one of the witches.

The film *Tough Guys Don't Dance* was met with sometimes negative or hostile reviews. But despite the criticism, Mailer in his first foray as director of a major commercial film shows his growth and virtuosity as an artist, and presents us with precisely what he described in *Maidstone*: a good movie made from a modest novel.

NOTES

[1]By contrast, Mailer's ambitions for many of his other novels were far less modest. As Joan Didion forcefully wrote in "I Want to Go Ahead and Do It," rev. of *The Executioner's Song* by Norman Mailer, *The New York Times Book Review* 7 Oct. 1979: 1,

> It is one of those testimonies to the tenacity of self-regard in the literary life that large numbers of people remain persuaded that Norman Mailer is no better than their reading of him. They condescend to him, they dismiss his most original work in favor of the more literal and predictable rhythms of *The Armies of the Night*; they regard *The Naked and the Dead* as a promise later broken and every book since as a quick turn for his creditors, a stalling action, a spangled substitute, tarted up to deceive, for the "big book" he cannot write. In fact, he has written this "big book" at least three times now. He wrote it the first time in 1955 with *The Deer Park* and he wrote it a second time in 1965 with *An American Dream* and he wrote it a third time in 1967 with *Why Are We in Vietnam?* and now, with *The Executioner's Song*, he has probably written it a fourth.

[2]Tierney's drinking kept him unemployable for many years. Tierney maintains in Gerald Peary, "Medium-Boiled Mailer," *Sight & Sound International Film Quarterly* Spring 1987: 104-07, that his career was sabotaged by gossip columnist Hedda Hopper, who would "print terrible lies" about him. Most of Tierney's early roles were as criminals in 1940s B-movies, including *Dillinger* (1945) and *Born to Kill* (1947). He also played Jesse James in *Badman's Territory* (1946) and *Best of the Badmen* (1951), and the villain who "derailed the circus train in Cecil B. DeMille's *The Greatest Show on Earth* (1952)." After Tierney quit drinking, he played in *Prizzi's Honor* (1985) and appeared in episodes of *Hill Street Blues* as, ironically, a police sergeant.

[3]If courage, the capacity to steel oneself and rise above immediate fear, is here (as throughout Mailer's work) perceived as the noblest expression of the *human* will, many of the characters are described in pointedly animal terms. Other animal imagery in the novel includes the moment when, facing a new challenge, Tim feels "a descent from man to dog" (97) before he musters the will to go on. Yet, ironically, the attributes of the true dog are shown to be positive when Tim's Labrador Retriever, Stunts, demonstrates courage, sacrifice and loyalty by giving his life for Tim, dying with Spider's knife in his heart. (Although this scene is incorporated into the movie, Stunts's appearance in the plot is sudden and unexpected.) The truly negative animal metaphors are reserved for Spider Nissen, in his hideous nickname, his "crablike mouth" (103) and Tim's observation that "he had a touch of the hyena...that same we-eat-tainted-meat-together intimacy that burns out of a hyena's eyes behind the bars of his cage" (101). John Snyder's portrayal of Spider in the film evokes a palpable distaste in the viewer, but this animality is only vaguely implied.

'This is clearly another echo of *An American Dream* (New York: Dial, 1965), in which Mailer posits the existence of a cohesive cosmic order, "An Architecture to Eternity," within which Mailer's Manichaean God and Devil struggle for men's souls:

> No, men were afraid of murder, but not from a terror of justice so much as the knowledge that a killer attracted the attention of the gods; then your mind was not your own, your anxiety ceased to be neurotic, your dread was real. Omens were as tangible as bread. There was an architecture to eternity which housed us as we dreamed, and when there was a murder, a cry went through the market places of sleep. Eternity had been deprived of a room. Somewhere the divine rage met a fury. (204)

WORKS CITED

Bowden, Mark. "Norman Mailer: The Prisoner of Celebrity." *Philadelphia Inquirer Sunday Magazine* 2 December 1984: 40-44.

Harmetz, Aljean. "Tracy Wynn Fighting to Get TV-Series Credit." *The New York Times* 15 January 1982: C8.

Leeds, Barry H. "A Conversation with Norman Mailer." *Connecticut Review* 10.2 (Spring 1988): 6-7. Rpt. in *Conversations with Norman Mailer*. Ed. J. Michael Lennon. Jackson: University Press of Mississippi, 1988. 359-77.

Mailer, Norman. *Advertisements for Myself*. New York: Putnam's, 1959.

_____. *Cannibals and Christians*. New York: Dial, 1966.

_____. *Maidstone: A Mystery*. New York: NAL, 1971.

_____. *Tough Guys Don't Dance*. 1984. New York: Ballantine, 1985.

Smith, Dinitia. "Tough Guys Make Movie." *New York* 12 January 1987: 32-35.

Doctorow's *Billy Bathgate*: Compelling Postmodern Novel, Retro-Realist Film

Michael Bruce McDonald

The film version of *Billy Bathgate* begins with the same evocative scene as the novel: Bo Weinberg, a gangster with sophisticated pretensions, has made the fatal mistake of double-crossing the vengeful Dutch Schultz. Doctorow's description of Bo's being hustled aboard the tugboat that will carry him to a watery death is memorably intricate:

> [Schultz] had to have it planned because when we drove onto the dock the boat was there and the engine was running...everyone knew where everything was, and when the big Packard came down the ramp...the doors were already open and they hustled Bo and the girl upside before they even made a shadow in all that darkness. And there was no resistance.... (3)

The narrator is young Billy Bathgate (the last name is assumed, taken from the avenue of his childhood), erstwhile knockabout from the Bronx streets who, having gained the attention of the notorious Dutch Schultz, has come to enjoy provisional status as a member of his gang.

Hardly coincidental to the novel's overall framework, this portrayal of Billy's initiation into the brutality—and oddly mannered decorum—of gang life decisively establishes the idiomatic manner whereby the rest of the novel will unfold. Indeed, the crucial elements of Billy's narrative are already well in place: the way that Billy's words are couched in long sentences whose parataxis suggests a refusal to order events hierarchically, insisting rather on dramatic but not necessarily explainable conjunctions between events;[1] Schultz's apparent omniscience as he plans "it all" without seeming to leave a trace of his scheming; and the frank realism that, verging on simple reportage, is nevertheless artfully combined with figurations (such as Bo and his girl moving too fast even to make a shadow) no less extravagant for their subtlety.

A strong sense of Billy's power of observation—the very quality Schultz finds so attractive—is introduced here as well, as Billy (Loren Dean)

169

witnesses the protracted humiliation of Bo Weinberg (played by Bruce Willis).
(See Figure 31.) His every gesture fraught with wide-eyed awareness, Billy
watches the laborious process whereby Bo's feet are encased in cement, and
then must helplessly await the execution that comes almost as a relief.

While these opening scenes have garnered praise from reviewers of the
film and novel alike, their crucial role in establishing the overall scheme of the
book tends to get overlooked. One notable exception is Alfred Kazin, who
not only calls the book's opening scenes "stunning" but also praises Billy as
"the Bronx's own Huck Finn":

> Like Huck, [Billy] is encased in a violence not his own. Like Huck,
> he is so sentient, self-dependent, and…self-"educated" that he
> brings a special style of his own to the book. This is quite lyrical at
> times and amusingly overdrawn in a style that rises at times to
> Joyce and descends to…Runyon. Billy…alone finds the clues in
> Dutch's last words that enable him to discover the millions that
> Dutch stashed away. With these Billy grows up to become an Ivy
> League graduate, a U.S. army officer in World War II, and a
> corporate entrepreneur. (41)

Just as Huck's story—its broad social context notwithstanding—is
unmistakably his own, so the strongly idiomatic nature of Billy's narrative
makes him all the more a modern-day, urban Huck.[2]

Figure 31. Billy watches the execution of Bo Weinberg (Bruce Willis).
Copyright © by Touchstone Pictures.

Conversely, while the film's reviewers have almost invariably singled out its opening scenes for special praise, they tend to lack enthusiasm for director Robert Benton's overall vision,[3] or for the stripped-down version of Doctorow's richly detailed narrative that is Tom Stoppard's screenplay.[4] The most dramatic contrast between the novel and film, however, lies in the manner whereby the latter largely eschews the burden of portraying Billy as a sort of supreme witness to the dramatic final days of the Schultz gang. Rather, in subsequent scenes he is depicted as merely one of several protagonists instead. Billy's role as witness is indeed displaced by the camera itself, whose single eye *sees* all—or enough—but which fails to lend any idiomatic flavor to Billy's story; for unlike Doctorow himself, the camera fails to take *Billy's* particular point of view. This substitution—for the sake of what thus becomes a starkly realistic, narrative-free story—of a dumbly omniscient, unblinking spectator for Doctorow's incisive and *flawed* witness marks the displacement, and undoing, of his uniquely rendered narrative. To put things a bit differently, the film, by serving up the novel's realistic elements alone, severely undermines its narrative; and insofar as that narrative is informed by the uniqueness of Billy's voice as both witness and storyteller, the film tells a different tale altogether.

Writing in *The Nation*, Stuart Klawans argues, on the other hand, that Billy's narrative is so infused with verbal brilliance that *no* voice-over could begin to do it justice anyway, and thus he finds no fault with Benton or Stoppard for failing to address this aspect of the novel in adapting it for the screen:

> They wisely choose to portray Billy from the outside, while encouraging the audience to identify with him. He becomes likable in a conventional manner, which he certainly is not in the book. (719)

But why, and for whom, is it desirable that Billy become "likable in a conventional manner"? If Billy, like Huck, engages us largely because of his striking *unconventionality*, why is it wise to strip him of the very qualities which make his character so memorable in the first place? If his narrative truly comprises the essence of the novel, where is the wisdom in divesting his story of the source of its ultimate meaning and significance?

This is the sort of question that Fredric Jameson might ask of the film. No reader has had higher praise for Doctorow's novels than Jameson; no one has acclaimed their political force more resoundingly. In *Postmodernism: Or the Cultural Logic of Late Capitalism*, Jameson asserts that Doctorow— virtually alone among contemporary American novelists—has created a fiction "nourished with history in the more traditional sense" (21), a foundation indispensable to his confrontation with certain problems haunting the American present. For Jameson, Doctorow's fiction plays an anomalous, and thus quite indispensable role as a sort of historical conscience for contemporary postmodern culture,[5] imparting, at least for those with "left sympathies,"

> ...a poignant distress that is an authentic way of confronting our own current political dilemmas in the present. What is culturally interesting, however, is that he has had to convey this great theme formally (since the waning of the content is very precisely his subject), and...has had to elaborate his work by way of that very cultural logic of the postmodern which is itself the mark and symptom of his dilemma. (24-25)

Jameson's comments suggest how the story of a poor picaro from the Bronx—a "capable boy" (3) who eventually finds not only an identity in the Schultz gang but a sizable fortune to boot—could yet bear significant implications for the politics of contemporary American culture. The explicit social critique absent at the level of content is effectively worked out, that is, in the disarmingly subtle form of *Billy Bathgate*.

For, despite possessing extraordinary capability, Billy finds economic and social opportunity only in the company of mobsters. The youthful Billy is indeed capable enough eventually to batten onto Schultz's seemingly lost fortune (a detail oddly missing from the film), but at the cost of a certain solipsism of the spirit, revealed not so much in the novel's content as in its form. For if the book's content is overwhelmingly focused on the dramatic events of Billy's youth, its form unfolds as the narrative of a much older, somewhat world-weary and guarded man, a man ultimately unwilling to entertain the larger implications of the very events he has so poignantly narrated:

> Who I am in my majority and what I do, and whether I am in the criminal trades or not, and where and how I live must remain my secret because I have a certain renown. (321)

By contrasting the capability that interests Schultz in the first place with Billy's somewhat subdued state at the close of the narrative, Doctorow shows how even the canniest aptitude for acquiring wealth can devolve into a state of spiritual impoverishment. Not coincidentally, he shows how capitalism itself—attended by its oddly exact ideological Doppelgänger, gangsterdom—tends to conspire in this process.

The film fails to impart *any* sense, however, of Billy's confrontation with—and eventual submission to—the ideological assumptions of his milieu. While admirably conveying, scene by scene, the vivid realism of the novel, the film ignores the book's formal implications by omitting any sense of the older Billy, the retrospective narrator who has exchanged the openness of youthful capability for the solipsistic comforts of a merely hoarded wealth. Doctorow's subtle critique of the manner whereby gratuitously garnered wealth can exact spiritual poverty[6]—certainly an issue which, in the wake of an era of overnight junkbond millionaires, remains germane for contemporary American culture—is thus absent from the film. Without the retrospective presence of the older, fairly cynical Billy, the film's story—unlike that of the book—lacks a sense of its own inner history.

Lacking this sense, the film can only "mystify," to cite John Berger's formulation, the relationship between past and present:

> ...fear of the present leads to a mystification of the past.... [that] entails a double loss. Works of art are made unnecessarily remote. And the past offers us fewer [ideas] to complete in action. (11)

The film enacts just such a double loss. Not only does it make the scene of Billy's story "unnecessarily remote" by stripping away the narrative voice that makes him such a memorable presence in Doctorow's novel; the film also omits any trace of the crucial notion subtly insinuated toward the narrative's close, the idea that the ideological exaltation of the self-replete individual—an exaltation so endemic to American thought—is finally inadequate to the challenges of modern life.

Fredric Jameson would argue that such omissions are inherent in contemporary American cinema, which, by offering little more than a "pastiche of the stereotypical past" (21), becomes acutely problematic *for* the present, fostering the sort of uncritical attitudes toward past and present history bemoaned by such diverse critics of contemporary culture as Allan Bloom, Alexander Cockburn, Robert Hughes, and Camille Paglia.[7] Precisely to the extent that it blurs the past, moreover, contemporary cinema tends merely to endow "present reality and the openness of present history with the spell and distance of a glossy mirage" (21), an idea whose importance is confirmed by John Berger's assertion that, "If we can see the present clearly enough, we shall ask the right questions of the past" (16).

On the other hand, Doctorow has asked precisely the right questions of the past in *Billy Bathgate*, especially inasmuch as the book subtly shows how certain aspects of life in the thirties have come to fruition in the present. Thus, Doctorow is able to expose the very qualities which *link* the problems of the past to one of the great dilemmas of the present: the role and nature of the individual in a complex modern society. Conversely, by ignoring the question of what Billy's story means for the present, the film is truly able only to imbue its vision of the past with "the spell and distance of a glossy mirage"; even the particulars of a past ruled by mob violence—and by a politics in collusion with such violence—thus merely amount, in the end, to the stuff of a virtual fairy tale.[8] If fairy tales are fiction, however, they are also always true documents of culture: stories, as the late Joseph Campbell might say,[9] that a culture tells itself about itself, about its otherwise secret dreams and aspirations.

In the essay "False Documents"—a forceful paean to the necessarily political character of fiction—Doctorow argues that novels, too, document certain truths of culture, even if the very nature of the novelist's art necessitates that he or she "lie" in the process. Distinguishing two kinds of "power in language," that of "the regime" and "the power of freedom," Doctorow links the former to the problematic status of realism in the novel:

> ...*the power of the regime* is...the modern consensus of sensibility that could be called *realism*, which...may be defined as the business of getting on and producing for ourselves what we construe as the satisfaction of our needs.... Therefore I have to conclude that the regime of facts is not from God but man-made, and, as such, infinitely violable. (17)

Insofar as the "regime of facts" is contingent—and thus forever under construction as well as "infinitely violable"—even writers of fiction perform an inescapably political role.

Doctorow argues, furthermore, that novels can and must intervene on behalf of the "language of freedom" whereby we envision ourselves and our world anew, rather than slavishly acquiescing before the status quo:

> There is a regime language that derives its strength from what we are supposed to be and a language of freedom whose power consists in what we threaten to become. And I'm justified in giving a political character to the nonfictive and fictive uses of language because there is conflict between them. (17)

The great power of Doctorow's novel derives from its depiction of the dynamic whereby the incipient language of Billy's freedom—the language of what he "threatens to become"—degenerates, in the end, into mere acceptance of the status quo, of the regime.

Billy's ultimate submission before the "power of the regime" intersects, curiously enough, with a seeming oddity—and true paradox—of "False Documents": the notion that novel-writing is "the only profession forced to admit that it lies," but that this very quality bestows a "mantle of honesty" upon novelists (26). Novelists are especially trustworthy, moreover, insofar as their documents tacitly admit to such lies:

> The novelist's opportunity to do his work today is increased by the power of the regime to which he finds himself in opposition. As clowns in the circus imitate the aerialists and tightrope walkers...we have it in us to compose false documents more valid, more real,

more truthful than the "true" documents of the politicians or the journalists.... Novelists know...that the world in which we live is still to be formed and that reality is amenable to any construction that is placed upon it. It is a world made for liars and we are born liars. (26)

While Billy too is a "born liar"—at least to the extent that he zestfully elaborates truths which, in less capable hands, might indeed seem mere lies—he eventually exchanges the false document that is the grand story of his youth for mere riches. By declining to enact it for the viewer, the film escapes the burden of this tradeoff. But the key to understanding the relevance of Billy's story for contemporary American culture lies in noticing precisely how the discourse of Billy's belief that he possesses special ability unfolds over the course of the novel.

The older Billy realizes he was a boy "capable of learning, and I see now capable of adoring that rudeness of power" (3). To be judged a capable boy by someone as *powerful* as Schultz is thrilling to Billy and does a great deal to explain how he comes to subsume even the gravest dangers of life in the Schultz gang under the rubric of an aesthetics of inwardness. This is to say that a very significant aspect—and liability—of Billy's capability lies in his tendency to euphemize the danger in his involvement with Schultz as a mere sign of his own singularity, as confirmation, indeed, of his own special fate.

The film, however, fails to portray the constant, lurking menace which Doctorow's Schultz embodies. In the novel, he is described as "short-necked and stolid" (12), compensating for an utter lack of elegance with "a certain fluent linkage of mind and body...both were rather powerfully blunt and tended not to recognize obstacles that required going around rather than through or over" (13). In the film, Dustin Hoffman not only lacks this quality of bluntness but, as Stephan Talty points out, is "more elegant than the book Dutch, [lacking] real menace" (35);[10] thus, he never becomes the man whom Billy describes as "the great gangster of my dreams." For whatever reason, Hoffman simply does not inhabit this role in the way that justly earned him fame in films like *Midnight Cowboy*, *Tootsie*, and *Rain Man*.[11] Furthermore, whereas in the novel Schultz's assessment of Billy's capability is everywhere attended by an air of impending menace as well as genuine praise, in the film, which glosses over this dialectic of menace and reward, Billy becomes just an opportunistic hanger-on; and the book's impressive psychodrama is thereby occluded and, finally, lost.

Schultz's prime directive to Billy—simply to pay close attention, to *watch* (see Figure 32)—is emblematic of the manner whereby the boy's status in the gang oscillates in uneasy tension between menace and reward. The nature of Schultz's directive suggests, moreover, that by quietly observing, Billy will participate in a special economy, one which supplements—but nevertheless stands in uneasy tension with—that of the rackets:

Figure 32. Throughout *Billy Bathgate*, Billy (Loren Dean) functions as witness. Copyright © by Touchstone Pictures.

> My instructions were simple, when I was not doing something I was specifically told to do, to pay attention, to miss nothing...[to] always be watching and always be listening no matter what state I was in...to lose nothing of any fraction of a moment even if it happened to be my last. (4)

This capacity for awareness—the value in Billy first recognized, and then commodified, by Schultz—is certainly germane to the numbers-wary economy of the rackets. But it is also fundamentally excessive to the strict requisites of that economy, for such awareness leads directly to the non-utilitarian clarity embodied in Billy's narrative, in a discursive act which, by its very nature, can never be of any use to Schultz.

Such excessive clarity contrasts nicely, moreover, with that of Otto "Abbadabba" Berman (played by Steven Hill), mathematical genius and executor of the Schultz rackets. Like Billy, Berman possesses a nearly devouring awareness that misses nothing, or *almost* nothing; as a hardened participant in gangland economy, however, Berman's role is most certainly not to maintain an exceptional state of awareness "no matter what." He simply cannot allow himself to stray from the necessities of the operations he oversees. Since Billy's essential role in the gang is to act as a kind of supreme witness, on the other hand, he is virtually encouraged to exercise a latitude of awareness that Berman can never afford. But Billy's very freedom in this regard marks his ultimate tangentiality to the rackets, to an economy which he aspires to enter into more fully, but from which, as a necessarily distanced witness, he is finally prohibited.

Significantly, Doctorow's portrayal of Billy's almost obsessive inwardness illuminates the ideological dynamic which Herbert Marcuse terms "affirmative culture." For Marcuse, such culture values states of inwardness above all others, even as it secretly despairs of harmonizing aesthetic with everyday experience (93-96). Indeed, this divergence between inner and outer realms of experience—a state simply assumed in much postmodern fiction[12]—shapes the underlying tension of Doctorow's *Billy Bathgate*. In his reading of Marcuse, John Brenkman asserts that, under capitalism,

> the very satisfactions that the inner world provides—be they spiritual, intellectual, or aesthetic—become justifications for the outer world as it is. Culture becomes "affirmative." The higher value attributed to the soul, thought, and art becomes an apology for reality.... (6)

Doctorow's novel of gangsterdom might seem readily to lend itself to appropriation by—and *as*—affirmative culture, inasmuch as it is Billy's sense of inwardness that enables him to survive in that milieu, and indeed to prosper despite the ultimate demise of Schultz and his gang. Billy's sense of the nearly transcendent value of his own inwardness enables him to apologize, however tacitly, for the injustices of his milieu. Even so, Billy's position is undermined just enough, in the end, to disclose an implicit critique of American life in the thirties.

Interestingly in this regard, those who praise the film most highly often seem to lack any particular concern for anything in the novel besides what it certainly is on the surface, a picaresque tale of American gangsterdom. For instance, writing in *Maclean's*, Brian D. Johnson notes that "the atmospheric expanse of Doctorow's novel has been distilled into a sharply evocative coming-of-age picture," yet ignores the crucial fact that Billy's narrative is not only informed by the complexity of the forces attending his coming of age but also shaped by their conflict. Rather than examining the fact that Billy is not simply or one-dimensionally virtuous, Johnson instead praises the film's "stark and unremitting realism" (87) and beautiful location photography.

Time's Richard Corliss, recognizing that "the trick of Doctorow's novel...was in its narrative voice," conveys a fuller understanding of the novel's complexity than Johnson's. Young Billy, he writes, is

> the ideal observer...a kind of underworld groupie who is appreciative of [gangsters'] style and implicated in their actions but still one ironic step outside their souls, and who is ready to analyze every movement and moment in 484 pages of headlong streetwise orotundity and subordinate clauses even longer than this one. (95)

But even Corliss misinterprets the film's central focus, asserting that it rests with "society dame" Drew Preston (played by Nicole Kidman), the object of both Schultz's and Billy's affections. "[T]his is at heart a movie about the power of a beautiful, fearless woman," writes Corliss, who "flies out of two men's lives...[like] an airborne goddess of artful deceit" (95).

Still other reviewers have decried the film for seeming to lack any focus. For instance, James Bowman mockingly praises the poster for "tell[ing] you more of what the film is about than the film does."

> Occasionally...the picture [attempts] to make an ironic point about the connection between legitimate business and gangsterdom, as when Dutch complains about...government interference by saying: "It's not fair! What does a man have to do to enjoy the fruits of his labor?" But it doesn't insist even on this idea, which was pretty thoroughly explored in The Godfather anyway, and you walk away wondering what it was all about. (62)

Indeed, such confusion helps to account for the film's relative failure to achieve popular success.[13] By comparison, the book's much greater success within its market may be linked to the reasons why some critics, noting its strongly realized visual aspect, have called it "cinema-ready."[14] In fact, the reception respectively accorded the novel and film suggests that the former already provides, as a novel, the sort of visual satisfactions usually associated with works of the cinema, while the film achieves little more than a certain redundancy in this regard.

My own criticism of the film version of Billy Bathgate seeks, likewise, a richer understanding of how such a well-intentioned film—a film benefiting from the efforts of an admirable cast, director, and cinematographer—can nevertheless have largely failed to engage its potential audience. If, as Gerhard Bach suggests in his essay on adapting Doctorow's work (specifically Ragtime) for the screen, Doctorow's novels in themselves confront the problems—and delights—of "visual literacy" (which Bach defines as "the critical reading of films" [165] and images), then it is indeed appropriate to examine the imagery which, though realized in the novel, is absent from the screenplay. The film's failure to include these very images may help explain why Bowman and others have been so confused—precisely at the level of visual literacy—about the actual subject of Benton's movie.

One such image has to do with Billy's juggling, a skill which, even before he meets Schultz, seems excessive to the interests of mere survival. But it is precisely this *seemingly* useless artistry that first gains him Schultz's attention, and which thereby ironically helps not only to ensure his survival but to be in a position to find the boss's treasure after his death. Truly an amazing juggler, Billy happens to be performing his most esoteric feat, juggling five objects of uneven size and weight, when he first catches Schultz's eye:

> I...demonstrated my latest accomplishment...a Galilean maneuver involving two rubber balls, a navel orange, an egg, and a black stone...assorted objects rose and fell through my line of vision like a system of orbiting planets. (25)

The tossing of such disparate objects calls forth an odd mixture of sheer dexterity and self-entrancement in Billy: "I was juggling my own self as well," he says, "in a kind of matching spiritual feat, performer and performed for, and so, entranced, had no mind for the rest of the world..." (25).[15]

Characteristically, however, the film omits this crucial detail, merely showing, and from a considerable distance, Billy juggling objects of apparently even size and heft, yet attracting Schultz's attention nonetheless. Thus, the film glosses over the very detail that prompts Schultz to refer to Billy as a remarkably "capable boy," and that foreshadows the manner whereby Billy will have to juggle a bewildering array of disparate bits of business for Schultz as he struggles to stay afloat in the unnerving maelstrom of gangsterdom. Generally, the tasks of the gang are strictly divided among its members. (See Figure 33.) However, Billy's juggling anticipates the relative ease with which he will assume a variety of roles, from posing as Schultz's Bible-studying "prodigy" in the upstate town of Onondaga, to serving as courier and spy while the gang is exiled from New York City, to shadowing special prosecutor Thomas Dewey, setting him up for assassination in the days just before Schultz himself is finally gunned down.

Even as Billy describes, in his juggling, a capability that exceeds the narrow strictures of gangland economy, he inadvertently clarifies the nature of Schultz's own symbolic position as he recounts their first meeting, which occurs just after his extraordinary performance:

> He stripped off a ten and slapped it in my hand. And while I stared at calm Alexander Hamilton enshrined in his steel-pointed

Figure 33. Dutch Schultz (Dustin Hoffman) and the members of his gang, including Billy, Otto Berman (Steven Hill) and Drew Preston (Nicole Kidman). Copyright © by Touchstone Pictures.

eighteenth-century oval I heard for the first time the resonant rasp of the Schultz voice, but thinking for one stunned instant it was Mr. Hamilton talking, like a comic come to life, until my senses righted themselves and I realized I was hearing the great gangster of my dreams. (27)

While the U.S. government would naturally seek to repudiate any perceived similarity between the capitalist economy it sanctions and the illicit economies of gangsterdom, Billy's auditory hallucination conveys the ultimate correspondence between the two. For this boy from the impoverished Bronx, it is money itself—not the authoritative discourse of the government that merely prints the money—that seems, if only for a moment, truly to speak.

Moreover, the fact that the voice of Alexander Hamilton "speaks" from—and only from—the dispensatory hand of Dutch Schultz illustrates a brutal truth of dire poverty: it finally does not matter whose hand dispenses the cash, so long as it ends up in Billy's own. The passage thus suggests the manner whereby capitalist ideology, while appealing to the rule of law, tends to blur the boundaries between legitimate and illicit enterprise. That is, while capitalism is nominally opposed to gangland entrepreneurship, that officially sanctioned enterprise—as Billy suggests—ultimately subsumes, and oddly sanctions, even the brutally illicit economies of gangsters like Schultz. The film, lacking anything like Billy's extraordinary narrative voice, fails to depict his conflation of Alexander Hamilton with Dutch Schultz, and thus elides the book's crucial blurring of the demarcation between government-sanctioned capitalism and the illicit economies of gangsterdom. In its rigid separation of what is everywhere conflated and confused in the novel, the film does a disservice to a narrative wherein the boundary between legitimate and illicit economies becomes so hard, finally, even to see.

Billy's uncannily vivid recollection of the affect of Schultz's words is quickly subsumed, however, by his evocation of the Social Darwinist ethos of American capitalism.[16] This ethos allows the older, simultaneously more refined and cruder Billy to repudiate his former peers, whom he calls "miserable fucking louts" and "poking predators of their own brothers and sisters":

> Oh...that you could aspire to a genius life of crime, with your dead witless eyes, your slack chins, and the simian slouch of your spines—fuck you forever, I consign you to tenement rooms and bawling infants, and sluggish wives and a slow death of incredible subjugation, I condemn you to petty crimes and mean rewards and vistas of cell block to the end of your days. (28)

Thus, looking back on his youth at the close of his narrative, Billy finally naturalizes himself to capitalist ideology. Such naturalization is embodied in the sheer rabidity—the intervening years notwithstanding—of his condemnation of his thieving peers (ironic because it condemns them to the status *already* bequeathed them under capitalism), even as Billy thinks that this condemnation is simply a way of standing up for his own inalienable rights.

Billy thus misses another irony, the fact that, by taking such a position, he has completely discounted the gratuitousness of the events which have enabled him, even granting his ability, to escape the very sort of condemnation he now almost gleefully heaps upon his former peers. In this respect, he participates, albeit unconsciously, in the great myth of American capitalism: the failure to rise above even the most grinding poverty *must* be one's own fault, a sign that one is truly a mere "dumbbell" or "lout." Clearly, the older Billy acts on the deeply ideological assumption that he has achieved his riches solely because he is uniquely capable; the gratuitous dynamic which has allowed that capability even to begin to work in his favor has conveniently been forgotten.

Everyday life with his extraordinary mother ought to have taught him better. Eking out her living in a hellish laundry (another important detail appearing in the film barely long enough to register upon the viewer), Billy's mother is a woman broken not only in body but in spirit. Hunching every evening over her "table of lights"—candles lit in ambivalent memory of the husband who abandoned her long ago, and whose picture she has carefully scratched out of the wedding portrait still holding a place of pride in her desolate apartment—she can barely acknowledge her desperately precocious son, much less respond to his needs:

> One night…Mama looked up…[and] said Billy, my name, Billy, something's wrong, what have you done? That was an interesting moment and I wondered if it would hold, but it was only a moment and then the candles caught her attention again and she turned back to her…table of lights.… Day and night winter and summer she read the lights, of which she had a tableful, you only needed one once every year but she had all the remembrance she needed, she wanted illumination. (28-29)

Her characteristic confusion temporarily allayed, Billy's mother is delighted when he gives her five dollars from the ten Schultz has awarded him; this tiny sum represents "about half her week's wages from the industrial steam laundry on Webster Avenue" (34).

In a world where a ten-dollar bill bears such value, Billy, as a sort of budding venture capitalist, learns to revel in the sheer danger intrinsic to entrepreneurial risk-taking, all questions of mere legality aside:

> How I admired the life of taking pains, of living in defiance of a government that did not like you and did not want you and wanted

to destroy you so that you had to build out protections for yourself with money and men, deploying armament, buying alliances, patrolling borders, as in a state of secession, by your will and wit and warrior spirit living smack in the eye of the monster.... But beyond that, contriving a life from its property of danger, putting it together in the constant contemplation of death...thrilled me... (67)

Insightfully, Billy likens gangland economy to that of the capitalist nation-state, a state organized around the imperatives of amassing and protecting private property. Indeed, his relish for the inherent dangers of gangsterdom recapitulates the Euro-American penchant for the mythic character of the pioneer-trader-conqueror, risking life and limb in search of new markets in unknown lands. For Billy as for Dutch, risk-taking enterprise is the great leveling force which links the illicit economies of gangsterdom with those of state-sponsored capitalism, and it is thus most appropriate that Billy's sense of the negligible differences between these economies—even though they are nominally mortally opposed—should be confirmed by Schultz himself:

> The law is not majestic. The law is what public opinion says it is. I could tell you a lot about the law.... When we had the important precincts, when we had the magistrates court, when we had the Manhattan D.A.? Wasn't that the law?...The law is the vigorish I pay, the law is my overhead.... judges, lawyers, politicians, who are they but guys who have their own angle into the rackets except they like to do it without getting their hands dirty? (209)

While it is important not to euphemize Schultz's brutal spurning of ethical considerations in his pursuit of capital and power, his denial of the altruistic and egalitarian pretensions of U.S. law curiously echoes Marx's insight that, under capitalism, the very notion of "political ethics" is an oxymoron:

> The ethics of political economy is *acquisition*, work, thrift, sobriety—but political economy promises to satisfy my needs. The political economy of ethics is the opulence of a good conscience, of virtue, etc.; but how can I live virtuously if I do not live? And how can I have a good conscience if I am not conscious of anything? It stems from the very nature of estrangement that each sphere applies to me a different and opposite yardstick—ethics one and political economy another; for each...stands in an estranged relation to the other. (97)

The era of Billy and Dutch Schultz embodies just such estrangement; if we see very little of the altruistic aspects of American life in the thirties, it is because the pretense of American altruism does little more—for Doctorow as for Marx—than euphemize the stark estrangement and desperate bravado epitomizing this milieu.

While Billy persists in the idiomatic parataxis of his narrative style, the spirit of his remarks becomes essentially hypotactic in the end, as he decisively asserts his superiority to the "scum" of his childhood milieu. No longer merely aspiring to gangsterdom, the older, reminiscent Billy has joined the ranks of the great captains of industry, robber barons, and mob bosses who must quash all evidence of past indiscretions in order to protect the integrity of the hoard. The excess of capability which made him so useful to Dutch in the first place—the capability embodied in his juggling and extraordinary mental agility alike—has devolved, in the end, into a mere capacity for secrecy. The reminiscent Billy finally seeks to suppress any outward evidence of precisely those outstanding personal traits which his narrative had sought, on the whole, to *celebrate*. Eschewing self-celebration, Billy finally settles for the self-imposed anonymity that can redound upon a life narrowly focused on hoarded property.

How, then, is this remarkable novel evocative of concerns dear to the American left? I believe that the answer lies in the very nature of Billy's career. Surely, his milieu is indicted by its inability to offer such an exceptional being a place *save* in gangsterdom, even if we must look in vain to Billy (or to Doctorow himself) to utter that indictment. Indeed, the very fact that the novel became a bestseller surely testifies to the light-handedness of Doctorow's articulation of political concerns. The book can be read, moreover, as a lively picaresque adventure without troubling oneself too much over the niceties of its politics, and this is precisely the reading offered by the film. Even so, a careful reader can discern Doctorow deconstructing nothing less than the most cherished of American myths, that of the fully self-empowered individual who triumphs over hardship regardless of material concerns and circumstances.

For Theodor Adorno, the state of inwardness elevated by such myths—the very state which, for Marcuse, is both highest aesthetic value and form of identity in affirmative culture—should

> be made transparent as a social function and its self-containedness...revealed as an illusion...vis-à-vis the real social process itself. The "individual" is a dialectical instrument of transition that must not be mythicized away, but...superseded. (119)

Doctorow's *Billy Bathgate* is nothing less than a revelation of the illusory nature of self-containedness. If the novel can *also* be understood as a picaresque adventure, this testifies not to its political weakness, but to the strength of Doctorow's refusal to "mythicize [his protagonist] away" in order to serve the needs of some explicitly political agenda. While Doctorow does not indicate how the individual is to be superseded, Billy's narrative calls, in the end, for some corrective to the sort of solipsistic isolation that is finally his lot. In this regard, the novel's politics may well rest with its negation, and subtle critique, of the idea that human life is determined by consciousness.[17] For Billy grows cynical, even reclusive, precisely to the extent that he fails to admit that his life has not been determined by his consciousness, so much as his consciousness, no matter how agile in its capability, has been shaped by his life.

Willfully excising the older, increasingly embittered Billy from the scene of its action, the film offers up yet another, ultimately mystifying portrait of the underbelly of American prosperity. Where Doctorow shows us an older man denying the fact that he has been profoundly touched, indeed shaped, by the events of his early years, the movie portrays young Billy walking away from those events unscathed, ready to glory anew in the plenitude of his capable youth.[18] Ignoring the novel's depiction of a consciousness convinced that its own plenitude shapes the world, the film omits Doctorow's exposé of the illusory nature of such consciousness. Thus, the film's practice is to substitute an evanescent *entertainment* for Doctorow's entertaining yet highly politicized narrative, a narrative that finds surprising ways to address pressing social concerns in the very midst of a postmodern era that is bent, it would seem, on escaping the burden of socially committed artistic praxis altogether.

NOTES

[1]The paratactic style, which places together—typically within long sentences—clauses not interrelated through subordination, was made famous by the work of Ernest Hemingway. Alfred Kazin aptly reminds us, however, that the sheer rush of Billy's discourse "rises" to something more like Joyce or—to take the example of another American author whose work is often strikingly paratactic—Faulkner (41).

[2]Anne Tyler, calling *Billy Bathgate* Doctorow's "shapeliest piece of work," asserts that its plot is "as tightly constructed as that of *Huckleberry Finn*" ("An American Boy in Gangland," Rev. of *Billy Bathgate*, by E. L. Doctorow, *The New York Times Book Review*, 26 February 1989: 1+). In a review that includes an interesting reading of the metaphoric resonance of Billy's juggling, Garry Wills elaborates on the comparison between Billy and Huck: "Doctorow, like Twain, like Dickens, sees adult possibilities in 'the boy's book'—the tale of an orphan, not yet socialized into ordinary adult life, who acquires an outlaw mentor.... Thus Billy, outside accepted moral systems, must create his own code of responsibility, as Huck does" ("Juggler's Code," Rev. of *Billy Bathgate*, by E. L. Doctorow, *The New York Review of Books*, 2 March 1989: 3-4). While Billy is not literally an orphan—his distraught mother remains very much among the living, and his father has simply fled—his mother's perpetual state of distraction effectually makes him one, and his

self-conception throughout the novel is shaped by a sense that he is very much on his own.

[3]Benton previously worked with Dustin Hoffman (Dutch Schultz in *Billy Bathgate*) in *Kramer vs. Kramer*, for which both won Oscars: Benton for Best Director, Hoffman for Best Actor.

[4]For instance, even as he praises Nestor Almendros as "one of the best" cinematographers in the business, Stanley Kauffmann's qualified praise for the film's cinematography—and his sense that, on the whole, Benton "greatly wastes" Almendros's talent—is fairly representative: "The opening shot, a tugboat moored at night with spotlight beaming to the left and the ocean lights speckling the darkness across the water, is breathtaking in its shades of light and night. But our breath is undisturbed by the rest of the film, which could have been shot by any competent person." See "The Sorcerer's Apprentice," Rev. of *Billy Bathgate*, Dir. Robert Benton, *The New Republic* (25 November 1991: 30-31).

[5]While a strikingly diffuse proliferation of competing, sometimes contradictory definitions has been offered for the term "postmodern," I have chosen to retain this term partly because of its currency in discussions of contemporary culture, but mainly because I find Fredric Jameson's usage indispensable. For Jameson, "late capitalism"—in contradistinction with its so-called "classic" mode—features "the emergence of new forms of business organization (multinationals, transnationals) beyond the monopoly stage but, above all, the vision of a world capitalist system fundamentally distinct from the older imperialism, which was little more than a rivalry between the various colonial powers" (xviii-xix). Just as Doctorow's vision of the thirties is keenly responsive to the material conditions of that milieu, so Jameson's exploration of contemporary life reflects an abiding sense that culture takes distinctive form in response to specific changes in economic organization.

[6]Since Billy's capability does factor in his acquisition of Schultz's wealth following the gangster's death—inasmuch as he alone deciphers the clues Schultz provides to its location in the course of his deathbed rant—my contention that Billy's wealth is gratuitously gained is somewhat arguable. Nevertheless, Billy's narrow escape from being massacred along with the rest of the gang—and the events which subsequently enable him to sit concealed in Schultz's hospital room, writing down the boss's final rants—suggests that a spirit of serendipity, quite as much as sheer capability, is at work here.

[7]The late Allan Bloom bemoaned, from a decidedly conservative perspective, the condition of contemporary American culture in his famously controversial *The Closing of the American Mind*. In his regular "Beat the Devil" column for *The Nation*, the unabashedly socialist Alexander Cockburn pens incisive jeremiads against the selective historical memory increasingly characteristic of contemporary American culture. The mordant wit and keen insight of art critic and historian Robert Hughes are prominently featured in his recently published *Culture of Complaint: The Fraying of America*. Having become something of a cultural phenomenon in the wake of the popularity—and notoriety—of her thorough and passionate study of the interrelation of Western culture and history, *Sexual Personae: Art and Decadence*

from Nefertiti to Emily Dickinson, Camille Paglia frequently seizes the opportunity to denounce various aspects of contemporary American culture.

[8]Doctorow's acute awareness of the odd collusion of political and mythic, even fairy tale, culture in popular American thought is poignantly evidenced in the concluding scenes of his most overtly political novel, *The Book of Daniel,* where the protagonist's final, desperate attempt to come to terms with his parents' execution for espionage is played out in—of all places—Disneyland! In this light, the irony of Disney Studios producing the film version of *Billy Bathgate* can only intensify.

[9]See, for example, "Myth and the Modern World," the first of several interviews with Bill Moyers posthumously published as *The Power of Myth,* Ed. Betty Sue Flowers (New York: Doubleday, 1988. 3-35). Interestingly for the present argument, Campbell explicitly likens the stories told by novelists to those embodied in myth (4).

[10]Talty's review is especially noteworthy for its citations of a pre-release phone interview with screenwriter Tom Stoppard. Stoppard, brilliant playwright though he is (*Rosencrantz and Guildenstern Are Dead*), rather comically eschews *all* responsibility for conveying any sense of Billy's narrative to the screen, thereby demonstrating his complicity in avoiding the obligation to deal with what is, after all, the novel's most interesting—and significant—aspect.

[11]It should be noted, however, that many reviewers have found Hoffman's portrayal of Schultz quite satisfying. See, for instance, Richard Corliss and Brian D. Johnson. In particular, Johnson calls Hoffman's performance "exceptional."

[12]For instance, compare the passion and sense of imminent danger informing Billy's narrative with the conspicuously self-anesthetizing narrative of Jack Gladney, the protagonist of Don DeLillo's superb novel *White Noise.*

[13]Following the film's first week in wide release, Lawrence Cohn could say that it "had a disappointing launch," and that it "did not benefit from its delayed autumn debut, despite the conventional wisdom that fall is a better season for serious pictures" (*Variety* 11 November 1991: 8). By the end of its third week in wide release, Cohn could confidently assert that *Billy Bathgate* had "hit a brick wall of viewer indifference," plummeting "a full 50%...to total merely $12.7 million; it probably will not earn enough to pay for its prints and ad campaign. With a $40 million negative cost, Disney will have a considerable write-down coming on this feature" (*Variety* 25 November 1991: 6). It remains to be seen whether the video will help Disney recoup such losses, but tracking the film's rapid descent as reported in the pages of *Variety* certainly attests to its failure to gain widespread popular acceptance.

[14]J. M. Blom and L. R. Leavis assert, for instance, that the novel comes "too close" to F. Scott Fitzgerald in its treatment of "the leading lady, the glamorous moll Miss Drew, a fantastic Hollywood vision. The final killing of Schultz and his side-kick is in a style ready for the screen. A lot of talent has been devoted to [making]...a super book of the film before the film has been made; not an easy task to write so polished a book, but too easy for a writer of Doctorow's ability" (Rev. of *Billy Bathgate,* by E. L. Doctorow, *English Studies* 71 (1990): 427). Compare Gary

Davenport's rather disparaging assertion that the "...sepia-toned appeal to movie producers with which Doctorow ends the book is scarcely distinguishable from blurb-writing: 'the gabbling old women carrying their shopping bags of greens and chickens, and the teenage girls holding white dresses on hangers to their shoulders, and the truckmen in their undershirts unloading their produce, and the horns honking and all the life of the city turning out to greet us just as in the days of our old happiness, before my father fled, when the family used to go walking in this market, this bazaar of life, Bathgate, in the age of Dutch Schultz'" (Rev. of *Billy Bathgate*, by E. L. Doctorow, *The Sewanee Review* 98 (1990): 706-08). This reading indicates a failure even to consider the possibility that whatever "blurb-writing" obtains here is *Doctorow's* only insofar as it is Billy's. Rather than confront the interesting likelihood that the above-quoted passage might be indicative of *Billy's* attitude toward his milieu, Davenport apparently finds it more convenient to mock Doctorow instead.

[15]See also Garry Wills's illuminating discussion of this scene in "Juggler's Code," Rev. of *Billy Bathgate*, by E. L. Doctorow, *The New York Review of Books* (2 March 1989: 3-4).

[16]The importance of the ideology of Social Darwinism for the development of American capitalism in the latter half of the nineteenth century has been widely discussed, but a concise account can be found in Eric Foner and John A. Garraty, eds., *The Reader's Companion to American History* (Boston: Houghton Mifflin, 1991. 999-1000).

[17]Marx asserted that, contrary to the assumptions of idealist philosophy, consciousness does not determine being; rather, social being determines consciousness. See "Marx on the History of His Opinions," *The Marx-Engels Reader*, ed. Robert C. Tucker, 2nd ed. (New York: Norton, 1978) 3-6.

[18]Indeed, the film closes as Billy, having escaped near execution at the hands of Lucky Luciano's henchmen, wanders desultorily off into the New York streets, lacking any apparent prospect of finding the immense fortune that his novelistic counterpart *is* able to locate. Rather, the film's last, rather anti-climactic scene depicts Billy, his back to the camera, walking away with the *relatively paltry* ten thousand dollars Schultz had earmarked as a bribe for a Tammany hack, and that Luciano has magisterially—if unaccountably—decided that Billy can keep.

WORKS CITED

Adorno, Theodor W. "Letters to Walter Benjamin." *Aesthetics and Politics*. Ed. Ronald Taylor. London: Verso, 1977. 110-33.

Bach, Gerhard. "Novel as History and Film as Fiction: New Perspectives on Doctorow's *Ragtime*." *E. L. Doctorow: A Democracy of Perception*. Ed. Herwig Friedl and Dieter Schulz. Essen: Die Blaue Eule, 1988. 163-75.

Berger, John. *Ways of Seeing*. London: Penguin, 1972.

Bowman, James. "Post No Billings." Rev. of *Billy Bathgate*, Dir. Robert Benton. *The American Spectator* Jan. 1992: 62.

Brenkman, John. *Culture and Domination.* Ithaca: Cornell UP, 1987.

Corliss, Richard. "Extra! Billy Bathgate Lives!" Rev. of *Billy Bathgate*, Dir. Robert Benton. *Time* 4 November 1991: 95.

Doctorow, E. L. "False Documents." *E. L. Doctorow: Essays and Conversations.* Ed. Richard Trenner. Princeton, NJ: Ontario Review Press, 1983. 16-27.

_____. *Billy Bathgate.* New York: Random, 1989.

Jameson, Fredric. *Postmodernism: Or the Cultural Logic of Late Capitalism.* Durham: Duke University Press, 1991.

Johnson, Brian D. "Love in Gangland." Rev. of *Billy Bathgate.* Dir. Robert Benton. *Maclean's* 11 November 1991: 87.

Kazin, Alfred. "Huck in the Bronx." Rev. of *Billy Bathgate* by E. L. Doctorow. *The New Republic* 20 March 1989: 40-2.

Klawans, Stuart. Rev. of *Billy Bathgate.* Dir. Robert Benton. *The Nation* 2 Dec. 1991: 719-20.

Marcuse, Herbert. "The Affirmative Character of Culture." *Negations.* Trans. Jeremy J. Shapiro. Boston: Beacon, 1968. 88-133.

Marx, Karl. "Economic and Philosophic Manuscripts of 1844." *The Marx-Engels Reader.* 2nd ed. Ed. Robert C. Tucker. New York: Norton, 1978. 66-125.

Talty, Stephan. "Inside 'Billy Bathgate.'" Rev. of *Billy Bathgate.* Dir. Robert Benton. *American Film* July 1991: 32-35+.

Contributors

Bruce Bawer is a poet and writer whose articles have appeared in *The Bennington Review, The New Criterion,* and *The American Scholar.* He is author of *The Middle Generation,* on the lives and poetry of Schwartz, Jarrell, Berryman, and Lowell; *Diminishing Fictions; The Contemporary Stylist;* and, most recently, *The Screenplay's the Thing: Movie Criticism, 1986-1990.*

Benedict Giamo is an Assistant Professor of American Studies at the University of Notre Dame. He is author of *On the Bowery: Confronting Homelessness in America* and co-author of *Beyond Homelessness: Frames of Reference.*

Jerome Klinkowitz is Professor of English and University Distinguished Scholar at the University of Northern Iowa. He is the author of sixteen books on contemporary American fiction and culture, including *Literary Disruptions, The Self-Apparent Word, Structuring the Void,* and *Slaughterhouse-Five: Reforming the Novel and the World.* He has edited twelve other books, including *The Vonnegut Statement,* and is also the author of numerous articles and essays and of works of fiction, such as *Short Season.*

Barry H. Leeds is Connecticut State University Distinguished Professor of English and Immediate Past Editor of the *Connecticut Review.* He has published more than one hundred fifty essays, articles, and reviews; his books include *The Structured Vision of Norman Mailer* and *Ken Kesey.*

Barbara Tepa Lupack, formerly Academic Dean at the State University of New York/ESC, directs a small literary press and edits *The Round Table.* Her essays have appeared in numerous journals such as *The Polish Review* and *New Orleans Review;* her books include *Plays of Passion, Games of Chance: Jerzy Kosinski and His Fiction* and the forthcoming *Inmates Running the Asylum: Insanity as Redemptive Response in Contemporary American Fiction.*

Michael Bruce McDonald, who recently received his Ph.D. from the University of Oregon, is currently Adjunct Assistant Professor of English at Iowa State University. He has published an essay on the aesthetics of dissonance in Joyce's *Portrait* in *Twentieth Century Literature* and has an essay on the Circe episode of *Ulysses* forthcoming in *James Joyce Quarterly*. His work in progress includes an essay on the special relevance of John Coltrane's music for American democracy and a book-length Nietzschean reading of Joyce and Woolf.

Robert Merrill is Professor of English and Chair of the Department at the University of Nevada at Reno. Author and editor of numerous articles and books, including *Joseph Heller, Norman Mailer*, and *Critical Essays on Kurt Vonnegut*, he was just named "UNR Outstanding Researcher."

John Peacock is Professor of Language and Literature at the Maryland Institute College of Art in Baltimore. His essays on American culture have appeared in *Literature/Film Quarterly, New Art Examiner, Art and Academe, Ethnohistory, The Canadian Review of American Studies*, and *ESQ: A Journal of the American Renaissance*. He is also a published poet and short story writer.

John L. Simons is Professor of Modern American Literature and Film at the Colorado College. He has published numerous essays in journals, including the *New Orleans Review, Western Humanities Review, Literature/Film Quarterly*, and *Modern Philology*, and is currently at work on a book on Sam Peckinpah, to be co-authored with Robert Merrill.